Michael Robert Gorman, MA

The Empress Is a Man
Stories from the Life
of José Sarria

More pre-publication
REVIEWS, COMMENTARIES, EVALUATIONS . . .

"José Sarria is a born story-teller. By using José's own words as a vehicle, Gorman has written an oral history of a little-known facet of gay life—the Court System. From the World War II closet to the first drag balls to the rising political consciousness, this slice of San Francisco life is told with vim, vigor, and vinegar as only a true Empress can."

Dell Richards
Author, *Lesbian Lists*
and *Superstars: Twelve Lesbians Who Changed the World;*
Dell Richards Publicity,
Sacramento, CA

"Thank heaven this bit of history has been preserved! We owe Michael Gorman a debt of gratitude, first of all, for recognizing that it should be preserved and secondly for bringing his wit and enthusiasm to it! Gorman's fresh and playful style assure this book will be read and enjoyed—a fascinating man and a fascinating era. José Sarria is *our* royal and one we can be very proud of!"

Nan L. Goodart, MA, JD
Estate Planning and Probate Attorney,
Sacramento, CA;
Author, *The Truth About Living Trusts*

"Michael Gorman captures the quintessential soul of one of America's most celebrated deviant divas. His stories from the life of José Sarria invoke the reality of a life of graciousness and goodness touched by fantasy and imagination.

The Empress Is a Man is a royal romp that demonstrates to the world that love is more than affection and that human sexuality at its finest shares a myriad of expressions. It professes that our lives are authenticated by the grace of God and limited only by our willingness to persevere in the face of pain and by our lack of imagination to appropriate with zest all of the possibilities of life. For the shy and the timid, read it. You'll discover that life is more than a cabaret. It's the whole blooming, outrageous world just waiting for you to enjoy."

Rev. Charles H. Lewis, MDiv
San Francisco Night Minister Emeritus

The Empress Is a Man
Stories from the Life of José Sarria

HAWORTH Gay & Lesbian Studies
John P. De Cecco, PhD
Editor in Chief

New, Recent, and Forthcoming Titles:

Barrack Buddies and Soldier Lovers: Dialogues with Gay Young Men in the U.S. Military by Steven Zeeland

Outing: Shattering the Conspiracy of Silence by Warren Johansson and William A. Percy

The Bisexual Option, Second Edition by Fritz Klein

And the Flag Was Still There: Straight People, Gay People, and Sexuality in the U.S. Military by Lois Shawver

Sailors and Sexual Identity: Crossing the Line Between "Straight" and "Gay" in the U.S. Navy by Steven Zeeland

The Gay Male's Odyssey in the Corporate World: From Disempowerment to Empowerment by Gerald V. Miller

Bisexual Politics: Theories, Queries, and Visions edited by Naomi Tucker

Gay and Gray: The Older Homosexual Man, Second Edition by Raymond M. Berger

Reviving the Tribe: Regenerating Gay Men's Sexuality and Culture in the Ongoing Epidemic by Eric Rofes

Gay and Lesbian Mental Health: A Sourcebook for Practitioners edited by Christopher J. Alexander

Against My Better Judgment: An Intimate Memoir of an Eminent Gay Psychologist by Roger Brown

The Masculine Marine: Homoeroticism in the U.S. Marine Corps by Steven Zeeland

Bisexual Characters in Film: From Anaïs to Zee by Wayne M. Bryant

The Bear Book: Readings in the History and Evolution of a Gay Male Subculture edited by Les Wright

Youths Living with HIV: Self-Evident Truths by G. Cajetan Luna

Growth and Intimacy for Gay Men: A Workbook by Christopher J. Alexander

Our Families, Our Values: Snapshots of Queer Kinship edited by Robert E. Goss and Amy Adams Squire Strongheart

Gay/Lesbian/Bisexual/Transgender Public Policy Issues: A Citizen's and Administrato 's Guide to the New Cultural Struggle edited by Wallace Swan

Rough News, Daring Views: 1950s' Pioneer Gay Press Journalism by Jim Kepner

Family Secrets: Gay Sons—A Mother's Story by Jean M. Baker

Twenty Million New Customers: Understanding Gay Men's Consumer Behavior by Steven M. Kates

The Empress Is a Man: Stories from the Life of José Sarria by Michael R. Gorman

Acts of Disclosure: The Coming-Out Process of Contemporary Gay Men by Marc E. Vargo

Queer Kids: The Challenges and Promise for Lesbian, Gay, and Bisexual Youth by Robert E. Owens

Looking Queer: Body Image and Identity in Lesbian, Gay, Bisexual, and Transgender Communities edited by Dawn Atkins

Love and Anger: Essays on AIDS, Activism, and Politics by Peter F. Cohen

Dry Bones Breathe: Gay Men Creating Post-AIDS Identities and Cultures by Eric Rofes

The Empress Is a Man
Stories from the Life
of José Sarria

Michael Robert Gorman, MA

Harrington Park Press
An Imprint of The Haworth Press, Inc.
New York • London

Published by

Harrington Park Press, an imprint of The Haworth Press, Inc., 10 Alice Street, Binghamton, NY 13904-1580

Cover design by Monica L. Seifert.
Cover photo by Brian Ashby.

The Library of Congress has cataloged the hardcover edition of this book as:

Gorman, Michael Robert.
    The empress is a man : stories from the life of José Sarria / Michael Robert Gorman.
      p.   cm.
    ISBN 0-7890-0259-0 (alk. paper)
    1. Sarria, José. 2. Gay men—California—San Francisco—Biography. 3. Female impersonators—California—San Francisco—Biography. I. Title.
HQ75.8.S27G67 1998
305.38'9664'0979461—dc21
                                                97-26364
                                                CIP

ISBN 1-56023-917-4 (pbk.)

CONTENTS

ABOUT THE AUTHOR

Michael R. Gorman, MA, has worked as an editor, journalist, and columnist for three different gay newspapers in Sacramento, California, and is a strong activist in the struggle for gay, lesbian, bisexual, and transgender rights. Michael is also a poet of some renown in northern California, the Sacramento gay community having dubbed him "the Poet Laureate of Lavender Heights." A former high school teacher of creative writing and folklore, he now teaches writing part-time at Cosumnes River College in Sacramento.

JOSE'S FAMILY TREES

Biological

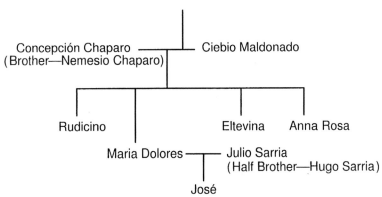

Concepción Chaparo
(Brother—Nemesio Chaparo) ——— Ciebio Maldonado

Rudicino   Eltevina   Anna Rosa

Maria Dolores ——— Julio Sarria
(Half Brother—Hugo Sarria)

José

Adopted

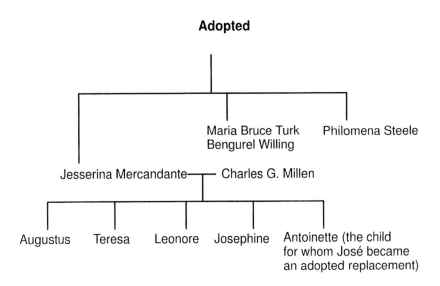

Maria Bruce Turk
Bengurel Willing   Philomena Steele

Jesserina Mercandante ——— Charles G. Millen

Augustus   Teresa   Leonore   Josephine   Antoinette (the child
for whom José became
an adopted replacement)

Preface

I have times when my perception of things becomes so precious to me that I am no longer able to see objectively. What I think ought to be ought to be, and reality be damned. Yes, I know that many people consider reality itself subjective—I went to college—but if I consider that, I will go even further than usual off the track and forget what my point was. I consider digression a kind of art form, if the truth be known. Okay, my point: I began writing this book with very clear preconceptions about how one goes about capturing a person's life story. In my mind was a kind of biographical style-book. (Not everything you learn in college is good.) Thanks to my little internal rulebook, I almost abandoned this project.

I could not figure out why I kept growing bored with my own work. I would sit enthralled for hours listening to Sarria's stories. I would share my own with him, pleased that I could get a delighted response from such a veteran storyteller. I thank my Irish roots. Our time together was just plain fun, but my attempts to chronicle the story formally seemed dry by comparison. I found myself wishing that my future readers could just sit down with me and listen to our sessions and get to know this fascinating man. Suddenly I had a revelation, an epiphany. As my son says when the starkly obvious is overlooked, "Duh!"

I have always loved the oral tradition, and I have always loved stories, telling them and hearing them. I decided to try to capture José's voice and add my own observer's rambling. To do otherwise would be untrue to the nature of our interaction. I set out to piece together the stories with an ear toward capturing José's unique way of speaking. Since stories told informally tend to be self-contained, I used my own voice to provide some transition and context, some-times historically, sometimes in the details of the telling, voice inflection, facial expression, and surrounding events and people. Of course, I tell my own stories as well; try to stop an Irishman from doing that! Sometimes, when José's stories came in bits and pieces over time, I took the liberty of piecing them together and retelling them, always, however, quoting him throughout to preserve his perspective.

Scattered here and there in the chapters you, gentle reader (I write that with tongue firmly planted in cheek. I don't know if you're gentle. You might be the most cantankerous person on the planet—in which case, I want to meet you.) will find occasional brief commentary on some seed of meaning in the stories. I believe that too is a part of the storyteller's trade: ". . . and the moral of the story is." You're free to disagree, of course.

All of this left me with a logistics problem. How does the reader know when it's my voice and when José is telling the story? Well, besides the fact that my part includes all those impressive, big words (Did I mention I went to college?) and grammar more correct than it ever is in my speaking, I have provided a visual clue: any language within quotation marks will be José's words unless otherwise indicated in the text. There, that was easy.

When I felt a particular turn of phrase or slang interfered with the communication of the tale, I altered the wording a bit for clarity, but I tried to retain as many of José's colloquialisms and quirks of speech as I could. Sometimes when a slang word from the gay subcultural dialect popped up, I interjected an explanation for those not familiar with that brand of English. At those times when I felt a need to inject an explanatory comment during José's narrative, I set it off in parentheses.

Although I researched to verify names and dates and other particulars in the stories, I was more interested in José's perceptions than in capturing precise historic detail. I let him go ahead and put his spin on events. Occasionally I would push for consistency or question him for clarity, but never so hard that he lost the magic flow of the story. A good storyteller always takes the facts and, shall we say, embellishes. That is the heart of folk stories, the thing that gives them soul. So read with a cautious mind but a heart of abandon.

The stories of José's life are presented chronologically, although anyone who has ever listened to a grandparent's tales knows that we tend to pick up pieces of the teller's life rather randomly. I have cut and pasted and arranged somewhat to telescope almost four years of interaction. The flowers grew wild, and I arranged them in a vase.

At times in the stories themselves and in the order of presentation, the present intrudes on the past because that is how, I think, we look at our histories. We can never avoid a bit of contemporary overlay on our past memories, nor can we escape our own limited perception. That is okay. The yarns are all the richer for it.

If there is a theme in this book, it was best stated by my son when at thirteen he first met José: "You know Dad, old people know a lot! I like listening to them. It's like a history class, only cooler. Old people rule!"

So grab a cup of coffee or tea, sit back on the deep couch, and hear the gentle voice of a man who is, in some way, a grandfather or father to each of us. Let me introduce you to José Julio Sarria.

Acknowledgments

I once believed that the universe occasionally brought forth an incredible human being, whether writer, political leader, shaman, or artist, who seemed to be able to make magic things happen with no help at all and against all odds. Yet the men and women we call heroes and saints are the first to point out their many unsung supporters and colaborers. Of course, we just call this humility and raise them even higher on that pedestal. We do so hate to abandon our myths. Unfortunately, this particular myth makes the rest of us mortals feel either inadequate or complacent in our usualness.

I have learned that no great work, or dastardly work for that matter, happens without an amazing amount of cooperative effort, starting, of course, with our mothers. (But I'll save that one for another book. . . . I heard that sigh of relief!) All of this is to say that I refuse to take full responsibility for this book. I'd like to introduce you to a few of my coconspirators, whom I refuse to let off the hook.

I'd like to thank my lover Dean and my son McGregor (Mack) for helping to create that safe but slightly lunatic place we call a home. It has been a rich environment in which to work and live and love. (Muchas gracias, El Gringo Loco. Grazie per la canzone, amore mio.)

Carol Reynolds, your transcribing was a lifesaver, but I mostly liked the way we could giggle together over Jose's stories. Thanks, girlfriend.

Cliff, you are the man who first dragged that slightly nervous, just-out-of-the-closet me to my first Coronation at the Court of the Great Northwest Imperial Empire. You are a good man . . . and you look great in heels! Thanks for the memories.

Thanks, Marghe, my tough dyke Italian momma sister and friend, for never wavering in your belief in my writing. Coming from a wordsmith I admire so much, your encouragement is powerful indeed.

Betty, Maxine, and Angie: thanks, girlfriends! You've made my day job a joy. You deserve medals for putting up with this emotional drama queen. You are a truly awesome trio.

Brian Ashby, my brother, thank you for the beautiful images. You're a true artist. Thanks for your part in my meeting José. Thanks also for not making me sleep in the tub when I snored in DC. Who knows the psychic repercussions that would have set off—to say nothing of the fetish possibilities! I never would have gotten this book done!

PART ONE:
WE ARE FAMILY

The Empire Begins

The Empire began silently, though even in its inception it spanned the continent. A letter mailed in San Francisco arrived in New York City in the hands of José Sarria, who was working at the World's Fair. The year was 1964, and José, singer, performer, female impersonator, social and political activist, "the Nightingale of Montgomery Street" according to San Francisco columnist Herb Caen, read the invitation. The Tavern Guild, an association of gay bars since the days of the infamous Black Cat Cafe, had decided to hold a summer ball, and they wanted José to return to the City by the Bay to be the guest of honor. Having been a part of the inception of the guild and having been for years the heart of the Black Cat and much of the city's gay community, José wanted to attend what the organization hoped would be a major social and fundraising event. Unfortunately his work at the fair prevented him from returning that summer. The guild wrote back that they would instead honor José at their Beaux Arts Ball at Halloween, an increasingly popular annual event begun in 1962.

"That night they declared me 'Queen of the Ball,' but they couldn't make me queen; I was always the queen. So I declared myself Empress José the First."

The Royal Court System that evolved around José from that night has been described as a kind of Shriner's Club for drag queens, where funny hats are replaced by fabulous gowns, big hair,

1

and flamboyant makeup. And titles. The system began raising money for various causes and organizations through benefit drag performances. The group that eventually emerged can match records in charity work with the best of community organizations.

It was 1970, and five monarchs had ruled the San Francisco Court since its inception. José, now the Dowager Empress to a lengthening line of successors, as well as dukes, duchesses, czarinas, and assorted Court dignitaries, was growing concerned about the strong-willed independence of the new empress. It had been months since the coronation of Empress Crystal, and despite the council set up to standardize the rules among the growing number of courts, the new monarch seemed all too willing to issue edicts independently. Empress José I saw the need for a gentle assertion of authority over the young court, and the opportunity came with an invitation to the first coronation to be held outside of California, the investiture of the second Empress of Portland.

As a nonprofit organization and as a political, social, and fundraising entity, the Court needed stability and continuity, yet in his characteristic spirit of mischievous campiness, José decided not to confront the errant empress directly, but rather to assert himself in character and in the context of the Court's royal chimera. Always good at a show, José decided not to make the long trip to Portland on the bus chartered by Empress Crystal. That decision alone served as a gentle reproof, but José had more planned. He would not make the trip as a man, but would dress in full empress traveling drag. He went to his close friend Rose Oldstein, costumer for the San Francisco Opera, and borrowed dresses, hats, veils, and traveling dusters from the 1890s. He informed his traveling companions, Lee Ackerman, Henry Vondekoff, Richard Cora, Carl Stafford (aka Lotta Crabs), and Gary McAdery, that they would all be dressed for the trip. Two guards rounded out the entourage, which left early on a cool San Francisco morning in two carriages (cars).

The rest stop on Interstate Highway 5 near the Oregon-California border looked much as it did on any typical day. Cars were parked in the special lot with the long parking spaces and the wide, easy-access driveways in front and behind so truckers could pull in and not have to back up when they left. A few families sat at the picnic tables eating casual lunches. Some drivers stopped only long enough to use the restroom before heading back to the highway. Others stretched their legs walking on the green lawns dotted with young trees or walked their dogs in the designated area. The day was balmy and bright.

Few eyes took notice of the two cars that pulled up alongside the picnic area around noon. The coming and going of strangers is hardly noteworthy at a rest stop. But when the front doors of the lead vehicle opened and two bearded men dressed in Victorian dresses, hats, and traveling coats stepped out, more than a few began to take notice. Ignoring the curious stares, the men lifted their veils, opened the trunk of the car, and began unloading the noon banquet for the Empress. The two guards stepped out and spaced themselves beside the carriages.

The bearded ladies of high position spread a lace tablecloth over a rough, wooden, graffiti-carved picnic table, and then began to set out fine china dinnerware and crystal. Silver utensils rattled musically while the cut goblets refracted the light of the warm California sun. By this time the other travelers were stopping to stare openly, as commoners are wont to do when royalty passes. Containers of fried chicken and potato salad followed the place settings, along with chips and sodas and other assorted picnic foods.

When all was in order, the two bearded duchesses and the royal guards returned to the lead car. A guard opened the door and assisted out of the car what appeared to be a woman of some importance. She stepped out regally, followed by another woman dressed similarly to those who had set the table. Noticing the stares from curious onlookers, the Empress nodded her appreciation and gave a slight wave to her subjects. One of the duchesses escorted the empress across the lawn to the table. The rest of the party followed at a respectful distance. Once the Empress was seated comfortably, the others joined her around the banquet table. By this time the other denizens of the rest area were not as focused on their own affairs as they had been. The party at the table ate as if nothing were amiss, as if, being royalty, they were used to the uninvited ogling of the common folk.

When the noon meal was over, the scene played in reverse. A duchess escorted the Empress to the carriage. The others cleaned up the banquet, packed up the cars, and joined their monarch. The carriages started up and pulled away from the curb, leaving the staring populace of the rest stop wondering what and whom they had just seen.

At every stop they made for the remainder of the trip, Empress José's small band of aristocrats played their parts to the unsuspecting travelers around them. They left a wake of curiosity, consternation, and amusement trailing behind. As it approached the outskirts of the Portland realm, the entourage pulled over and called the Empress of Portland to inform her that the Dowager Empress, Her Most Royal Majesty, José I, Widow to His Royal Majesty Joshua Norton I, Emperor of North America and Protector of Mexico, was approaching the gates of the city and expected an escort worthy of her most royal personage. The Portland Court, recognizing the power and authority of high camp and unabashed but humorous derring-do, immediately fell into the spirit of the charade, meeting José with a great winged Cadillac and a long line of cars as escorts from the appointed freeway exit. The procession of the First Empress became the talk of the Coronation weekend in Portland.

The arrival of Empress Crystal's chartered Greyhound hardly made a ripple. After the events in Portland, her reign in San Francisco took on a much more conciliatory tone. Empress José the First said not a word to reassert her authority. There was no need.

The Cemetery

I first met José Sarria when my friend photographer Brian Ashby and I decided to do an article and photo essay comparing the contemporary drag community with the older, pre-Stonewall drag queens. (Actually, Brian was more of a "sister" than a mere friend. We slept together in Washington, DC—actually slept, although he threatened to banish me to the tub and close the bathroom door because of my snoring.) As we looked for people to interview and photograph, José's name kept coming up. I had seen the PBS documentary *Before Stonewall,* which featured José. My first lover was involved in the Royal Court System and performed in drag, so I was familiar with José's name there as well. In addition, most people familiar with the gay world of female impersonation to whom I mentioned our article idea immediately suggested José.

But how does a relatively obscure journalist from the Sacramento Valley go about contacting and meeting a gay icon living on a hill in San Francisco? I mean, the man's name is in the indexes of the gay history books! I imagined layers of protective friends and business associates demanding to know my mother's maiden name. If I did penetrate the guards (Hmm,) what would I say? "Hello. You don't know me, and I've only been out of the closet for a few years, and you have been a courageous mover and shaker since before I was born, but I really think you should let me come into your home, take your picture, and ask you intimate details of your life." I was a little starstruck.

I took a deep breath and reminded myself that public figures need the media, whatever their personal feelings about the profession. I steeled myself with the knowledge that I did indeed have something to offer a man like José. Other articles of mine had been published nationally, and there was a good chance this one would be, too.

How to find him? In my research for various investigative pieces, I've usually tried to eliminate the obvious possibilities first. It is such an embarrassment to take some elaborate, circuitous route to a nugget of information only to find out you could have called Information. I called Information. They gave me José's home phone number. If I were billing my research by the hour, I'd have been starving so far. I called; José answered. So much for the guards.

"Oh, my dear, of course. It sounds like a wonderful idea."

He then invited me to the cemetery.

*   *   *

"Brian, I got the interview and photo op with José Sarria."

"Great!"

"But we have to meet him at a cemetery first."

"Come again?"

"The cemetery. It's a big memorial service."

"What cemetery? What?"

"I forget. Something with 'memorial' in it."

"Oh, that narrows it down! Sometimes you're such a ditz!"

"Wait, I wrote it down. The Woodlawn Memorial Cemetery. In Colma. It's a memorial ceremony. Apparently, there are lots of cemeteries there."

"Who for?"

"The cemeteries?"

"The memorial service, smartass."

"Some crazy ex-businessman from the Gold Rush period. I'm not sure. But there will be a free Continental Breakfast."

"At the cemetery?"

"Yeah."

"That's twisted!"

"Yeah, I know."

"I like it."

"Me too."

*   *   *

Although the little town of Colma, south of San Francisco, is home to countless cemeteries that accommodate the deceased by the bay, it was relatively easy to find the Woodlawn Memorial Cemetery that day. There were limousines and other cars parked nose to tail in the curved drive, not an unusual state of affairs at a memorial park, but there were also men in black mourning drag contrasting with those in outrageous, campy makeup standing beside musicians in bright red marching uniforms carrying gleaming gold tubas and trumpets and sleek black clarinets. There were leather queens in black chaps and caps and leather dykes leaning against their shiny black and chrome motorcycles. There were bright rainbow-colored gay pride flags fluttering above the crowd and on automobile aerials, as well as frozen in bumper and window stickers. There was a minister in flowing lavender robes. There was a colorguard dressed in black leather carrying the gay pride flag along with the flags of Mexico, the United States, and California. And in the midst of all of this seeming pandemonium was a short but substantial woman in a huge black mourning dress over crinoline petticoats from the turn of the century, complete with elaborate black hat and veils, black elbow-length gloves, and oh-so-tasteful jewelry. We surmised that this was José.

We were unable to approach José initially, given that he was surrounded with people asking last-minute questions about the ceremony. Being good and responsible journalists, we went for the food. Pleased to host such an auspicious yearly event, the management of the cemetery took pains to create an enviable continental breakfast for the mourners. Several long tables held miniature mountain ranges of grapes and apples, cantaloupes, croissants, sweet rolls, and sandwiches. Pretty young men in smart white coats served coffee and juice. They smiled in polite deference and barely suppressed amusement, seeming to enjoy this job immensely. The crowd was friendly and the conversation easy.

Eventually, we were able to work our way into the throng and introduce ourselves. José reacted as if he were meeting long-lost friends, a reaction that I subsequently learned is common for him; he sincerely likes people and loves meeting new ones. We made arrangements to talk after the ceremony and the brunch to follow at a leather bar where the principals were meeting afterward.

Shortly following our brief encounter, the procession began. The San Francisco Lesbian and Gay Freedom Marching Band fell into its formation and struck up a rousing "San Francisco, Open Your Golden Gates." The drum major and the baton twirlers led the way through the stone archway and into the cemetery. Curious visitors stopped to stare as the parade proceeded up the hill toward the grave of Emperor Joshua Norton.

Joshua Norton was a prominent merchant in San Francisco at the time of the Gold Rush. In the midst of his success, he suddenly lost everything. Some say it was a love of gambling that stripped him of his wealth. Others say it was simply bad business decisions born of overconfidence. After his devastating losses, Joshua disappeared for a time. One version of the story says that he went out to the gold fields to try to recoup his losses. In any case, Joshua disappeared for a number of years.

Norton showed up again in San Francisco after his mysterious absence, but his cart was obviously a few bricks shy of a load. Wherever he had gone, he had left a piece of his mind behind. Soon after his reemergence in the City by the Bay, he marched into the office of the *Bulletin* newspaper wearing a feathered top hat and a blue military-style tailcoat and declared himself "Joshua Norton the First, Emperor of North America and Protector of Mexico!"

Now in most cities in the world, Joshua's declaration would have ended up as an amusing footnote to a dreary workday, followed by a call to the police to have the crazy coot removed from the place of business he had interrupted. But this was San Francisco. Amused editors and writers treated Joshua with all the deference due an emperor, and then they ran the story of his declaration of rule. The novelty of having an emperor in San Francisco caught on with the citizens, and for the rest of his life, Joshua was treated as the ruling sovereign in all social matters. Restaurants served him free meals. The Board of Supervisors appropriated funds each year for his clothing. Children would flock to him on the streets, largely because of his tendency to duck into candy shops and order "his good subject" to give a piece of candy to each of the young ones.

Ironically, it was San Francisco's crazy emperor who first suggested a bridge across the bay between San Francisco and Oakland. In fact, he decreed that one be built. Perhaps for fear of unwanted consequences of the bridge building, he also decreed that Oakland must always stay on the east side of the bay.

Following his death soon after the turn of the century, Joshua's story began to fade. He would occasionally show up as a brief historic anecdote in guidebooks and articles on the history of the city. His grave at the Woodlawn Memorial Cemetery had only a small marker with his name, and even that fell into disrepair. Joshua rested in relative obscurity until the mid-1960s, when José Sarria was busy founding the Court System. He had already been declared Empress by the Tavern Guild during a fundraising ball. (They had tried to declare him Queen of the Ball, but he said he was already a queen and they'd have to do better than that.) To the new title, the ever-clever and campy José added, "Her Royal Majesty, Empress José the First, the Widow Norton." In the slightly off-kilter world of bohemian San Francisco, José thus legitimized his claim to the title Empress. He was, after all, the loving widow of the Emperor.

José soon began holding an annual memorial service for his dear departed husband Joshua out at the cemetery in Colma. It became an occasion for fun and frolic with a satiric edge. The mourners mixed campy humor with a biting yearly assessment of the state of gay lives and civil rights. It was both cathartic and entertaining, serious and lighthearted, political and social, much like drag itself. The Woodlawn Memorial Cemetery was so pleased that José was keeping alive the legend of Emperor Norton that they erected a new marker over the grave, a handsome marble obelisk declaring the plot to be the final resting place of Emperor Joshua Norton I, Emperor of North America and Protector of Mexico.

When the AIDS epidemic began to devastate the ranks of the Imperial Court's family in the early 1980s, the annual ceremony took on the added pathos of a memorial for and celebration of those who had succumbed to the disease. They were José's children, his family, his fellow monarchs. Honoring them there was an appropriate tribute to Joshua Norton, the crazy outcast transformed into beloved royalty.

On the day we attended the memorial service, chairs had been arranged at the grave site, and the band positioned itself off to one side as the royal family took its seats. As the band finished, the Lesbian/Gay Chorus of San Francisco stepped forward to sing, introduced, of course, by the Dowager Empress José.

As the voices of the chorus faded, José introduced the Court's official chaplain, the Reverend Charles Lewis. The reverend's invocation and tribute to Emperor Joshua Norton was a rollicking mixture of biting satire, sincere compassion, insightful commentary, and outrageous humor. More conservative ministers would no doubt have blushed.

After the song, the Widow Norton continued with introductions and expressions of gratitude. All of José's descriptions of personalities and introductions were filled with wild exaggerations and overblown praise. The titles came fast and furious. It was like the flattery of the Academy Awards times ten. A keyboardist punctuated many of his statements with humorous scraps of songs and musical exclamations.

After several more musical pieces by solo artists, José presented special rings to the retiring monarchs of the previous year. He then made official the elevation of the new year's emperor and empress.

A line of seven handsome men dressed in "leather drag" (black leather vests or chest harnesses, chaps, pants, hats, and boots, usually accompanied by mustaches, beards, or goatees) raised rifles to their shoulders. Three times they fired heart-vibrating volleys above the heads of the crowd in a twenty-one-gun salute to the monarchs.

As the men marched off to the side, the Vestal Virgins, a group of eight men dressed in flowing white, gossamer gowns with flowers in their hair, took positions center grave site. José made a comment about the difficulty of finding eight virgins in that crowd. Various members of the crowd expressed doubt about the authenticity of the claims of purity. The virgins began a circular dance and a less-than-pure song parodying the Widow Norton and her children. Once done, they floated off cemetery right.

At that point, the current empress stepped forward in full drag and very high heels, carrying the urn of ashes from one of the past empresses, Empress Sissy Spaceout, who had died of AIDS. She had left very specific instructions for the scattering of her ashes. The current empress opened the urn next to the gravestone of Emperor Norton. As the keyboardist began playing an airy rendition of "The Dance of the Sugar Plum Fairy" from *The Nutcracker Suite* by Tchaikovsky (a trés gay composer, by the way), she began a kind of sweeping dance around the gravestone, scattering the ashes. The remains had been mixed with glitter, so as the ashes floated in the air, the sun created a rainbow of sparkles. It was a funny, sad, wonderful moment such as only gay boys in dresses can deliver. We smiled and giggled through our tears, the water in our eyes reflecting the clear coastal sunshine and matching the shimmering of the ashes.

After another song from the chorus, the trumpeter played taps, and José led the crowd back down the hill.

I never quite felt like I had really come back down the hill completely after that day. That ceremony was the beginning of a brand new character in my life. As always when something touches me profoundly, I had to write. I had to write about José. Little did I know how much.

The Disturbance

"My mother used to sit on her stool and darn, and she would tell me about when she was a young girl in Colombia. It was so fascinating! She would always end her stories by saying, 'One day you will go to Colombia and see where I was a little girl.'"

José fulfilled his mother's prediction in 1972 when he made a kind of pilgrimage to Colombia to learn what he could about his forebears and their lives in that northwest corner of South America.

When José talked about his family history, I felt myself transported to a time and a culture that I found exotic and enigmatic. Except for a few vague but proud references to Spanish aristocrats long ago, José's knowledge of his family begins during a revolutionary uprising at the turn of the twentieth century. I have never experienced war firsthand (I turned eighteen soon after the Vietnam draft had ended), much less a civil war in my own country. José's deep sense of cultural and familial pride gave him a special emotional tie to relatives he never met and their troubled times, and sometimes as he talked it almost seemed as if he had been there in Colombia during those turbulent years of social upheaval. José speaks with pride about his Spanish aristocratic heritage, and yet his family belonged to the more liberal political faction in Colombia that wanted to minimize ties with Spain and its governmental and religious institutions. This seeming conflict in José's paradoxical reverence for both his aristocratic roots and his heritage of revolutionary defiance reflects the discord that plagued Colombia from the time the Europeans first stumbled upon it.

Soon after Columbus's fourth voyage to the Americas in 1502-1504, during which he sailed along the coast of what is now Colombia, Spain established settlements in Panama. From there the Spaniards explored the Colombian territory. Eventually New Granada was established as a colony, with Bogotá as its capital. The colony included the area that is now Colombia, Ecuador, Venezuela, and Panama. In 1819, Simón Bolívar led a revolution that defeated the royalists, and a new congress established the Republic of Gran Colombia. Bogotá remained the capital. Internal conflicts between liberals (who supported religious tolerance, public education, acceptance of the native peoples, and an end to slavery) and the conservatives (who advocated a strong central government and loyalty to the Catholic Church) led to the secession of Venezuela in 1829 and Ecuador in 1830. In Gran Colombia, two parties emerged: the Liberal Party and the Conservative Party. Most of the century was marked by repeated civil war between the two factions.

Between 1884 and 1886, the Liberals were defeated in a bloody civil conflict by a new coalition of Conservatives and centrist Liberals called the Nationalist Party. The victors established a constitution that created a very centralized, authoritarian government for what was now called the Republic of Colombia. The Liberals continued to try to overthrow the new regime. The bloodiest of these revolts happened between 1899 and 1902, and is the conflict José calls "the revolution," and which many of the people he talked to on his trip to Colombia in 1972 called "the Disturbance of 1,000 Days." It served as the backdrop for his family's story.

"My mother was born on a street named La Calle San Marcos in the capital, Bogotá. She was born in the house where my grandparents lived. The street is now called 13th Street. I went to Colombia in 1972, after my mother had died. I retraced everything I could. During the revolution, a lot of things were destroyed, old records. The hall of records in Bogotá was burned. After the revolution, the streets were given numbers instead of names. That made the search difficult. A lot of the places nobody could remember. Some old records of that time in Colombia are held by the church. One of the only people I could find who could talk about that time was one priest who was in his seventies or eighties, an historian who kept records of the street names and the locations of important buildings. He knew many stories from Colombia's history. He told me how Simón Bolívar, at seventy, was supposed to have jumped out of the window onto his horse as people were coming to his rescue. Crazy things like that this priest knew. He helped me find where my mother's house had been. There is another building there now."

José's mother, Maria Dolores, was the second born of Concepción Chaparo Maldonado and Ciebio Maldonado. Their firstborn was a son, Rudicino. After Maria came two more daughters, Eltevina and Anna Rosa. Concepción, always the matriarch of the family, ran a business in Bogotá. The family owned a coffee plantation near Buenos Aires as well. José jokes that the area is now a cocaine growing district, and that maybe his grandfather was a pioneer in that business.

"No, I'm joking. Actually I remember just before the Depression my mother would receive a big sack of coffee beans, and my godmother (the woman for whom José's mother worked) would take it down to the Piggly Wiggly store and get it ground. The beans were from relatives in Colombia. It's still my favorite coffee."

José's grandfather, Ciebio, developed a debilitating sickness in Bogotá, and the family, hoping for a healthier environment, moved to the small, rural town of Utica, sixty miles northwest of Bogotá. José's mother described a large house that took up an entire block and was surrounded by a wall and trees. He found it during his 1972 trip.

"The house in Utica was exactly as my mother said. It was a block long with a fence around it and beautiful trees. I didn't ask to go inside. I should have, but I didn't."

For a short time the family lived in relative peace and happiness in the house in Utica, but the calm was soon to end, and the Maldonadoes would never again be together as a family. Eltevina, the third child of Ciebio and Concepción, died of a childhood disease soon after the move to Utica. Ciebio himself died soon after. It was following his death that the bloodiest of the Liberal uprisings took place. The conflict ultimately split the family as it did the country.

"Down there they don't call it a revolution. They call it 'The Disturbance of 1000 Days.' When I asked people in Colombia about the Revolution, they would say there was no Revolution; there was a disturbance. And they were so serious about it. It was like the 'police action' in Vietnam. Yet it was a revolution by the true definition of the word. The president came out of the palace, and they chopped him up into pieces, and they fought all over the countryside, but it was just a 'disturbance.'"

After the death of her husband, Concepción tried her best to protect what remained of her family. She was a strong woman, and a politically savvy one as well. Her efforts in support of her family and her liberal beliefs gained her the respect of most of her neighbors, as well as many in the forces fighting the government. Yet despite her determination to preserve the well-being of her brood, tragedy struck again soon after the uprising began. Her daughter Anna Rosa went walking by a lake one cool morning, slipped on the lush grasses by the bank, and fell in. She drowned.

After the death of Anna Rosa, Concepción's determination to save her two remaining children from the cruel whims of fate strengthened into a stubborn resolve.

"Now my grandmother, Concepción Chaparo, was well known to all the good people of Colombia. She was a real political activist. I think that's where I got it from. They knew that she was not on the government's side in the fighting. My family were very progressive people. At the time of the uprising, my mother's brother Rudicino was around fifteen or sixteen, and my mother was younger. Concepción believed that one day the country would be in good hands, that the liberal reformers would win, so she took risks to keep her son around to protect her and her remaining daughter Maria Dolores rather than let the government draft him into its army.

"To keep the government agents from finding him, she would hide him out in the fields. One time while he was out there hiding, he snagged his leg on a cactus, and it got infected. The doctors almost had to cut off his leg. My grandmother kept him home and nursed him. Home medicine cured him. He didn't lose his leg, but he was left crippled. He walked with a limp after that. He had to walk with a cane."

Concepción managed to keep her small family intact as the war raged, but she was growing old, and feared that she would not be alive long enough to personally ensure her children's safety. She worried most about her daughter Maria. Not one to let even death thwart her intent, she devised a contingency plan involving her brother Nemesio, who was off somewhere fighting with the Liberal antigovernment forces.

When José traveled to Colombia in search of his roots in 1972, he petitioned the National Department of Defense Secretary of the Archives for information about his mother's brother, Nemesio Chaparo Ramirez, a sublieutenant in the Liberal forces.

"You see, my mother told me the story of Nemesio. It is important because it is how my mother got out of the country. My great uncle Nemesio was part of the revolution. My grandmother Concepción told my mother that if anything should happen to her, my mother should locate her Uncle Nemesio, and he would help her.

"This one morning my grandmother got up and said, "Dolores, I am not feeling well. Would you fix my breakfast for me and call me when it's ready?

"So my mother made the breakfast, but when she called her mother to breakfast, her mother said, 'Oh, I don't feel like eating. I think I'm going to die. Go and get your brother and bring him here.'

"My mother went and got my uncle Rudicino and brought him in to Concepción. She gave them her instructions: 'You must pay attention. Now there's only two of you left. When I am gone, you must divide everything, and Maria Dolores, you must leave Colombia. For you to stay here would be very bad. You have to go to General Uribe, who is leading the forces here, and you must tell him that you are the daughter of la Doña Concepción, and that you place yourself in his care. He is a very close friend of mine. He'll take care of you so that nothing will happen to you. He will help you find your uncle Nemesio. You must divide everything between you and your brother: the chest with the money, the jewels, the land. You divide everything. Rudicino, you take the land, because you are strong. You are a man. You can farm the land. Dolores, you take the jewels and the money. You are a woman.'"

Concepción died that very day.

Because she had no coffin, and none were available due to the war, Maria Dolores was forced to prepare her mother's body and lay it out on a table in the parlor. She then promptly did what her mother had asked her to do. She went into the surrounding countryside and sought out the general. She approached the stern military leader and announced, "Doña Concepción has died. I am her daughter. She told me to find you."

The general reacted with sadness over the news and with tenderness toward the daughter of his good friend. He spoke of Concepción's help in housing and feeding his men when they fought in the area near her home. When Maria told him about having to lay her mother's body out without a coffin, the general immediately ordered his men to procure one of the coffins prepared for his men. He arranged for the delivery of the coffin to the house, and when it came time for her burial, he arranged a military escort and a horse-drawn wagon. He paid for her plot in the town cemetery.

Nearly seventy years later, José visited the cemetery in Utica.

"I found the cemetery where my grandmother was buried, but I couldn't find her grave. Years after she was buried they redid the entrance to the cemetery, which happened to be almost on top of her grave. They moved the gate over her grave. So she's hidden by the gate. She's probably right under that damn archway! Otherwise, I would have found her grave. But she's there; I did find records in the church.

"The priest who showed me the records had a girlfriend. See, the priests down there did not practice the priesthood the way they do here. The priests down there had girlfriends who lived with them. They were not celibate like they are here. And this one was more uncelibate with each visit. He lived off the fat of the land, and the church looked the other way. There are thousands of them like that."

After the funeral, Rudicino and Maria split the family holdings as their mother had instructed. Rudicino inherited the properties, but he did not remain in Utica. José was able to trace his uncle's fate on his trip to Colombia, even finding someone who had known Rudicino.

"When I went to Colombia, I was able to find out about my mother's brother, my uncle, because of his limp. I would ask people if they knew about Rudicino Maldonado, but I did not tell them about the limp. Of course everybody wanted to be related to me because I was an American. Many many people claimed to know Rudicino. Some said they were related to him. I said, 'Could you describe him?'

"And they would say, 'Oh yes, we knew him very well!' And then they would describe him. But none of them would mention the limp. So when people would come to me and say that they were related to me, and say that my uncle was five foot two with eyes of blue, I knew they were not relatives.

"One woman in the town said, 'If he is the same person that I am thinking of, there was a young girl here in Utica, who later became a madam, and he was very partial to her. And she still lives. She is a very old woman now. She will tell you about him.'

"She told me where the old woman lived, out by the river, El Rio Negra. I went down there. There I found this older woman, but you could tell that in her prime she had been very pretty. I asked her if she knew Rudicino. And she said, 'Yes. You know, he was hidden in the cactus, and he had his leg damaged.'

"I knew that she knew him.

"She told me that he had married and that he and his wife had gone to San Marcos, the Riviera of Colombia, with his son, his daughter, and his son-in-law. They were massacred there by government soldiers."

The Liberal uprising that had served as such a catalyst for the rending changes in the Maldonado family ended in defeat for the Liberal Party. The conservative Nationalist Party remained in control of Colombia until 1930. In the years after the uprising of 1899-1902, many of the party's enemies were executed. José's uncle was among them.

"In my big hunt for information about my uncle, I really stirred up a lot of people. One of them was a columnist at the paper *La Prinsa*. He was very interested in trying to help me. He ran ads, and he found that in San Marcos on a certain date, there was a massacre. My family had land like the Conservatives, but they wanted a free democracy. They were Liberals. They wanted change, and the government was out to get their ass. Anyway, the journalist found that there were pictures of the family before they were hatcheted to death.

"There was a book that included those photographs which was published at the time. We tried to get it, but we couldn't find it. He advertised for it. Some people who lived in the mountains had a copy. They said they were related to me, but they probably weren't. They told me my uncle and his wife and my first cousins were massacred, but my cousins' children survived. I contracted an infection there and got very sick."

Unlike her brother, Maria Dolores survived the political upheaval at the turn of the century. The decision by Concepción to send her daughter to General Uribe proved to be a wise one. After the funeral, the general took Maria into his protection. He searched the troops and located her uncle Nemesio, who in turn took his niece to the American Consulate. Given Maria's difficult position in her native country, the American officials agreed to accept her as a ward of the American government. Using the connections he had through his family, Uncle Nemesio found Maria Dolores a position in Panama working for a German family.

There was a precarious political dance going on at the turn of the century between the United States, Panama, and Colombia. In 1903 Colombian negotiators agreed to give the United States a ninety-nine year lease on a ribbon of land across the Isthmus of Panama. The United States intended to build and administer a canal across the narrow piece of land in order to connect the Atlantic ocean with the Pacific and avoid the treacherous shipping lane around Cape Horn at the southern tip of South American. When it came time for the Congress of Colombia to ratify the canal treaty, it refused to do so.

Washington became angry. Business interests in Panama feared that the loss of the canal would be a severe financial blow to Panama. With the support of the United States, a small group of revolutionaries declared Panama's independence from Colombia on November 3, 1903, only ten months after the failed treaty between Colombia and the United States. The U.S. military blocked any armed response from Colombia's government, and the American government officially recognized The Republic of Panama on November 6, 1903. At the end of the month, Panama signed a treaty with the United States in which the United States promised to guard Panama's newly declared freedom, and in return, Panama offered the same canal deal that the United States had sought with Colombia. It was truly one of history's shortest struggles for independence.

Following Panama's break from Colombia, the relationship between the United States and Colombia remained cool until the return of Colombia's Liberal Party to power in 1930. The liberal revolution that José speaks of finally succeeded almost three decades after the bloody civil disturbance. But even before the return of the Colombian Liberals, the newly independent Panama became a safe haven for a young woman forced to leave her native land because her family was on the wrong side of a century-old political conflict.

"My mother got to Panama with directions to the home of a family named Kopp. He was the chairman of the big German beer company there. They were very wealthy. She went to work for the

Kopps. I have a picture of her with the kids upstairs. The woman had a household full of servants, ten or fifteen of them: a cook with a kitchen staff, food servers, maids, a servant who did the laundry, nannies for the children. My mother was the upstairs maid, and she took care of the children. She did all of the ironing. Mrs. Kopp was a very good woman, I understand. My mother said that when the traveling music companies, like the Merry Widow, came to play she would buy them all tickets, and they would get dressed up and go down to the opera house to see the musical productions from Europe.

"In Panama my mother's health suffered. She was having terrible headaches. She would collapse at the ironing board. Mrs. Kopp sent her to several doctors who suggested ocean air. Mrs. Kopp helped her to travel for short periods looking for a place to move that would be better for her health. She returned for a time to Colombia, first to the seaside town of Buenaventura. It was there that doctors first suggested that she cut her hair. The weight, they said, caused the headaches. She refused. She tried other seaports in Colombia, looking for sea air that would cure her headaches as the doctors suggested. No place solved her problem. She would always return to Panama and the Kopps. My mother made very good money there. Once the Kopp family had some problems, and my mother lent them 30,000 pesos, which was quite a bit of money."

Maria Dolores was happy working for the Kopps, but fate had other plans for the young Colombian woman. Those plans entered her life in the person of the proprietress of a house of ill repute.

"While she was in Panama, my mother became friends with a madam who had one of the biggest establishments in Panama."

("A restaurant?" I asked. José chuckled and continued his story.)

"Her name I can't remember, but my mother became very good friends with her. On my mother's days off, she used to go and visit the woman and spend the day with her. Edwina, I think, was her name. She was the mistress of the chief of the electrical installations for the canal. Goforth was his name. He was an electrical engineer, and he was putting it in."

(José smiled sheepishly and glanced at me to see if I had caught his intended double entendre. I had.)

"My mother used to go and visit the madam, and she met Goforth there. They would talk, and he would leave my mother his laundry. She would take the clothes and darn them and wash them and then bring them back. Meanwhile, the mistress took care of other needs.

"Sometimes when he would come to the house, he would be drunk, you see, and he had a lot of money on him. So that he wouldn't be rolled later, Edwina would take all of his money away, and she banked it over the years.

"Now, during the work on the canal, lots of the workers found jewels in the diggings. One of those workers, an Indian, found an emerald of fair size, and he gave it to Goforth. Goforth had two rings made out of it. When his tour in Panama was all done, and he was getting ready for his next post, Edwina gave a dinner party, and that's when he gave her one of the emerald rings and then gave the other to my mother. He said, 'These are thank you notes—one for my wife in the daytime (my mother) and one for my wife in the nighttime.'

"I still have the ring he gave my mother. I would say it's a good carat."

According to José, Edwina had her own surprise to spring at that fateful and fortuitous dinner party in Panama. She strode over to a locked drawer, opened it, and withdrew a thin booklet. Smiling conspiratorially, delighted with herself, she walked coyly toward her engineer lover, who had a drink in his hand. She handed him the mysterious book. It was a bankbook. Goforth opened it and read the record of thousands of pesos saved in his name. He looked up, confused, and to the delight of the assembled guests, Edwina explained her benevolent subterfuge.

Raising his drink, Goforth announced that any woman who loved him enough to take such good care of him, even when he didn't know it, deserved to be his wife. He proposed on the spot.

In short order, the American engineer married his frugal mistress.

Goforth's next assignment was to install electricity in Guatemala City. The new couple, expecting to need the help, and hoping to soon start a family, asked Maria Dolores to come with them to their new post. She agreed, anticipating that the weather farther north might be better for her health. The logistics of her move would be easy since she was a ward of the United States. She contacted her brother Rudicino and made the final arrangements for the division of the family estate in accordance with their mother's wishes. With her ties thus severed, and with an inheritance of jewels and cash added to her own savings, she left with her new employers. However, according to José, she did not go as a submissive servant. On the first day of her stay in Guatemala City, her family's flair for defying convention surfaced in the surviving daughter.

"Now when they arrived, they were shown the house they would live in by the 'alma de casa,' the general manager of the house. She commanded the roost. My mother said that she welcomed Mr. and Mrs. Goforth and showed them their rooms. Then she showed my mother her bedroom, which was right off the child's room. There was no bed—just a mat. My mother asked, 'So where is my bed?'

"The woman looked surprised and said, 'Servants don't have beds. In Guatemala the help sleep on the floor.'

"My mother turned to her and said, 'That may be the law of the land in *your* land, but where I come from human beings sleep in beds! Even the poor have beds, and I want a bed.' The woman looked at my mother sternly. My mother looked back proudly and said, 'I will speak with the Señora, and you will find that I will have a bed and a chair.'

"It was that way in Guatemala at that time. You either sat at a table, or you served people. There was rich and poor. My mother did not like living in a society with no middle class. Today it's different.

"My mother stayed there in Guatemala until Mr. Goforth's job was done. They only stayed there for six months. It was 1920."

Goforth's next professional stop was Washington, DC. Because he viewed Maria Dolores as an employee and not a servant, yet recognizing that he could not leave her to her own devices in a new country, he gave her a choice of destinations and offered to help her resettle in the United States. If she wished, she could have gone with the couple to Washington. He also suggested New York City, San Francisco, or New Orleans. In José's words, his mother weighed the options by saying, "San Francisco was not too far away and had a nice large colony of Latins, whereas in New Orleans were the French, and New York was too big with too many Puerto Ricans."

When José recounted his mother's reasoning about the resettlement plans, I remember thinking, "José, that is so *not* politically correct!" Though he makes these types of comments now with a touch of self-deprecating humor, and even teasing affection for the group he is seemingly pigeonholing, the remarks echo his early years and his family's perceptions. His people were very proud of their Spanish heritage and spoke the Castilian dialect of the upper classes. They made clear cultural distinctions, as does José now, although they treated everyone well. José is not Hispanic, and he is not Mexican; he is "of Spanish Colombian descent." He is not a drag queen; he is a female impersonator. He is not a queen; he is the Grand Empress.

José's cultural pride is evident, even through his satiric, sometimes profane, always campy demeanor. Yet he remains always a man of the people, loving them all, the little people, in his quirky, tongue-in-cheek, humorous, uncompromising way. And even in his sometimes paradoxical way.

José's mother, Maria Dolores Maldonado, sailed to San Francisco at the dawn of the Roaring Twenties on a ship called, perhaps prophetically, the *San José*. It was on the *San José* that she met a handsome young man who would become her son's father. The ship sailed into the waters of San Francisco Bay through the narrow opening not yet gated with the magnificent bridge that would, years later, capture the imaginations of people across the world. At the foot of the hills upon which the city stirred and bustled, the ship came to port and docked, discharging its passengers to begin their individual adventures in that most unique of cities. Not long after Maria stepped ashore, the *San José* returned to the waters of the bay—and sank.

For Unto You Is Born This Day
in the City of San Francisco

I remember the houses of my New Jersey aunts when I was growing up. For a curious little kid like me, they were wonderful places. They smelled of old furniture, aging wood, stale perfume, and the salty ocean air of Atlantic City, and every shelf and mantle had brightly colored knickknacks, browning post cards, framed black and white or tinted photographs, and a thousand other mementos of a long life remembered in moments. Being the youngest of seven children in a large Irish Catholic family, I had aunts, lots of them, who were the age of the grandparents of most of my friends. They still had antimacassars on the chairs when most people I knew didn't even know what antimacassars were. And they all had very big hair, many of them redheaded, and very brassy voices.

I thought of my aunts the first time I visited José's apartment in San Francisco. His place was like theirs, filled with old-fashioned beauty and comfortable clutter, except that in the *casa de José* there was also a subtle touch of old-world elegance mixed with a genuine gay sensibility of camp and humorous irreverence. But for the touches of the profane (one of his saint statues is actually a dildo) his could be the home of a transplanted European matriarch. He was, in fact, the first of his family to be born in the United States.

"Now on the boat coming to this country is where my mother met my father, Julio Sarria. He came from a very large, wealthy family, very well known. He was the youngest of seven children. His father was Benito Sarria and his mother was Alejandra Sarria. His grandparents came from Spain. I would like to do more research on my family. It seems I might have a relative who was a president of Nicaragua; he would be my second cousin."

The cuckoo clock went off as José spoke, somehow striking me as appropriate punctuation to the crazy, serious, fascinating world about which I was learning.

Maria Dolores Maldonado's former employer, Mr. Goforth, and the American authorities arranged for a family in San Francisco to sponsor her into the country, promising her a job and a place to stay. There she became known as Dolores, the name José uses when speaking of her.

"My mother, Dolores Maldonado, arrived here with one trunk. She did not speak English. She had money, and she came with jewelry. She had nowhere else to put it, so she kept it in the trunk.

"When she arrived in San Francisco, she went to the home of the woman who had sponsored her into the country. In return for her passage, my mother had to work for the woman for a year. She had her home on Clay Street between Franklin and Van Ness Avenue. Today, there are modern apartments there. My mother worked for her, although the woman was not very nice, and my mother was not happy there. She was given a job as the upstairs maid. This woman was evil and wanted to get her help cheap. She was a bitch. My mother didn't trust her. I have a picture of my mother and my dad in front of the stairway of the house.

"The company that used to deliver the milk was the Maron Dairy Company. One of the daughters of the Maron family married into the Pisanis, an Italian family, who had the Bonita Market, a big produce market. It was located at Filmore and California streets. And the dairy was next door to it. It is now the Goodwill. The milkman, Mr. Frank Maron, liked my mother very, very much. Evidently my mother was a flaming beauty. He would come and give her extra goodies; I think there was a little bit of something more that went with the cream between Mr. Maron and my mother! He was very, very nice to her.

"Another of the Maron daughters, Frank's sister, married George O'Brien, who was a police officer who later became assistant chief of police with the city of San Francisco. They were Irish girls. The daughter of the sister who married into the Pisani family married Camberi, who was sheriff here for so long. Camberi's wife and I used to play together as children. They owned a lot of property in the Filmore area, which was a very nice area in the twenties. It was his bar we bought and ran as the Magic Garden out on the Haight. It used to be called Emerald Isle. It's up from Stanyan Street. Its a bar —just a bar."

The milkman came to see Dolores quite often, while at the same time the man who was to become José's father was courting her. Julio Sarria was the maitre d' at the Palace Hotel, and he was a bit of a dandy. He came from old money and considered himself a member of the higher class despite his service job. His clothes were always fashionable, and his grooming was impeccable. He knew the woman for whom Dolores worked, and agreed with her reputation as a difficult woman. Yet with his charm and verbal dexterity, he never faced opposition to his visits.

With learning her way around her new city and learning the new language, as well as balancing the attentions of two handsome men, Dolores found her first year passing mercifully fast. Frank Maron knew of her unhappiness in her position at the house on Clay Street, so as her year-long obligation drew to a close, he began searching for another position for her.

"When my mother was finally allowed to leave that first job, Mr. Maron found her a job with the Jost family. Mr. Jost was the chief interpreter for the Superior Court of the State of California. The Jost brothers came from Costa Rica, where they were accused of selling millions of dollars worth of oil rights that never existed, phony-baloney oil rights on the beach. The scandal brought them to this country. Mr. Jost was a very brilliant man who spoke sixteen or twenty languages. A brilliant man. They lived on Washington Street in a very, very elegant house. The house is still there. He had a lovely family. He married a very well-to-do woman and had three daughters. He also raised his niece.

"Mrs. Jost's sister became a famous singer and actress on the French stage in the twenties, and she had a daughter that was born deaf and dumb. Jost's sister died a very, very bad death, and the father, who was a drunk, did not want to raise the child, so Mrs. Jost took her and raised her as her own. The little girl was called La Mudita, the little mute, because she couldn't speak. My mother was hired to care for this little girl and to be the upstairs maid."

Dolores knew very little of the financial workings of the American system, and she worried about her financial security. Her health problems continued to plague her in San Francisco, and she wanted to know that she would have the resources to survive if she became unable to work. She turned to her new employer, Mr. Jost, for help.

He convinced her to take her money out of the trunk and put it in a bank. He offered to invest her money for her and act as her advisor in all things financial. She agreed, turning over her cash and what gold she had to the man. She also recommended Mr. Jost to others who came to her for financial advice.

Typical of her family's activist leanings, Dolores became involved in San Francisco's Latino community almost immediately upon her arrival in the city. She particularly enjoyed working with young women, helping them find jobs, providing support when they became pregnant out of wedlock, and accepting the money they wished to set aside for the care of their children should anything happen to them. Dolores would turn that money over to Mr. Jost to invest as he had invested hers.

The time Dolores spent at the Jost house was pleasant for her. She genuinely liked her employers, and though the work was rigorous and her health still precarious, she felt safer and more comfortable than she had in many years. She even made a close friend within the household, Nanita Santos.

Both Mr. and Mrs. Jost's families could trace their genealogies back to the early settlers who came from Spain and established themselves in Costa Rica. The families had brought indentured servants with them to the Americas, and they continued to have such servants while in the new world. The last remaining one of these was Nanita Santos, who had been wet nurse to Mrs. Jost and whom the Josts had brought with them to San Francisco when they fled their native country.

Nanita Santos was the child of a tribe of people indigenous to Costa Rica, and three generations of her family had been indentured servants to the Spanish families who settled in her country. She was almost ninety years old when Dolores came to live and work in the Jost household, yet she continued to work, cooking and caring for the children. Her sternly proud demeanor belied her physical stature; she was four feet tall. As José put it, "She was the only one who could stand up and tell the Josts what to do and where to go. She knew where all the skeletons were buried. Her name meant 'saint child.' My mother remembers her wearing long dresses and a Pershing Campaign hat that she dearly loved."

Dolores spent her work days cleaning and ironing upstairs and caring for the deaf niece. She worked to teach the girl how to speak, as was the accepted custom at that time, consulting often with Nanita Santos in order to draw from the woman's long experience with children.

Julio Sarria continued to see Dolores when she moved to the Jost house. In her eyes he was sophisticated and playful and immensely charming, with a disarming smile. He was handsome, he had money to spend, and he came from a good family with a highborn history like her own. She found herself falling in love, and he seemed to return the feelings. She fell deeper and deeper under his spell as the months passed. After a time of passionate courting, she began to feel changes in her moods and in her body that could not be explained by the excitement of her infatuation. She was pregnant.

When she announced her condition to the family, Mrs. Jost shared news of her own. She too was going to have a child.

As the women's pregnancies progressed, Nanita Santos began to grumble about Mrs. Jost having given birth to too many girls. Three was quite enough of that gender as far as the old nursemaid was concerned. She informed the lady of the house that it was high time she had a son. Nanita had already raised Mrs. Jost, her three daughters, and her niece. She had never raised a boy.

As the pregnancies neared their ends, Nanita walked purposefully up to Mrs. Jost, almost eye to eye, though Mrs. Jost was seated. She shook her thin, wrinkled finger at the woman who once nursed at her breast and said, "You've already had three girls. I want you to have a boy before I die. If you have another girl, you will take care of it by yourself, because I will not. I have raised all the girls I am going to raise."

Both Mrs. Jost and Dolores were taken on the same day to St. Francis Hospital, the choice of many of the society women in the city at that time. They had their babies within hours of each other. Nanita came to the hospital when the women were relaxing with their newborns. Dolores was pale and weak from the ordeal of birth. Mrs. Jost had come through the event with a stronger constitution and was looking well. Nanita strode to her employer and lifted the swaddling sheets to peer at the child's genitals. She lowered the white cloth, patted the child delicately, looked at Mrs. Jost, and said, "This one is yours."

She repeated her actions with the infant in Dolores's arms. She smiled brightly when she lifted the sheets and proclaimed, "Ah, this one is mine! This one I will care for." She lifted the child from his mother's embrace and began to rock him and coo quietly.

José said of his homecoming from the hospital, "Nanita Santos picked me up and wrapped me like a papoose, put me on her back, and off she went! She carried me on her back when she did her housework."

Dolores did not regain her strength as she should have following José's birth. The doctors feared that if her physical decline continued, she might die. When she complained of severe, debilitating headaches, the same headaches she had suffered with for years, the doctors insisted that she cut her long, heavy hair. Her reddish -brown locks grew to her calves, and it had always been a source of great pride to her that scissors and razor had never once touched her hair. The doctors pressed her with dire warnings of the physical consequences of letting the headaches continue. With great sadness, she complied. She had her hair cut so short that for a time she wore a wig. To her relief, the intense headaches that had plagued her with weariness for so long subsided. Over time, her health gradually rebounded.

"She sold her hair to Mr. Boxer, who was one of the biggest wigmakers in the country. He paid her nine hundred dollars for her hair. I still have one wig made of my mother's hair. It's a chestnut color. Very pretty."

The arrival of the two babies at the Jost house caused an excited stir among the neighbors. Hearing a rumor that the upstairs maid had no bed for her baby, the next door neighbor, Mrs. McAllister (her family is the namesake of the street in San Francisco), took a large, soft pillow off her chaise lounge and offered it to Dolores, saying, "This is for the baby."

"That was my first bed, and I still have the pillow downstairs. It's pink and satin. It's beautiful, with a ruffle all around it. It's got all of my pee stains on it yet. And my mother said that was my pillow."

Very little fuss was made over the arrival of the Jost's third girl. The infant José was the talk of the neighborhood. The two older Jost sisters were seemingly more excited than anyone else about the arrival of a new baby boy in the house. They treated him like a treasured doll, played with him, dressed him, and carried him in their arms whenever they could find him somewhere besides Nanita's back. They spent every spare moment with the infant José, and even some not-so-spare moments.

"The girls attended an elite school for girls on the site of what is now Presentation College. And that was a school for the very elite —the very, very wealthy. One morning they packed me up like I was a doll, and off they went to school. I was very small. I didn't weigh four pounds. I fit in a shoebox. I cried because I was wet and hungry, and I caused a real a disturbance at the school.

(If it's not one disturbance from this family it's another!)

"The Sisters (the nuns that is) had to call the Jost family, and the Josts sent out a chauffeur to pick me up and bring me back to the house. But that didn't stop the girls. They took me to school again, and again the limousine had to hurry to the school."

(José is still being chauffeured around in limousines. Early training sticks.)

"The nuns insisted that my outings cease, and the girls were told not sneak out with me anymore."

Because she was busy working upstairs and assumed Nanita Santos was watching the baby, Dolores learned of José's trips to school only after the family sent the chauffeur to retrieve him. It was no use complaining to Nanita Santos; she was growing very old and unaware of her own unintentional neglect of the child. Her senses were no longer keen, and she often could not tell when he had messed his diapers or hear his cries when he was hungry. The baby was not receiving the proper nourishment, and he remained dangerously small. Dolores found herself at a loss for solutions. Her duties at the house left her little time during the day to care for an infant, and the Josts offered no solution. Hiring a nursemaid for a maid's child was just not done.

"Living nearby, just down the street, was a lady named Maria Bruce. She was married to a police officer who was very high up in the Masonic Order. She was the woman I later called Aunt Maria. She had six husbands altogether. She was very much a society lady. It was her third marriage at the time. She heard of the plight of the upstairs maid, that she needed to find someone to take care of this little baby boy. It just happened that her sister had recently lost a little girl to diphtheria. She had already had four children and one miscarriage. She went a little bit off her rocker with the loss of this child, who had been a gorgeous and well-behaved child. So Maria went to my mother and said, 'You know, I understand you have a problem. You need someone to take care of the baby.'

"My mother said, 'Yes.'

"Maria said, 'Well, my sister just lost a little girl, and the doctors recommend that she find another child to take of.'

"So they made an appointment to meet, my mother and this lady, whose name was Jesserina. She and my mother, more or less, hit it off. So my mother said, 'Fine. You take care of the little boy, and I will pay you.' The arrangements were made."

José thus went to live with the people that he came to consider his adopted family.

Kidnapped!

War is a force that displaces people, uproots them and sends them off to places they would not otherwise have considered living. Sometimes people migrate as refugees of war, as Maria Dolores did. Sometimes, however, people simply follow the economic spoils of war, the jobs created out of wartime necessity or those jobs abandoned by the men and women who left to fight the war more directly. Such was the case with José's adopted family during World War I.

In 1917, soon after the United States declared war on Germany, Jesserina and Charles Millen left San Fernando in Southern California and moved to San Francisco to seek jobs in the shipyards that were bustling with the war effort. As with all of his familial connections, José is quick to recount the impressive roots of the Millens.

"Jesserina came from early California stock. Mercadante. They migrated to California in 1849 and married into the Bernal family, a noble California Spanish family. Her husband Charles's father migrated from Scotland the same year and married into one of the Spanish land-grant families. They were the founders of Wilmington, California, and helped found Santa Monica. They came north with their children. They had Augustus, Theresa, Josephine, Leonora, and Antoinette. They first lived on Shotwell Street, and then they lived for a short time with Jesserina's sister, whom I eventually came to call my Aunt Maria. She had a house on Balboa and 33rd. Aunt Maria was an Eastern Star, a wealthy woman married to Mr. Bruce, who was a police officer on the Divisadero beat at Divisadero and Sutter Street."

When Jesserina and Charles were finally able to move into their own place they settled in an largely middle-class Irish district called the Castro. Their home was on upper Castro Street in the floors above a bakery. It was there that José came to live with the Millen family. Whether by destiny or coincidence, the Castro would later become a world-famous center for gay culture in the 1970s and beyond, and José would be famous there.

Soon after the move to Castro Street, eight-year-old Antoinette contracted diphtheria and died. Jesserina's other children were in their teens, and Antoinette had been her baby, the final fruit of her childbearing years. The loss of her youngest devastated Jesserina. She was inconsolable. Suddenly her years of motherhood, an integral part of her identity, were cut short. She could never again have a child of her own, and the only one of her brood who was still a young child was now gone forever. She alternated between weeping and numb quietude. In an attempt to end her severe depression, her doctor recommended that she take in another child to raise.

Maria Bruce worried about her sister Jesserina's condition. She knew of the doctor's recommendation, so when she heard about the plight of the upstairs maid at the Jost household she determined to speak to the woman. She made an appointment to meet with Dolores and explained her sister's dilemma. She offered to arrange for Jesserina to take Dolores's son José into her home and care for him. Mrs. Bruce insisted that such an arrangement would solve the problems of both Jesserina and Dolores. She asked Dolores if she would approve of a meeting with Jesserina to see if they could work together for the child's welfare.

Dolores was nervous as she approached the Millen flat above the bakery at the top of the hill on Castro Street. She struggled with mixed feelings about leaving her infant son with another woman, yet she was determined to find a better, healthier, and safer situation for him. Maria Bruce ushered the Colombian maid into the house and introduced her to Jesserina. The women smiled politely and sat down to talk. They discussed the living arrangements for José, and learned that they held similar beliefs about childrearing. The other Millen children seemed polite and respectful to Dolores. Soon the women had relaxed and found themselves enjoying each other's company, discussing their family backgrounds and Spanish heritage, their adjustments to the city of San Francisco, their children.

Not long after the initial meeting, Dolores brought her four-month-old baby boy to the Millen home. Jesserina was enchanted by the child, and the women decided that José would live with the Millens. It was 1923. Except for one short and very tumultuous separation, José would call the Millen home his own for the remainder of his childhood. Jesserina and Charles became his godmother and godfather, and their children were considered his adopted sisters. As he learned to speak, José called the couple "Ma and Pa."

Following José's move to the Millen house, Dolores's situation changed as well. Frank Maron, the milkman, had a sister who was married to George O'Brien, a police officer whose career in the police department was rapidly rising. He was on the fast track to the job of assistant chief of police, and his political and professional rise necessitated a great number of social engagements. Mrs. O'Brien had recently given birth to her second child and found herself struggling to meet her social obligations while caring for an infant. To help his sister, and possibly to situate Dolores more closely to himself, Frank proposed a solution.

"I believe that Mr. Maron, the milkman for all of these families in the area, had a deep, abiding love for my mother. After my mother had worked for some time at the Josts', his sister gave birth to her second child. He contacted my mother and said, 'My sister just had a baby, and she needs a nurse because she has no time to care for it with her social obligations. It will be better pay and less work than your job at the Josts'.' My mother thanked Mr. Maron for the tip and went and interviewed. Mrs. O'Brien hired her.

"My mother worked for the O'Brien family for fifteen years. George O'Brien eventually became the assistant chief of police, serving as the acting chief whenever the chief of police was out of town. Mrs. O'Brien's first child was Alouisius. The second boy was George, and then came a sister, Annette. I have pictures of George dressed in a girl's costume. My mother dressed him like a girl. Annette became a nun, George became an attorney, and Alouisius was a gardener for the city. I think it's interesting that the daughter who became a nun, Annette, was called by the nickname "Sister" when she was young. I guess now she's Sister Sister. The gardener, Alouisius, died when a tree fell on him. My mother raised them all. That's why my mother was known in City Hall, because she was the nanna of the children of the chief of police.

"This is where my mother was all through the Depression. She had a good living there. But it was very, very hard work. My mother was the maid and the cook and the nanny and the kitchen help. My mother had to do everything."

Though Dolores worked hard to provide a good life for her child, José's father Julio had little involvement in his son's life. He made a decent wage as maitre d' at the Palace Hotel, but he paid nothing to support the child. Aunt Maria, being a woman with a strong sense of moral correctness and familial obligation, decided that if Julio would not marry Dolores, he would at least contribute to his son's keep. Yet when Dolores would ask for money, Julio consistently refused to pay. José was well cared for, but she considered the money a matter of principle; fathers should care for their children. Though Dolores never went beyond simple entreaty and appeal to Julio's sense of obligation, Aunt Maria decided to take a firmer approach.

Maria discussed the matter with her husband, the police officer, and with George O'Brien, Dolores's employer and the future police chief of San Francisco. A warrant was issued for Julio Sarria for failure to pay child support. A paddy wagon rolled up to the Palace Hotel in the middle of Julio's shift, and officers arrested him and escorted him off the floor. They drove him in the paddy wagon to city hall, where a local judge ordered him to pay five dollars for his release. The money went for the care of José, and Julio went back to work.

When the first of the month again rolled around, and the money again was not forthcoming, the paddy wagon made its way to the Palace Hotel, the arrest was made, the five dollars was charged and paid, and Julio returned to his job.

"On the first of the month, they'd get the warrant out and go through the whole thing. I came across the court receipts in my mother's trunk. They did this every fucking month! Finally his mama told him to get his ass back home to Nicaragua sometime before the Depression. I must have been about four years old."

Given what seemed to her the tenuous nature of José's relation-ships with those who cared for him and her own fading prospects for marriage, Dolores was determined to secure her son's future well-being. She made the major financial decision to buy a house on Broderick Street. Because her work was a live-in position, she did not move to the house. Instead, she moved José and the Millen family into it.

"There I can remember Christmases, and all kinds of things. We had a big house, a huge house, with a big formal dining room and a huge kitchen. I remember the kitchen had one of those hot water heaters—a cylinder water heater. Oh, wow. And off the pantry was a big room, and that was our room, me and the other children. You see, after the older children were gone, so that I would not be raised by myself, my godmother took in children from poor mothers, and she took care of them. There were always three, four, five, or six kids. We were all raised together so I wouldn't be spoiled. But it didn't work. The kids were Billie, Anna Marie, Olga, and there were the twins. The twins were the last. That was most of my childhood up to the Depression. So that was the family home, and that was everything."

Many of the members of the Latino community in San Francisco assumed that Maria Dolores Maldonado had a great deal of money squirreled away. After all, she had bought a house, an investment beyond the means of most domestic servants, and she made other investments as well. Rumors also circulated about a trunk of jewels and gold that she had brought with her from Colombia. When asked, she smiled and spoke of hard work and frugal living, but the talk of her wealth persisted.

In fact, Dolores had not had to withdraw her savings to buy the house, nor had she used her jewels. Her trunk was in safekeeping at the home of a couple she had met soon after arriving in San Francisco. One day she went to check on the trunk and her jewels and papers, and the woman claimed that there had been a fire, and the trunk was gone. Dolores grew suspicious and demanded to be allowed to retrieve her trunk. The woman brought her husband out to discuss the matter with an angry Dolores.

"So the husband came out and told my mother that the trunk was no longer there. So then my mother grabbed hold of him and beat the shit out of him, and he screamed for mercy. My mother stormed into the house. The man called the police. In the meanwhile, my mother found the trunk and threw it down the stairs. The police came, and my mother was arrested. She went to court, and they charged her with assault and battery; however, it ended up that my mother told her story, and the court told her to go and settle it on her own. But the judge told her she just could not go around beating up men."

Dolores was able to take her trunk back, but much was missing, including her birth certificate. The couple had apparently broken the lock and begun to help themselves to its contents.

"I had a hard time with not having her birth certificate, not knowing when she was born. The only thing we had for a date was when she came to this country. That was on her passport. My birth certificate was not issued until 1932, because of my illegitimacy. My birth certificate was gotten finally by Mr. Jost. I got a fancy one with a big star. When the birth certificate was issued, my mother put the dates on it that she wanted. I think I was born in 1922 because I can remember people speaking of President Harding being alive after I was born, and he died in office in 1923. My birth is listed as 1923 on the birth certificate, so legally you have to use that."

José and his mother lived in relative peace during the next few years. She felt at home in her job at the O'Brien home, and she was able to keep up the payments on the house and provide well for José. There were forces, however, that even her determination and diligence could not tame. In 1929, the stock market crashed and the nation went into an economic tailspin. With so many in the Latino community living on modest means, the subsequent Depression caused an enormous amount of tension between neighbors and friends.

Dolores decided to take out a second mortgage on the house, which Jesserina and Charles considered ill-advised. Yet they had no say about the home in which they lived, since it belonged to Dolores. In the midst of this economic tension, Jesserina approached Dolores with a request that she be allowed to adopt José. Dolores had again begun to fight her old illnesses, and she was growing weaker. Jesserina wanted to secure José's situation should anything happen to his mother. Dolores, already frustrated that she had been able to spend so little time raising of her son, refused Jesserina's request angrily. The women argued bitterly, and the tension between them increased.

Into this volatile situation came Natalia Marroquín. She was a member of the Latino community who had known Dolores for some time, though not intimately. She had heard the rumors about Maria Dolores's hidden wealth, of the trunk full of jewels and gold, and believed the stories. She saw Dolores as a simple solution to her own Depression-bred financial woes.

Natalia set out to befriend Dolores, giving her a sympathetic ear for her angry words about Jesserina. She shared time and conversation and what little she had in the way of food for entertaining her "friend." She encouraged Dolores to stand up to Jesserina. She warned Dolores that Jesserina was trying to take José away from her. Thus she stoked the fires of distrust and resentment.

Like any good general, Natalia did not fight her battle on one field alone. Even as she was drawing Dolores toward herself, she began spreading hateful stories about Jesserina. She hinted at abusive treatment of José. She painted Jesserina with her own mercenary colors, claiming that José's godmother wanted to enrich herself by using the child. She placed her stories strategically to assure that they would be heard by José's father Julio, who was himself not enamored of the family that kept dragging him into court every month.

Julio began to pressure Dolores to place José with a different family. Others in the community, having heard the stories that Natalia planted, did the same. Never one to give credence to rumors, Mrs. O'Brien admonished Dolores to stop listening so much to the wagging tongues of others and trust her own judgment. Despite her employer's misgivings, Dolores decided to take José away from the Millens and place him under the care of Natalia Marroquín.

"I remember my godmother saying, 'Josésito, you must go with your mother, now. You cannot live here anymore.'

"My mother packed my trunk. I still have that trunk. I cried and cried. I didn't want to go. I remember I fell onto the bed and hit my head on an iron railing on the headboard. She put everything in my little red wagon, and we pulled the wagon down California Street. She dropped me off with Mrs. Marroquín on Post Street and Steiner. It was terrible. Mrs. Marroquín said, 'I am your new mama. You must call me Mama.'

"That is where I was when my father came and bid goodbye to me before he went back to Nicaragua. I remember he was wearing a very, very fine fedora hat, and he had a full-length camel-hair coat. He was very tall and nice-looking. Very, very smart. He came, and I remember that I was all cleaned up, and Mrs. Marroquín said, 'This is your father,' and he bent down, and he kissed me, and he held me.

He talked to me, and we had ice cream and cookies, and that is the only time I ever saw my father."

Julio Sarria had made the critical mistake of mentioning to his mother in Nicaragua that he was considering marrying Maria Dolores Maldonado.

"See, his mother, who was the head of that family, called him back. He was her favorite. He was allowed to travel around the world without an escort at a very tender age while all the rest of his siblings could not. She often let him do what he wanted, but she wanted to control who became a part of the family. They came from Spain with the conquistadors; one family member was the Archbishop of Granada. They were listed as one of the ten most important families of the New World. We have a descendant who is buried with Father Junípero Serra. My grandmother did not approve of my mother. She knew nothing about my mother's family. She said, 'No, Julio. You come home, and you will marry who I say.' And that is exactly what he did. He went home and got married to a woman who she picked. Her name was Magdalena."

After José's father left for Nicaragua, Natalia Marroquín wove more thickly the web with which she intended to entrap José and Dolores. The Marroquíns had a daughter the same age as José, by now five or six years old. In the natural innocence of childish curiosity, the two explored each other's bodies, wondering at the differences. Mrs. Marroquín caught José and her daughter one afternoon beneath the dining room table. She lifted the long white tablecloth when she heard their giggles. There were the two, José with his pants at his ankles and the girl with her skirts lifted high.

In an attitude of solemn concern for the welfare of her child and Dolores's son, Natalia called Dolores to the house and sat her down for a serious discussion. She announced that José had violated her daughter and ruined her chances of a good match in the future. The only solution was to sign a legal agreement to have the children wed once they came of age. In serious tones, Natalia discussed the details of the proposed marriage.

Though Dolores often believed the best about people who did not necessarily deserve her trust, she was not the simpleton that Natalia Marroquín apparently took her for. The absurdity of forcing a marriage because of natural childhood exploration of the body awakened her to Mrs. Marroquín's scheming ways and nefarious motives. Her answer was unequivocally no. She left the Marroquín house wondering if there was anyone she could trust when it came to her young son. She vowed to put an end to all of the bickering and nonsense. She would trust no more neighbors and friends with her child.

Dolores made arrangements within a few days, and then went to the Marroquín house to retrieve her son. She packed all of his clothes in a trunk, just as she had packed her own possessions in a trunk years before. She added a few things from her own trunk as a kind of dowry to ensure his care. She dressed him in traveling clothes and took him to the little lumber town of Ukiah in the wooded coastal mountains a hundred miles north of San Francisco. There she dropped him off at the gate of an orphanage run by Dominican nuns. She watched as a calm and austere woman in traditional habit escorted José onto the grounds.

When Jesserina learned what Dolores had done, she felt a mixture of pain and frustration. Her own mother had sent her brother off to military boarding school at a young age and her sister to a convent. She grew up hardly knowing her siblings, and always resented the separation. Memories of her own childhood loneliness flooded back, and she ached for José. Unable to leave things as they were, Jesserina drove to Ukiah to visit José. She did not call ahead, because she wanted to see the true nature of José's treatment at the orphanage. What she found there broke her heart. José was listless and sad. He had lost weight and appeared sick. He wore none of his own fine clothes, but rather baggy, stained, ragged clothes that appeared to have covered many a child's body before José's. His hair was dirty and limp and his body unwashed. Not wanting to arouse suspicion about her motives, Jesserina said nothing to the nuns, but rather pretended to enjoy a pleasant and spontaneous visit with her godchild.

When she returned to San Francisco, José's godmother immediately contacted his mother. She pleaded with her, "Dolores, that is no place for the boy. You must go up there and get him. We'll make amends. Let me have him back."

Dolores was adamant. She insisted that the good Sisters would take care of José. She would have no more problems with him or with those who sought to exploit him. Unsure what to do next, Jesserina went to her sisters to ask their advice.

"Well, Jesserina discussed this with her two sisters, Maria and Philamena. Philamena came up from Los Angeles to help my godmother. 'The Three Graces,' I used to call them. My aunts called my godmother 'Jessie.' We all called Philamena 'Mena.'

"Aunt Maria and Aunt Mena and Jesserina said, 'We're going to have to make that woman understand, and we're going to get that kid back.' Together they asked my mother to go back up to Ukiah to see me, to see my condition for herself.

"She said, 'No!'

"So Aunt Mena said to Maria and Jessie, 'Fine. We'll kidnap her, and she'll have to go.'

"After a moment of surprise, Maria agreed.

"Jessie said, 'Yes, that's what we should do. But how?' "

Aunt Mena and Aunt Maria sat down to develop a plan. It did not take them long to devise a plot that was simple enough to work. On the following Sunday when they knew that Dolores would have a day off, they packed a picnic lunch and gathered some blankets. They packed the family's Essex touring car and dressed for an outing. They did their best to make everything look authentic. Once they had their props and costumes in place, they piled into the car and drove to the O'Briens'.

Doing their best to laugh and sound carefree, the three women knocked on the door. They asked for Dolores, giggling like schoolgirls on vacation. To their relief, Dolores was home and had made no plans for the day. Explaining that they felt terrible about the tension that had come between them, and wanting to entertain their visiting sister, they pleaded with her to come and join them on a Sunday drive and picnic. A part of Dolores wanted very much to reconcile with her friends, and, too, she was pleased with the prospect of a day in the country. She agreed. She hurriedly dressed in traveling clothes and joined the sisters in the car.

Chattering gleefully, the women drove off.

"So this is the famous kidnapping. They said they were going for a Sunday ride. They got my mother in the car and drove and drove. By the time my mother guessed where they were going, there wasn't anything she could do about it. They went putt, putt, putt, all the way to Ukiah. My mother was irritated with them, but not angry.

"Of course she was furious when she saw me at the orphanage. My nose was runny. I was in tattered clothes, dirty, old, ragged clothes. I was very, very thin. Malnourished. Well, my dear, she yanked me out of there, grabbed my trunk, and said to Jesserina, 'He comes home to you. There will be no more monkey business. You will keep this child forever. You are not going to have any more problems.'

"So I was brought back to San Francisco.

"My mother brought charges against the religious order in Ukiah for maltreatment and abuse of children. The church did an investigation of child abuse and financial shenanigans. By the time they settled that suit, the church had the orphanage staff dissolved because that convent was dissolved. That ended that nonsense.

"My godmother took me back to where I was born, the Saint Francis Hospital, to be treated for the rickets and asthma I had developed at the orphanage from malnourishment. I have seen pictures of me there. I was quite the little Buddha, but there was no strength in my bones. Now as a little tiny baby, because of not having the right kind of nursing when I was born, I was very susceptible to problems. They told my godmother that I could not stand because my legs would not carry my weight. I would be completely bowlegged. She bandaged my legs until my body began to correct itself, and now I have rather straight legs. Very nice legs."

Enquiring Mind

Nanita Santos continued to play a role in the life of young José. In his mind, she was as much a part of his extended family as any blood relative could be. Though she lived an exceedingly long life, her death was not a natural one, and were his story a novel, her death could serve very well as foreshadowing for the story of José's first great love some years later.

"I continued to see Nanita. When I was eight or nine years old, I remember she was celebrating her 100th birthday. My mother had bought her a beautiful new blouse. They remained friends through everything. She was going to church on California Street and Presidio Avenue, and she was hit by a drunk driver. She died."

José grew into a precocious child. He had heard the stories about his mother's hidden funds, and he became curious about the extent of them. The year after Nanita Santos's death, at the age of ten, he approached his mother and asked about the estate. She explained patiently that he needn't worry about any of that; Mr. Jost was taking good care of their savings and investments. Unsatisfied, José asked her how much money they actually had in the bank. Dolores said she was not sure, and dismissed the question lightly. Yet José's query sparked a question in his mother's mind. She began to wonder how much worth she had accumulated over the years. She told herself that it was only right that she should know. Keeping abreast of her family's finances was the responsible thing to do.

She took José with her the day she visited Mr. Jost to inquire about the accounts. It was not too early for him to begin developing a feel for money and how to use it to advantage. When Mr. Jost learned the purpose of their visit, he seemed evasive. He smiled and reassured Dolores that all of her finances were sound and well guarded. Thinking that Mr. Jost was simply patronizing her, she asked firmly to see the bank books. He tried again to dismiss her concern. Feeling a vague unease, she demanded again to see the books. As José and his mother watched, Mr. Jost reluctantly and slowly retrieved the books and set them on the desk.

Mumbling something about his intention to talk to her, Jost stood nervously. Dolores opened the books and began to trace the progress of her money over the years. There were entries showing substantial deposits in a savings and loan. Yet the final balances were extremely low. Jost explained that the savings and loan had lost a great deal of her money in bad investments. In those years there were no federal guarantees for money in savings and loans.

Continuing her perusal of the books, Dolores noticed several of the investments that showed returns. There were also numerous withdrawals with no record of where the money went. Many of the balances were at zero. When questioned, Jost made vague references to other investments for which he would have to find the records. Dolores announced that she would borrow the books to study them more carefully.

Dolores walked home in a grave mood. "Mama, I think that Mr. Jost has stolen our money. We should tell Mr. O'Brien." Dolores thought of all the young women and families who had trusted her recommendation and had turned their earnings over to Mr. Jost for safekeeping. She could not believe he had violated her trust, that he had knowingly hurt so many people. There had to be another explanation.

Dolores probed the columns of the bankbooks at home, but the mystery gained no clarity. No sudden explanations flickered between the numbers. José pestered his mother until she did indeed bring the matter to the attention of the police. The police agreed that there was strong evidence to suspect the money had been misappropriated, and when Mr. Jost failed to produce records of the other investments to which he had referred, Dolores decided to press charges.

Mr. Jost was arrested and charged with embezzlement. He was convicted and deported.

"So Jost was deported. The family stayed here. La Mudita, through the efforts of my mother, was able to learn to talk. She married a very wealthy man. Just after World War II, Mr. Jost developed cancer. He needed to come to the States for an operation. They contacted my mother and asked if she would agree to let him return. She did. He came back to the States and died in Texas."

Though there was a measure of satisfaction in the conviction of Mr. Jost, Dolores and those to whom she had recommended Jost received no compensation for their losses. Not satisfied with the outcome, Dolores contacted the president of Hastings Law School, whom she knew through her work in the community. She asked for the names of top graduates from the previous year, and from that list she chose a young lawyer named Francis O'Connell. She gave him his first major case. He sued the savings and loan for her.

"At that time the president of the savings and loan was also part owner, with a corporation, of the Clift Hotel and the Beverly Plaza Hotel. They wanted to settle out of court for something like thirty-five cents on the dollar. My mother said, 'No. I paid a dollar, I want a dollar back.'

"Finally there was a court settlement, and she got something like ninety-eight cents on the dollar. All the rest of the little old ladies got something back on their money. The last check came just before World War II. 1942. I remember it was a check for eighteen dollars and seventy-some-odd cents. The other money, what Mr. Jost embezzled, she never got back."

Largely due to the Great Depression, Dolores's financial situation did not improve, even after the lawsuit. Finally, in 1932, unable to pay the heavy mortgages, Dolores lost the house. She and Jesserina worked together to sell what possessions they had.

"My godmother sold paintings, silver, gifts that my mother had given her—my mother had given her a sable wrap. She had old photographs of her ancestors in California which she sold to the De Young Museum. With everything that my godmother sold, and with a little money my mother loaned her, they bought a property with a house in Redwood City. I was about eleven or twelve when we moved down to Redwood City."

The new home in Redwood City provided a measure of insulation from the ravages of the Great Depression. The family had enough property to plant an extensive garden, the California climate and rich soil making it possible to grow a wide variety of fruits and vegetables that could be staggered throughout most of the year. They also raised small livestock, particularly chickens. For the duration of those dark days, they had shelter and food. And later, thanks to an unexpected liaison with a transplanted European aristocrat, they had more.

A Voice for All Ages

In spite of the many financial and familial struggles in José's life in the twenties, all was not somber contention. José's mother and his godmother both doted on him. They never reacted in anything but amused affection when they found him trying on their dresses and shoes. José was allowed to be José, a fact that made it difficult for him, years later, to understand gay men who lived the double life of the closet. José's mother loved the idiosyncrasies and the creative flair evident in her son. It helped too that the accepted school curriculum of the day included training in the arts for all children. School recitals were important events, and outside of school, families that could afford it enrolled their children in tap dancing and ballet for the development of poise, and voice lessons and drama for elocution.

José remembers his first dance recital being held at the Princess Theater on Fillmore Street. I laughed when José told me this. "Now, *that* is appropriate!"

"Maybe then," José responded with a smile, "but now it would have to be the *Empress* Theater."

José remembers dressing in traditional Mexican folk dress and dancing the Jarabe Zapatío, the national dance of Mexico. His performance was a hit, and he was asked to perform with his partner several times after the initial recital. Perhaps José would have continued dancing were it not for the fact that his family's cultural pride centered on Colombia and not Mexico, as was true for so much of the Latino community of San Francisco, and his mother's purpose for the lessons was primarily for José's personal development. Besides, Dolores wanted José to be well-rounded in the arts, and her tastes were more classical than folk.

Following on the heels of his brief dance career, Jose took up the violin, an instrument his mother particularly loved. Not one to scrimp when it came to her son, Dolores paid for lessons from the concertmeister of the San Francisco Symphony. Much to his mother's disappointment, José did not take to the delicate stringed instrument. In fact, he seriously damaged several violins. Finally his teacher approached his mother and said, "Dolores, you can spend all the money you want, but he will never be a violinist. He may learn to play the violin, but he will not be a violinist. This is a waste of your money, my time, and certainly his time. Let him find what he truly does well."

Recognizing that José loved to sing and that he had a reasonably powerful voice for a child, Dolores decided to try voice lessons for him. She enlisted the services of a retired opera singer, Madame Faulk. José took to the lessons and to his teacher. He demonstrated a considerable natural talent, and he worked hard to develop an impressive youthful expertise.

"At this time, in Hollywood, there was a young star by the name of Bobby Greene, who was a child prodigy in voice. Hollywood had discovered him and was working him night and day. They finally worked him so hard that when his voice began to change, it cracked and failed. He was in the middle of a motion picture. They had to find someone with a voice to continue making the picture or all that money was lost. So they sent scouts out. At that time I was in high school, and they saw me, heard me, and went and contacted the family. They wanted to use me and give me a screen test, to see if they could substitute my voice for that of Bobby Greene, whose voice was a very naturally high soprano. I had a high tenor voice, lyric tenor. Well, that was very exciting and all."

In the middle of José's dreams of Hollywood stardom, his voice teacher approached Dolores with a recommendation that was a great disappointment to the boy, but that later proved to be words of wisdom.

"My teacher said, 'I was going to talk to you, Madame. I have reached as far as I can go with José's voice, because his voice is young. You must now stop to preserve the quality of his voice. If you continue, you are forcing the voice to crack, and he will never have a voice. He has to learn to rest until his body changes.'

"This was on the eve of the war. My mother said, 'I'm sorry. No Hollywood!—No movie star!—No singing!—No nothing!'"

Despite his disappointment, José acquiesced to his mother's judgment. He did not sing seriously again until after he returned from his tour of duty during World War II. He has never regretted that decision.

"And then the war broke out, and I never sang until after I came back. When I finally opened up my voice to sing, I had a beautiful, natural tenor voice. I could reach high C, not in falsetto, just in a normal voice. Even today I can sing. My voice has lasted. However, now with the smoke, and all this malarkey (in the bars), it's not as good as it once was. Now my voice is more raspy. It could be a woman's voice. They have said that my voice sounds like Sally Leander, the German star, and Lotte Lehmann, the woman in the *Three Penny Opera*. So I never had to camouflage my voice to sing as a woman in my shows.

"And that is how that began and ended. Thank God I had my voice to rely on!"

Thank God, indeed. José's voice gave him options when his first choice for a career fell victim to the prevailing attitudes toward gay men at the time. He was to grow famous, some would say notorious, for challenging those attitudes and the social conventions to which they gave birth. It was his voice, his magic ability to disarm through entertainment, that gave José the opportunity to defy the antigay prejudices and practices of his time.

The Mexican Dancer

I truly enjoyed listening to José tell his life story. I particularly liked his penchant for mixing historic detail with wry commentary on the past and the present. At times his habit of skipping between decades was maddening, and perhaps he sometimes sacrificed historic detail for the sake of a good line or a pithy comment, but that is a part of his style. Like Shakespeare, he considers the value of the story and the sensibilities of his audience over the dry facts of an event. Of course, his manner of storytelling sometimes made my job rather difficult. For instance, I asked him one evening about a Mexican dancer he had mentioned briefly. He nodded, smiled, and began talking about his roommate, the female impersonator and mistress of ceremonies at the club called Finocchio's in the North Beach section of San Francisco.

"I usually go to work at five in the morning and come home at two. My roommate, Beverley Plaza (Beverley's 'boy name' is Scott Lyons), diva of Finocchio's, is always very, very kind, after she arises, to take my messages."

I was not sure what taking phone messages had to do with the Mexican dancer from his youth, but José would always tell his stories in his own time and in his own way. I think he genuinely enjoyed the confusion he caused me when he seemed to go off-topic. This was one of those times. I decided to comment on Beverley, thereby taking the reins of the conversation, and then ask a question to gently prod him back to the story I wanted to record. It was an interview technique I had used well many times before.

With a look of sincerity (I thought) I said, "Yes, Beverley is the ideal roommate. She's always so polite to me on the phone. It must not be easy living with an Empress: the calls from around the country, the adulation, the stories. I bet she's heard most of your stories several times, but she always listens graciously when you tell them. I know my son and my lover tease me about telling the same stories over and over. Speaking of stories, you were going to tell me about the Mexican dancer."

José smiled, as if at an impatient child, and continued, "Yes, Beverley does a good job of taking my messages and making people who call feel very comfortable. That reminds me. There was a message here from the empress of New York. Where did I put that?"

José stood and walked to the end of the dining room table, which was filled with flyers and mail, and began shuffling through the papers there. Resigning myself to being on his time clock and not my own, I relaxed and waited. After a ten-minute search of the table and surrounding furniture, during which he found and commented on several other important notes and cards, José found the message. He placed the message by the phone and returned to his chair. "Now, where were we?"

"Well," I thought to myself, "You were just demonstrating that an empress tells her tales in her own time and does not succumb to pressure from others."

Aloud, I said, "You were discussing Beverley."

José smiled, satisfied, and continued.

"Yes. Beverley. She is very good about taking messages and making sure I get them. And she understands the whole message. But at the time of this incident, Beverley was not living with me. I had a prize idiot here who never got any of the phone messages right. So when I came home at two o'clock in the afternoon, there was a message for me to call a Tony Rodriguez in reference to a Consuelo who knew me when I was seven or eight years old. Well, you can imagine my surprise; my dear, that was over sixty years ago! I couldn't imagine who this Tony was. I dialed the number, but I kept getting a hospital, and nobody there knew of a Tony Rodriguez. I was beside myself. How was I supposed to contact this person if I had the wrong number? And here was a chance to make contact with someone from the past. I thought to myself, 'He might be listed in the phone book.' Well, sure enough, I went through information, they gave me a phone number, and there he was."

I smiled to myself, thinking of my first attempts to contact José for the story Brian and I wanted to do on him. Without telling me who Tony Rodriguez was, José began reminiscing about the woman Consuelo and her family. He met them during the Great Depression.

After José's mother lost the house on Broderick Street, his godparents moved with him to a flat at the corner of Noe and 18th Streets. It was during their stay on Noe Street that the family worked to liquidate its material assets, selling furs and paintings and old photographs, accumulating what would be the down payment on the house in Redwood City. Above them lived a Mexican family headed by a woman named Chavalita. With her lived her daughter Consuelo, and Consuelo's two sons, Jorge and Jaime. Consuelo was a dance instructor, and the responsibility for watching the boys often rested on Chavalita.

Just entering his early teen years, José was old enough to look after the boys when Chavalita needed a break from her grandsons. José would often take the boys to a movie theater, and the three of them became good friends despite the differences in age.

The boys had an uncle, Consuelo's brother, who did not live with the family because he was pursuing a career as a dancer in Hollywood. He was a young Latin sensation when he first hit the big screen in the early 1930's. He went by the name Paulo Fox. One day, on the way to see a movie, Jorge and Jaime informed José that their famous uncle was going to be coming to San Francisco to dance. The boys were excited though they were too young to have known their uncle very well before he left for Hollywood. They looked forward to introducing José and Paulo.

Paulo did indeed come to town to dance. He performed a limited engagement at a club called the Sinaloa, which had one of the biggest Mexican revues at the time. He also dance at the Xochimilco, another very popular Latino club.

"Another person that danced there was Lupe, a high-class prostitute and dancer. In later years she used to come to the Black Cat all the time, and she never wore any pants. She'd do high kicks with me, and she was just a riot. She was a beautiful woman. She was very, very nice."

Paulo took naturally to the image of the romantic Latin lover on screen, but like other men in Hollywood then and now, he kept a secret from his fans. He was gay. His sexuality, however, was not a secret to his family. Consuelo doted on her brother, and worried about his need to live a double life. She hoped that he would meet a nice man and know love. Like many a sister with a gay brother she loves, Consuelo developed a savvy understanding of sexuality and could recognize other gay men without having to be told of their innate attraction to their own gender. When José moved in downstairs, Consuelo recognized the young man's sexual orientation, though the family never discussed it.

When Paulo came to San Francisco for his dance engagements, his sister made a point of introducing him to José, her handsome young neighbor who treated her sons so well. As she had hoped, there was an immediate attraction. Unfortunately, her dreams of happiness for her brother were not to be.

"She introduced me to her brother, and we had an affair. It was a wonderful affair. He was a very, very, very handsome man. We saw each other every day while he was in San Francisco. After a while he got a new contract in Hollywood, and the studio he signed with told him to return south. He went back to Hollywood, and I didn't see him again."

In the early years of the twentieth century, openly gay love and Hollywood success were not a combination that was allowed by the powers that shaped the images of the men and women on the silver screen. It would be many decades before the Hollywood closets began to creak slowly open. Whatever might have grown between José and Paulo ended before it could take root. Hollywood called. Yet, it seems the Tinseltown closet was difficult for Paulo, and he never did achieve either the dream of love or the dream of lasting success.

"He became a very heavy drinker. His drinking lost him his work, and he died of cirrhosis of the liver, poor and destitute. Consuelo said it was a pathetic sight. He was six feet tall and had been very well built. When he died, he was absolutely skin and bones."

José and his men and the tragedies born of alcohol; this was to become a common motif in the life of the future empress.

When Jesserina had finally accumulated enough money for a down payment, she bought the property in Redwood City. José had never lived in such a rural setting, but his ties to San Francisco were strong and he rarely felt isolated from the bustle of his previous years. His mother remained in the city, initially working for the O'Briens, and his godmother, Jesserina, kept in close contact with friends there, including Chavalita and Consuelo and the boys. The family prospered, at least by Depression-era standards, and José and his godmother made frequent trips into San Francisco to share some of the bounty of their land.

"When we moved away, my mother kept in contact with the family on Noe Street. She would go every Saturday and Sunday, loaded down with vegetables and wines and clothing and blankets. My godmother was known for always visiting and taking gifts to people. She was a very generous woman. It was Depression time, and Chavalita barely had enough to pay the rent. Nobody had anything. My godmother's visits were very welcome."

Even after World War II began, Jesserina kept in contact with Chavalita.

"While I was away at war, Consuelo and Chavalita left San Francisco and took the boys back to Mexico to raise them. It was easier there. The father, who was a wealthy Basque man, took the children in and raised them. I promised my mother and godmother that if I came back safely from the war, we would take a nice trip. When I came back, I bought a new car, and we loaded it up and headed off to see Mexico, including a visit to Chavalita and her family in Guadalajara. We crossed the border at Nogales. We wanted to drive down the center of Mexico and into Guadalajara. I remember their address: 771 Calle Hildalgo. Chavalita had a beautiful, big home with a central courtyard. She ran it as a guest house in later years until she died. That was the last trip that my mother and my godmother ever took out of the United States. They always talked about what a wonderful time we had. I think we were gone for two months. But that's another story, that trip."

As José paused in his narrative. I knew at last who the Mexican dancer was, but I still did not know the identity of Tony Rodriguez or the connection of the story with the phone call that the "idiot," who was not Beverley, had so inadequately relayed. As if reading my mind, José looked at me, smiled, and continued.

"So now to get back to the phone call: I phoned up Tony. He said, 'You don't know me, but I remember you. I took dancing lessons from Consuelo.' Tony had become one of her best dancers, and he eventually began dancing at Finocchio's in its heyday. He used to come down to see me perform at the Black Cat Cafe. His theatrical name was Tony Di Molino. Mr. Finocchio did not want his people coming to see me at the Black Cat. I was the competition in town, and I took business away from his shows. But all the entertainers would come down to see my show anyway. I was good.

"Tony is a property manager now. Anyway, he was in contact with Consuelo, and one day my name came up. She said, 'I wonder if he's still alive. I knew him when he was just a little tot. He used to take care of my boys. His mother was so good to my family. If it was not for his mother, we would not have had the good food we had.'

"He tried to find me for a long time. If he had known to look in the telephone book under the Widow Norton, or Empress José I, he would have been able to find me. He finally did hear about the Widow Norton and he looked me up in the phone book by that name. He gave me Consuelo's number.

"She is living now in Los Angeles near 8th and Belmont. She's there taking care of her sister who is paralyzed. As for the two boys, the younger one died of cancer. The older one is in Mexico, a very prosperous businessman with a chocolate place. She is eighty–seven years old and was so excited to hear from me! On my next trip to Los Angeles, I'm going to see her and take pictures with me.

"Tony is going to show me how to apply for Section Eight, which is for people with a low income, to reduce their rent. We reminisced about the people that worked at Finocchio's who used to come down to see me at the Black Cat. Of course, ninety percent of them are all dead, but some are still living. Elton Paris is in Arizona. Laverne Cummings works at the Emporium in the furnishing department. He has a white beard and white hair. He was billed as the Most Beautiful Woman. He had his own hair. Beautiful hair. Beautiful hair. Lester Lamont, the Paper Fashion Plate. Tony and I haven't gotten together yet, but I'm looking forward to it.

"The irony is that Tony lives just around the corner from me on Leavenworth."

It seems the farther we move away from the past, the closer it comes.

The Baron

A unique delight washes over me every time I see the skyline of San Francisco from Highway 80; like being in love and seeing that special face again after an absence. My windows are rolled down to let the bay air wash over me, extracting the valley heat from my skin and replacing it with a coastal cool. The highway signs have become as familiar as old friends: University Avenue, Ashby Avenue, University of California Berkeley Next Exit. I keep glancing over my right shoulder at that incredible city across the gray-green water of the bay, as if I'd just picked up my lover from the airport and want to memorize his features all over again. Be patient. Watch the road. There will be time to gaze over cappuccino later. Never enough time though.

The majestic rise of the Bay Bridge toward Treasure Island speeds my pulse every damn time, just as surely as the first look at the roller coaster did when I was a kid. Some of my San Francisco friends roll their eyes at my unsophisticated excitement as I drive over the span, but that's okay. I'm content for now to be the valley boy thrilled to have another day in the Emerald City. Perhaps I am even at an advantage. My memories of the city are not mundane: rising for work, taking out the trash, forgetting to buy light bulbs. The collage in my head as I listen to the metallic hum of the bridge below my tires is made up of clam chowder in French bread rolls with my son on the wharf, collecting sand dollars on the beach, a free sample of raspberry fudge at Rococo Chocolates on Castro, interviews with fabulous and famous people performing or opening movies in the city, bragging about my sense of balance just before I entertain everyone by slipping onto my butt in the pool below the waterfall at Stowe Lake in Golden Gate Park, Dykes on Bikes roaring down Market Street, fires in Federal Building windows during the protest-turned-riot after the AB101 veto, dropping change in a homeless woman's styrofoam cup on Haight

Street, holding a warm hand against the cold wind on Twin Peaks as I marvel again at the carpet of lights spread out around the bay, sitting in José Sarria's Victorian living room and listening to stories of the city and of my people.

July 8, 1995. I think of it as the day José talked of love. His politics, his performing, his crazy antics, these are easy to discuss, but the Dowager Empress shies a little from talking about the intimacies of love.

I picked José up from his job at the printing house on Second Street at two in the afternoon. I had arrived an hour early. My son Mack and his buddy Tyler were with me. They had skateboarded the hour away under a piece of the old Embarcadero freeway (the one that had been coming down section by section since the earthquake of 1989). Long stretches of smooth pavement with occasional cement parking blocks shaded by that massive section of a freeway to nowhere: Mack said he had found his skater nirvana. While the boys skated, I went for coffee at a funky wooden lunch joint down by the yacht club, a kind of seaside greasy spoon with gourmet coffees. Cool.

José was in good spirits and talkative when we picked him up, and I looked forward to hearing what tales he had to weave about his past. The boys alternately watched television and hung out on the steps outside on Bush Street, "cruising chicks," eating candy from the corner market, and generally watching the world go by.

As we settled in at the dark wooden dining room table decorated with mail, periodicals, invitations, and assorted other papers, José began telling me about his exploits while he was training for the army during World War II. When he mentioned the baron in passing, something about his tone of voice and demeanor told me here was a good love story. I wouldn't leave José alone about it, and he finally settled into telling the story.

"Now Paul Kolish was an Austrian baron whom I had met through school. He was an executive with the National Bank of Austria, and he had made some very derogatory remarks about Hitler. He was very outspoken and had Jewish ancestors. Because of his position, he saw what was coming. He started sifting his money bit by bit into Switzerland. When Hitler marched into Austria, Paul marched out. Actually, he and his family left in the middle of the night and drove to Switzerland. He had a wife who was asthmatic and tubercular, and he had a little boy, Jonathan, who had inherited the same diseases. So they weren't able to come directly to America. He decided to stay in Switzerland where he could keep an eye on his money. There he was taking care of his wife and the little boy, but the wife got worse and worse, and she finally died."

After the death of his wife, Paul Kolish began making plans to emigrate to America. He could afford the trip, and the transfer of his money posed no difficulty, but his greatest logistics problem was the health of his son. The immigration authorities at Ellis Island strictly surveyed the health of those attempting to enter the country. Paul knew that his son's respiratory illnesses would be more than enough to bar his acceptance into the United States. Using his influence, and more than a little of his money, he persuaded a Swiss doctor to provide medications that would mask Jonathan's symptoms.

The trip across the Atlantic was difficult for the boy. His coughing and wheezing and his frail and labored movements made it clear to anyone nearby that Jonathan was not well. Other passengers would look at Paul and his son with sad sympathy, knowing the two would soon be sailing back toward war-torn Europe. When the dramatic climax of the journey came, and other passengers gathered excitedly on deck to watch the New York City skyline grow larger on the horizon, Paul Kolish slipped into an empty room and quietly administered soothing drugs to his boy. He decided to forego the chance to see the majestic and motionless greeting of the Statue of Liberty in order to remain below deck, holding his son and keeping him warm and calm.

There was a deep tension etched on Paul's face as he waited with his son on Ellis Island for the medical screening. He winced at every cough and sniffle. The drugs had made Jonathan sleepy, and he leaned heavily against his father, but his breathing was not labored. When the doctors examined the boy, they assumed any lethargy was the inevitable weariness of a young one after a long journey. Paul smiled and talked to the doctors, doing his best to create an atmosphere of optimistic anticipation—and health. They failed to notice the furrowed brow when Jonathan coughed once or twice. Finally, with a smile at the son and a nod to the father, a tired physician opened the gate to America for the former Austrian baron and his heir.

Paul had heard in Europe that San Francisco was a sophisticated town that would fit his worldly style, and, being a seaport, it was likely to provide more business opportunities in difficult times. It was the late 1930s, before America's entrance into the war, and Paul Kolish settled on the shores of the ocean.

Paul had another reason to settle in San Francisco. He would be relatively close to his one other living relative, a younger brother whom he had sent to America for dental school in the late 1920s. José was to later have dealings with the brother under extremely difficult circumstances, and he was less than fond of the man.

"His brother graduated and became a dentist in Hollywood. He was a society doctor. A horse's ass."

While Paul Kolish and his son were making their way to America and then establishing themselves in San Francisco, José was experiencing some upheaval as well. Tension arose between José and his godparents, though he refuses to discuss the details. He was a teenager, and perhaps that is all the explanation needed. He had been visiting his mother in San Francisco often on weekends and during holidays since the move to Redwood City. Dolores had lost her job at the O'Briens' when the family was forced by the tight finances of the Depression to let their domestic staff go. For a while she worked for the family of the president of Wells Fargo, but that position too ended. She found a job in the kitchen at the Saint Francis Hotel, but that, of course, was not a live-in position such as she had been accustomed to all her working life. Fortunately, the O'Brien family owned an apartment building on Sacramento Street, and they set her up in a small basement apartment with a kitchen, a bath, a bedroom, and a small garden out behind the building. It was her home for the rest of her life.

Unable to manage his frustration with his family, José ran away from home for a time. His sojourn into teen street life did not last long, because he did not adapt well to the harshness of life on his own.

"I lived on bananas and corn flakes. It was not a good time."

After a short time, José went to live at his mother's new apartment in San Francisco. He enrolled in Commerce High School. Gradually the tension that had led to his move subsided, and José visited the farm in Redwood City often, spending a large part of his summers there.

José was always a good student, and he distinguished himself in high school. He was particularly adept at language, and was in advanced classes in both German and French. With these added to his fluency in English and Spanish, he became the language department's star pupil. Consequently, he was the logical choice when a new businessman in town came to the school looking for a tutor in English. It was rumored that the man had been an aristocrat in Europe and had fled the Nazis. José was to tutor the gentleman and compose a paper each week that outlined his strategies and his new student's progress. His grade in language was to be based on those papers and the success of his tutoring. The student's name was Paul Kolish.

Paul had been thriving in his new city. His investments had been calculated and clever. A better command of the English language was a part of his determination to make the best of his forced flight from his native country. He intended to transplant his prosperity as he had transplanted his small family.

"What he did when he came to this country was figure out what was the most important thing for people to buy. Food. Transportation. And naturally, housing. So he bought a wholesale food supply house. He bought a chain of gasoline stations, so he had gasoline stamps. He bought a couple of used car lots, so he had automobiles. And then he bought some property.

"If you go down Geary Street between Steiner and Pierce, you'll see a park. On the corner of Pierce and Geary is a high school. At one time in that park area by the high school were tiny Victorian houses. He bought four of them.

"Paul and I got along very well. Very well. When I tutored him, he paid me a little money. By the time the war broke out, we were old friends. Oh, he was very, very nice."

José and Paul grew very close indeed. In a short time, they began seeing each other outside of their official student-tutor relationship. They went to dinner in the evening and began attending the theater together. Paul Kolish found himself falling in love with his young teacher.

Not one to hide any part of his life from his family, José introduced Paul to his mother and to his godparents. The family was charmed by the baron's old-world manners and his aristocratic charm. They found his son a delight, though Jonathan continued to live a very sedentary life for a child. He too was kind, like his father, and he deferred always to his elders. The family knew that José and Paul were much more than good friends, and although none of them found the relationship disturbing, it was never discussed as a love affair. Such things were simply accepted silently.

When Paul visited José's family members, he always brought gifts. He provided them with gasoline stamps, and he would bring food from his store. He would step into the entryway of the house in Redwood City, click his heels, and bend to kiss Jesserina's hand. In turn, Jesserina would give Paul meat from whatever had been recently slaughtered. As summer approached and José made plans to move down to Redwood City for a time, Jesserina expressed a desire to give back something more than an occasional chicken to Paul for his kindness and generosity. With some thought, she came up with an idea. When Paul and José arrived with José's things, she approached Paul and said, "I must do something for you. You bring the boy down here and let me take care of him for the summer."

Paul's son loved the farm in Redwood City. He would watch the animals for hours and stroll the property despite his weak condition. He particularly enjoyed feeding the chickens and milking the cow. Paul approached Jonathan with the idea of a summer on the farm, and he enthusiastically agreed. Paul made the arrangements with Jesserina, and brought his son down the peninsula from San Francisco to Redwood City.

"So he came down, and my mother put him in a pair of trunks and made him run around in the sunshine. Your son Mack makes two of him; that's how little he was." (My son had accompanied me often on my trips to San Francisco to meet with José, and the two of them have grown to like each other very much.) "Paul's boy *never* had another attack of asthma like he was having before. He was living outside, and he was just becoming healthy and growing up. Paul was so happy. For the first time he could watch his son play and climb and run. He was so pleased. He couldn't do enough for my family because of what we had done for his son. The boy spent the summer months in Redwood City and went back to the city for school."

After that summer, Jonathan referred to Jesserina as "Mama." His attacks of asthma grew so infrequent that he ceased to worry at all about physical exertion. His life of caution seemed long ago, as if it were someone else's life. He would run or jump with the other boys without a thought of his former condition. And always, he looked forward to his next visit with Mama.

Although Paul continued his generosity with the family, José sometimes remembers those years as selfish ones on his part, perhaps simply the selfishness of a youth unaware of the struggles his older beau had endured to preserve his life and his lifestyle.

"Oh, I treated him very mean sometimes. After we became lovers, when something would happen in town like the theater or a big show, I'd say, 'I want to go.'

"He'd say, 'Okay Zhoezay . . .' Zhoezay . . . he'd always call me Zhoezay. And we'd go. He was a little bit chintzy, and he'd buy a ticket maybe in the first balcony.

"And I'd say, 'I don't want to sit in the first balcony! You turn those tickets in and you get tickets downstairs!'

" 'No, Zhoezay, we can see . . .'

" 'I won't!' And I'd throw a fit.

"And he'd say, 'Oh, Zhoezay . . .'

"And I'd say, 'If you don't buy the tickets, you don't get nothing!'

"And he would buy the other tickets, oh immediately.

"I'd say that I wanted to go to a restaurant and have dinner. He'd find an inexpensive restaurant. I'd say, 'I want to go to something nice. I want tablecloths and napkins. I want to be served.'

" 'The food is the same. Sometimes it's not as good at the expensive restaurant.'

" 'I . . . don't . . . care.'

"Today I feel very bad, because I was so evil to the poor man! A lot of times he'd say, 'Oh, Zhoezay, just a little bit?'

" 'No, I've got a backache. I've got a headache. No . . .' and I gave all kinds of excuses. And I feel bad today about that. One should not do that. But you see, I was no different than the young people of today. I thought that my youth and my beauty were going to last forever. And you know there comes a day when you are not that pretty seventeen-year-old boy anymore."

As if sensing that his tone had turned too serious, José smiled with a twinkle in his eye and added a footnote.

"So if you're going to be a bitch, you have to be a bitch at an early age, and do it as long as you can."

Paul and José continued to see each other as America entered the war. Their relationship deepened, and Paul began to indulge his young lover more. One Christmas early in the war, Paul showed up in Redwood City with a Cadillac tied with an enormous red ribbon and bow. Although José loved to be pampered, he felt that the car was too extravagant. Paul insisted that José needed a car for his trips between San Francisco and Redwood City. José refused.

After José graduated from high school and the war intensified, he found himself wanting to join most of his friends in enlisting to serve his country. He did finally enter the Army, serving a tour of duty in Europe that eventually took him to Berlin. He corresponded with Paul during his absence from San Francisco, and it became clear that time and distance would not diminish their love for each other. When José returned in 1946, they continued their love affair as if he had never been gone.

Having been married once, and being very conscious of the wealth of his estate, Paul found himself frustrated with a legal and social system that would not allow him to name as his partial beneficiary the person that he loved most besides his son. It was not until the 1980s that any country in the world legalized gay marriage, and even as the millennium approaches the number of countries that do allow same-sex marriage still does not surpass that of the fingers on one hand. The United States is not among them. Like so many gay men and women before and since, Paul looked for a solution within the discriminatory laws and practices of his time.

He proposed marriage to José's mother Dolores.

In his practical businessman's mind, Paul had it all worked out. Dolores knew of his relationship with her son and would not misread his intentions. She too wished to see José's financial future secure, and would be willing to go along with a necessary ruse to make that possible. Should anything happen to Paul, she would inherit his money and businesses, and José, in turn, would receive them from his mother. In the meantime, Dolores would be free to cook and clean for her own household without the necessity of outside employment. They would all have a secure, orderly, loving home together. The plan also meant that Jonathan would always be able to stay with the family that had treated him so well. Paul had considered all of the angles and elements of the situation—except one: José's personal integrity.

Despite the prevailing silence and shame surrounding the subject of same-gender love in the American culture of his youth, José had already begun to develop a strong sense of his unique personhood, his right to be proud and honest about himself in all his facets. Perhaps it was the cultural pride with which he was raised, his sense of connectedness to his ancestors and his Colombian heritage. José was simply not willing to deny who he was, even for the guarantee of wealth and security. To do so would be a violation of his personal code of ethics. He was determined to stay out of the closet before the world even had the slang term *closet* to describe the phenomenon of a double life that so many gay men had been forced to live for so long. José preferred to keep their relationship honest and take their chances with the future.

"I said, 'I don't think that's a good idea, Paul. We'll just continue as we are. People think we are very good friends, but we know.'"

As José told this story, one of the deeper chimes from one of his many clocks began its somber knell. Coincidence?

"'Ah, but Zhoezay . . .'

"'No. You have your son, and it would not be good. What would you tell him?'"

Left with no other option, Paul contacted his brother in Hollywood and gave him detailed instructions as to how his estate should be divided should anything happen to him. He clearly outlined the things he wanted to leave to José and his family.

Paul and Jonathan continued to live as a part of José's family though the plan to marry ended with José's adamant refusal to live what he saw as a charade. At Christmas in 1947 the family decided to hold a large Christmas dinner at the house in Redwood City. José and his mother traveled down to the farm early on Christmas Eve. Paul had plans to attend midnight mass that night, and said he would come down early so that he and Jonathan could be with the family on Christmas morning.

"They went to midnight mass on Filmore and Hayes. The church is called . . . the Sister . . . Saint . . . oh . . . Saint Bernard. Saint Bernard Church . . . no, Sacred Heart Church, operated by the Sisters of Charity that have the big wings on their heads.

"They went to midnight mass, he and his son. And they had the mass, and then they came out, got in their car. They were driving, driving up Hayes Street to cut over to get to Geary Street, going home."

Paul intended to go home so that he and Jonathan could catch a few hours of sleep before making the drive to Redwood City. The gifts for the family were wrapped and waiting to be loaded into the trunk. Though tired, Paul and his son were in good spirits. Life had been filled with love for them for the past few years. This would be a good Christmas. Jonathan thought about the chickens and the Christmas tree that would be surrounded with presents.

Down in Redwood City, the sun rose on a clear, cold Christmas morning. The rooster crowed and the animals stirred, but the air remained still, as if waiting. José and his mother and his godparents rose and prepared for breakfast. They were not sure what time Paul and Jonathan would arrive, but there would be ample food all day, and they would not suffer missing breakfast. The brightly wrapped gifts sent out vibrant colors in the morning light that shone in through the window. While he ate, José glanced now and then at the door in eager anticipation, like a child waiting for Santa Claus, except that it was love he longed to see walk again through the door of his country home.

Breakfast ended, and the dishes were cleared. No sound of a car broke the morning stillness outside. The women began working in the kitchen, preparing the Christmas feast. José wondered why Paul was waiting so long to come. Jonathan would surely be anxious to open his gifts.

Time inched slowly toward noon, and José began to worry. When he could wait no longer, he telephoned Paul's house. No answer. He must have left by now. José carefully noted the time it would take for the drive, perhaps interrupted by a stop for a quick breakfast on the road. Then he waited. Time enough for the trip passed. Time enough for breakfast. Time enough for a potty stop. The possibilities began to force their way into José's worried mind. The car broke down. There was an emergency at one of the businesses. Paul changed his mind about coming. Why? Jonathan was sick.

José began to call the people he knew in San Francisco who might know where Paul was. After one of the calls, he fell as silent as the air outside.

"They were driving, driving up Hayes Street to cut over to get to Geary Street, going home."

José told the story quickly, in a matter-of-fact voice, as if to keep the past from getting a grip on the present, as if to keep it at a distance.

"They were driving, driving up Hayes Street to cut over to get to Geary Street, going home, Paul and his son. A drunk driver came around the corner and smashed into them. By the time they got to the hospital, they were dead."

I remember hearing those words from José and seeing a curtain draw back in his eyes, as if by a hand from behind. I saw a sharp pain there. I felt as if I were entering a place few were privileged to see. As suddenly as I saw it, the curtain fell back and José spoke in a very calm and even voice about the difficulties of aristocratic inheritance.

"Now the problem was, because of the inheritance, to determine who died first. Had the son died first, the father would have kept all of the estate. Then Paul would have died, and the brother could inherit since Paul had no other heir. Had Paul died first, the son would have inherited, and the brother would have gotten nothing. Because of the title, see? Paul had the title, but his brother did not have a title. The brother was just Doctor Kolish, whereas Paul was Baron Paul Von Kolish because he was the firstborn son. And everything would pass on to his firstborn son, Jonathan.

"I understand that Paul had a beautiful home, a palace, in Vienna, and a beautiful country home. He married very well. He had to sneak out of Austria, and all he took was a suitcase with the most valuable things he could fit in it, like jewelry. Everything else was left as it was to buy them time and avoid suspicion. He told some of his friends to go over after a while and take paintings and this and that before the Germans got there. And that was the end of it. The Nazis confiscated everything else. He never got anything back. Not long after the war, he was dead.

"The coroner said in his report that the son died first. And then Paul died, and the brother inherited everything. I was supposed to get some things from him. Paul had told his brother that I was to get certain things if anything happened. But Paul never wrote those instructions down. Or if he did, the brother kept it hidden. He didn't listen to Paul's wishes. The brother knew we had a relationship, and he didn't approve, but there was nothing he could do about it while Paul was alive. I would have gotten one of the houses, but he gave me only a little money and one ring. He claimed that was all Paul wanted me to have. He was so evil. He said afterwards, 'If you expect anything else, you're not going to get it.'

"He ignored his brother's wishes, and what made me upset was the fact that he wouldn't have what he had if it weren't for his brother. Yes, he had intelligence to know what side his bread was buttered on, and he built a very wealthy clientele in the Los Angeles/Hollywood set, but had he not been made to study by Paul and made to go to school to become a dentist, he never would have had a fucking thing. I figure he'll get his. He'll get what's coming. I don't know what ever happened to him."

José's family mourned bitterly at the passing of Paul and Jonathan. He was as much a member of their family as he would have been by marriage. Theirs was a family bound more by love and mutual care than by blood. Paul and his son had been another wonderful extension of that family, and they were deeply missed.

The intractability of Paul's brother, his refusal to acknowledge Paul's new American family, was yet another bitterness to endure along with the bitterness of untimely death. Had Dolores agreed to marry Paul, and had José concurred, the inheritance would have stayed in San Francisco and Redwood City. But it was not to be.

Despite the dearth of material reminders, José's years with Paul remain a shining moment in his life. He has memories of love and laughter and warm nights. He also has sad but gentle regrets.

"It was very sad. I have known some wonderful people in my life, and he was one of the best. He was good to me. He was good to my family. He was so fun. He was a fine man." (Jose smiled enigmatically.) "I was so evil to him, but I thought I was going to be young and beautiful and tight all my life."

Hermano a Hermano

Often when we think of our lives, we look back at the chronological progression and feel a bit of security in knowing that, in retrospect, we can understand the events of our past. First this happened, and then this, and then that, and there you have it. Memory can be like a bookshelf; everything on it is neatly stacked and arranged and in control. We can scan the familiar contents and reassure ourselves that all of the events are in the same neat order as when we reviewed them last. Yet the past is not always such a submissive creature. It scurries out of its assigned place and intrudes on the present like a hamster that won't stay in its cage. It forces the nice, neat chronology of our lives to break down and seem almost irrelevant. Any parent who has grown angry over a child's mistake that echoes a past mistake of the parent's knows this process all too well. So does the person who sees a stranger's face in a crowd that sparks a memory and a sudden upsurge of long-forgotten feelings.

Are our stories ever completed? Are they ever as neatly told as a novel? We may wish them to be, and we may fool ourselves into thinking they are, but in our private moments of remembering, in our silent tears and sudden smiles out of nowhere, we know that the past is as alive as it ever was. The gardens that are our lives, like the gardens out in the yard, change their look with the shifting of the light as the day matures. So it has been with José and his understanding of his life.

The story of José's childhood and adolescence was not completed for him when he entered the service, nor when he turned twenty-one, nor even when Paul died. A decade later he found a piece of the story, small in the scope of years: a statement uttered briefly by his father. Yet those words for José became central to his life's story. And out of those words came a renewed connection to his ancestry, adding significance to other events even later that clarified a bit of that history. They also led to a meeting with a brother he had never known. If these recollections of José's seem chronologically out of place, such is life.

"I almost had a chance to meet my grandmother on my father's side. She was ninety-seven or ninety-eight when she died in Los Angeles. I didn't know she was there. That wasn't so long ago. But I am in contact with my half brother from my father's marriage. His name is Hugo Anthony Sarria. He married, and it was not until 1953 that I met him. Hugo gave me pictures of the family. He told me that, before my father died in 1945, he acknowledged me as his firstborn. When my father went home, his best friend told the family that he had sired another son. My father finally admitted it. 'Yes, I have a son by Dolores Maldonado. He lives with her in San Francisco. His name is José.' He left in his will that his wife and son would find me, to give me some things. Some pictures of my dad, etc. My father died of a cerebral hemorrhage in 1945. He is buried in Nicaragua.

"So they all knew. It was his friend who snitched on him. It was not until 1953 that the family found my mother, nailed her down with the help of the FBI. And that is when I met Hugo.

"When I met Hugo for the first time, we double–dated. He was a graduate of the University of California. He was a buyer for the Emporium. This was my real brother. He was working for the Emporium and then the Grace Line, and then he went back to Nicaragua where he got married and he had two girls and two boys.

"One boy is a doctor, and one is an up–and–coming student, very handsome, very handsome. One girl married a banker, and the other is courting a high political figure, the minister or president of something.

"At first, Hugo knew about my life and my work as a female impersonator, but the rest of the family did not. Then in 1965, when I appeared in *Life* magazine, they knew who I was: 'the most notorious homosexual.' That's what they called me in the magazine. That was my title. So anyway, they all know who I am, what I do, and they believe I have my right to it."

As always, José's heritage, his connection with the noble people of the past, was tied closely to his feelings about his family and himself. As his ties to his Nicaraguan family grew stronger, so did his pride in that half of his ancestry. In the 1960s José met a man named Pierre, who subsequently became one of his best friends.

Pierre ran restaurants at world's fairs and expositions, and José went to work for him during several of the international events. José spoke to Pierre often of his noble ancestry, and, although Pierre loved and respected his good friend, he doubted his nobility.

"When I told Pierre that I was from a noble family, he had his doubts. But he should have known it was true. See, Pierre was in Barcelona riding on a bus on the main boulevard sometime after meeting me. Different stretches of the road were named after different people and families. At one point, the bus driver said, 'And now we have the section of the boulevard called Avenida de Sarria, one of the oldest noble families of this area. Their castle still stands as the monastery outside Barcelona.' Pierre sent me a card with a picture of the street sign.

"Still he had his doubts. Or maybe he was just teasing me. Anyway, at the World's Fair in San Antonio, Texas, Spain allowed the royal archives to be taken out of the country for the first time and displayed. They set up a booth with Spanish books of heraldry and family ancestry. Pierre said, 'Now we're going to find out if your family really is nobility.'

"So one day we went over to the heraldry house. Pierre went in and said that we were trying to find my family.

"The man asked, 'What's the name?'

"Pierre said, 'Sarria.'

"The man said, 'Oh, that's a very, very fine name. The family goes back to the 1500s in our records.'

"We learned that the Sarrias were always a very noble people. They were counts and marquises. One of my ancestors got religious and gave everything he had to the Franciscan order and became a Franciscan priest in Spain. He later came to the new world. His name was José, and he was about third in command with Father Junípero Serra in the founding of the missions. He's buried under the altar at San Antonio de Padua. When they dedicated the church again, the Hearst family invited my mother to go down there to help officiate. It was a blasted hot day. She went into the confessional and took off her corset, and came out with her corset in hand.

"The records at the fair showed that José Sarria, my ancestor, not me, became involved with the Franciscans around the late 1700s. On December the fourteenth, 1817, two days after my birthday—

not in that year, however; I'm not that old—the mission of San Rafael the Archangel was dedicated. For a time the management of that mission was under the mission of San Francisco. Later it became independent. It was known as a place of healing. Indians from San Francisco would go there. I read in an article that the mission has the names of the founders on a bronze plaque over the entrance. Sarria, Abella, Yobada, and Durán.

"It was my ancestor, Father Sarria, who helped found the mission. He got in trouble because he would not take the oath of allegiance to the Constitution of Mexico. The government officials of Mexico were very, very angry about this. They had him transferred to another mission, Soledad. It was a very poor mission. He never complained. He worked with the Indians and shared what little food there was. The church sent him no help at all. He became skinny and ill. Still he refused to take the oath. He believed his oath was to God only. He kept refusing. Finally, he got so sick that he fainted and died at the altar of the church. He never did take the oath. The Sarrias have been rebellious and stubborn all along!"

PART TWO:
THEY SAY THAT IN THE ARMY

The Boys from Texas

It was a cold morning and the earth still smelled rich from the last rain. The air was clean and the golden browns and evergreens of the northern California winter were washed and bold. José and his mother and godparents had been to church in Redwood City and were gathered near the kitchen where the women were preparing homemade waffles on the heavy waffle iron. José's sisters, Leonore and Teresa, both of whom lived in Redwood City, had come over to share breakfast. It was a favorite Sunday breakfast of the family. The sweet bread smell of waffles filled the room and warmth radiated from the kitchen. The radio was on, and soft music played in the background. The family casually discussed the day, the sermon, the approaching holidays. Would Dolores be coming down for Christmas as in past years? Maybe a menu change this year? Or not.

Suddenly the music stopped and did not start again. José briefly wondered if the awkward silence was the handiwork of a new radio host learning the ropes. Maybe the radio went out. No, there was the familiar scratch and crackle of the station connection.

"Ladies and gentlemen, we interrupt your program to inform you that the Imperial Government of Japan has carried out a surprise bombing attack on the United States base at Pearl Harbor. Details of the attack are still . . ."

The family froze in shocked silence. The steaming waffles, the plates, a stirring spoon thick with batter, men seated in their Sunday suits, the table with its intricate lace tablecloth, aprons on the women, prayer missals on the end table: they were a still portrait of mid-century Americana, but for the looks of horror and stunned disbelief on their faces. America had been attacked. United States soldiers and ships had been bombed. Suddenly the great foreign war was on the doorstep through an act of naked aggression by a country that had, minutes before, been far from people's thoughts.

"Well, my goodness gracious, that was the end of the world! We were attacked! We sat stunned. Everybody wondered what was going to happen. There were interruptions all during the day about the disaster that had befallen. Nobody had been prepared, and there were questions as to why the Japanese were able to make a sneak attack."

José and his family spent most of the day near the radio. They ate their meals mechanically, and talked little. As evening approached, José and his mother returned to San Francisco, because there was nothing else to do but continue the routine that they knew. José talked briefly with Paul, for whom the attack was déjà vu. On Monday, José went to school, not knowing what to expect. A part of the answer came when the students were called together to listen to an address by the President of the United States, Franklin Delano Roosevelt. It was not to be his usual fireside chat. He spoke somberly, and he called December 7, 1941 "a day that will live in infamy." He announced that the United States had declared war.

Although Roosevelt had reinstituted military conscription even before the country's entrance into the war, José did not immediately have to concern himself with being drafted. He was young and in high school. He would be able to finish his senior year before deciding what to do about his part in the war. Yet the war seemed to invade every conversation. The boys at school alternated between nervous fear and youthful bravado. All of the young men spoke of the coming time when they too could serve their country as their older brothers, or uncles, or fathers already were. No boy dared speak of avoiding military service.

There were whispered conversations at José's school about the "4-Fers," the men who, for one reason or another, had been rejected by the military services. 4-Fer became the code word for shame and disgrace among the young men. Stories circulated about men who wanted to stay out of the service and who showed up at the draft board in dresses. There was talk of deferments for college attendance. Many of the young men José knew continued to expound upon their intent to "go show those Nazis and Japs what for" even as they began studying hard to raise their grades and prepare for college.

José was a good student. He had been a student body officer in his junior year and was again in his senior year. He was popular, and the few students who may have known about his relationship with Paul Kolish never treated him any differently than any other student leader. No one who knew ever reproached José about his sexuality, and no one ever associated him with the 4-Fers in dresses. José had fully intended to enter college after graduation, and he still made plans. At the same time, he did not want to face the dreaded 4-Fer label, and he talked often of joining the service. He sincerely wanted to serve his country, but like so many young men in school, he was quietly torn.

"Naturally all of us fellows were ready to go to war and fight. The United States was a united country. Everybody forgot that they were Republicans and Democrats. We all had a common foe. I graduated, and I started college. In order to stay in college, you had to enlist in the Reserves and keep a C or above average. If you went below a C average, they would nab you and put you on active duty. Everybody wanted to stay in school and get as much college in as they could before they had to go to war. We all knew that we would eventually go to war. Nobody wanted to be rejected and become a 4-Fer. That was very disgraceful. You were a 4-Fer for many reasons. Some men would not want to go to war, so they would put on a dress. People did crazy things."

After graduating from high school, José enrolled in college. He intended to concentrate his studies on home economics. Once enrolled, he made his obligatory trip to the recruiting offices to sign up for the Reserves.

"I went to the Navy recruiting office to hear what was being offered. I liked the uniform, and I thought it would be exciting. The recruiting officer talked about how clean the Navy was, and that we would see the world. But academically you had to take sciences and very heavy mathematical courses. I thought, 'Oh Jesus! I'm a home economics person.' I wasn't about to take trigonometry and physics and chemistry. I got up and walked out."

Disappointed that he would not be able to wear the stylish uniform of a sailor, José went to investigate his second choice, the Marine Corps.

"So then, I walked into the Marines. I said, 'I'll be a Marine.' The Army was always everyone's last choice because they were the dog soldiers. It wasn't glamorous. The uniform was very simple. And that's who you heard about getting shot all the time. I walked into the room at the Marine recruiting station. Before I had gotten very far, the enlisting officer stopped and said, 'I want to tell you that there are certain restrictions before you can consider becoming a Marine. That is, you must weigh at least a hundred and forty-five pounds and be at least five feet tall. We don't take people under those requirements.' Well, I barely weighed ninety pounds and I was a little under five feet. The recruiter could see I did not fit the bill."

Rejected by a second service, José began to worry that his small stature would make him a 4-Fer. With no other choice, he headed for the Army recruitment center. He sat listening to the recruitment officer who expounded upon the advantages and opportunities of Army service. José showed little interest until the officer began outlining the requirements for entrance into the Army. There was no special requirement concerning the types of courses to take in college as long as the student earned passing grades. That pleased José; he would be able to continue his liberal arts courses. He could keep his foreign language classes, which eventually served him well in the Army.

Then came the more problematic entrance requirement. Army soldiers had to be at least five feet tall and weigh one hundred pounds. José fell short of the mark. Yet, rather than worry about becoming a 4-Fer, José simply smiled to himself. He was hatching a plan. He knew that he had a special "ace in the hole" that only he and one other person knew about. He was quite certain he would be accepted in the Army despite the physical prerequisites. He was more worried about procuring his mother's signature on the paperwork.

"Being that I was not quite eighteen, I had to have the signature of my mother. I went to my mother and I said, 'Mama, will you please sign so I can get into the service and be like the rest of the boys?'

"She said, 'No. I will not sign. You are too young. You can wait.'

"But everyone in college will think I'm a 4-Fer! They might not let me stay in college!'

"She said, 'I don't care. I will not sign.'

"Well, my godmother understood my problem. She said, 'You bring the papers home, and I will sign them as your guardian.'

"My godmother vouched for me, which made my mother mad. She wouldn't talk to me for a while. But I got what I wanted. Of course there was still the problem of the size requirements. That's when I used my ace in the hole."

There was a major working with the enlistment offices in San Francisco whom José had met years earlier—at various gay parties. In the 1940s gay parties were relatively secretive affairs. Guest lists were carefully controlled, and those who attended agreed to an unspoken rule to guard the identities of the attendees in the outside world. Being identified as gay in the straight world more often than not led to loss of job, discharge from the service, shunning by parts of society, and often loss of family. There was a tight bond among gay men based on shared experience, but also on the vulnerability that each had to the others.

The major had taken a liking to José from the first time he met him at one of the parties. José was no wallflower, and the combination of his youthful beauty and his playful gregariousness charmed the military man. José flirted with the major as he did with most men at such affairs, and the major finally asked José to spend the night with him. José was flattered and a little interested, but he preferred to play hard to get. Despite the man's repeated requests over a few years' time, José continued to refuse. That, of course, was before he decided to join the Army.

"There was only one thing to do, and that was finally to give in to him. So when I came up to San Francisco to enlist, I went up to Fourth and Market where the enlistment station was, and got in line like everybody else. The major had the last say whether you got in or not."

José called the major after he had an appointment at the recruiting station. He explained to the major that he wanted very much to be allowed to join the army, and he was willing to be very good to anyone who would help him accomplish that goal. The major asked

José to meet him for lunch so that they could discuss his enlistment. The lunch was a fine one at the Saint Francis Hotel. When they were finished eating, the major paid the bill and led José up to the room he had rented. By the time they emerged some hours later, the major had promised to see that José would be in the Army soon.

José reported for his induction screening at the recruitment center on Market Street prepared to go through the motions of the physical examination.

"They told me to bend over and they looked into this and that. They weighed me and took my measurements. I was very small at the time. My body was really a woman's body.

"By the time I got to the major at the recruiting station, he was prepared. He had put down on a copy of the form that I was one hundred pounds and five feet tall. So anyway, I got through the first part.

"Then I went through this psychological thing where you stand there with your cock and balls hanging out, and you're jumping up and down and they're talking about girls and pussy and all this, and it's supposed to make you excited. And then they talk about men. They did all kinds of things to try to break you down. But I knew what the hell the story was, and nothing excited me. I was too smart for them. Consequently I got in. The major signed the papers, and I was sworn in at eight o'clock at night. I came home, and I went back to school, but I was in the Army Reserve.

"So you see, I screwed my way into the Army."

José returned to school, but he was only there for a short time. As the war intensified, the Army began calling many of its reservists to active duty. José was one of the young men called, but as he was preparing to leave for induction into the regular Army, tragedy visited Redwood City.

It was 1942, and José's godfather was as active and seemed as strong as he had always been. It was Charles Millen who had taught José how to enjoy the work and life of the farm. In social situations he always seemed overshadowed by the women, but he was always there, providing a strong security and a quiet love. When Jesserina took José in, and later Paul's son Jonathan, he never complained about an extra mouth to feed. He simply enlarged his circle of protection to encompass them. Suddenly, days before José's scheduled departure for the military, he suffered a heart attack and died.

José contacted the Army and asked for a delay of his induction date in order to attend his godfather's funeral and to help comfort the family. He was granted a month's extension. With the war and the death of Charles, it seemed to the family as if they were leaving behind a life that they would never recapture. José worried about leaving Jesserina alone, but, although his leaving would mean losing both of the men in her life within a short time, she assured him that she would be fine. Josephine and and her husband Cushman were close by; her other daughters, Leonore and Teresa, lived in Redwood City.

The month passed in sadness and reminiscing. Paul and Jonathan came to the funeral, and spent as much time with Jonathan's Mama as they could. Paul assured José that he would take care of Jesserina while José was serving his time in the Army. He hid his trepidation about José leaving for war. At the end of the month, Jesserina went with José to the train station in Palo Alto. She stood and waved as the train pulled out, and she kept waving until it was out of sight. José leaned out the window and waved until he could no longer see the station. He pulled back inside the train car with tears in his eyes. A man he had never seen before or since came up to him and said, "You can't cry now son. You can't cry anymore. You're a soldier now."

The train took José to Fort Ord where he was sworn into the regular Army and ordered to Sacramento to undergo his basic training with the Signal Corps. He did well, especially in marksmanship—not that he could easily envision himself actually shooting a real person.

During basic training, José found himself housed in a barracks building with a group of men from Texas. He was the only Latino in the company of men who considered Mexicans the absolute bottom of the social ladder . . . if they were on the ladder at all. The fact that José was Colombian made no difference to the young men. That was a distinction that meant little to them, Latin of any variety being a synonym for Mexican in their vocabularies. Many of them were university students, a few from Texas A&M, but they refused to associate with José in any way despite his college-level education.

"They were all very Texan, and of course, Mexican people were on the bottom of their list; they did not associate with them. I was just as intelligent as they were, but for the first month they did not talk to me. They would have nothing to do with me, and I would have nothing to do with them. We did our training. I was an expert at marksmanship. My marks were good. I passed the training."

When basic training came to an end, the new soldiers were given a short leave for "R&R," rest and relaxation. A group of the young men from Texas decided to take advantage of being in California and go visit the famous city of San Francisco. They had heard so many stories about the great times single soldiers could have there. However, when they made a few inquiries, they learned that a simple ninety-mile trip to the City by the Bay was not so simple in wartime. Gas was rationed. Food was rationed. Hotel rooms in San Francisco were at a premium if they were available at all, and none of them knew anyone there who could help them. The Texas boys almost gave up on their plan.

While they were discussing the improbability of seeing their trip through, one of the boys reminded the others that José Sarria was from San Francisco. Maybe he would give them some suggestions. They looked at each other with doubt. They had not spoken a cordial word to José since coming to Sacramento. Why would he help them? Someone suggested they pay him to show them around. He probably wasn't from families like theirs, and he would surely need the money.

"So they approached me and asked, 'You are from San Francisco?'

"I said, 'Yes.'

"'We would like to know how much you would charge us to show us San Francisco.'

"I said, 'Number one, I won't charge you anything because I'm very proud of my city. I would like to show it to you. You can be my guests.'

"They said, 'Well, it's going to cost you some money to do that. We'll pay you at least that.'

"I said, 'No, I don't think so. It will cost less than you think.'

"So they agreed. The first thing I did was call up my godmother and tell her that I was coming down with eight or ten boys from my unit.

"She said, 'Fine, we'll put them up when you get here.'

"I said, 'Well, would you phone Paul Kolish?'

"She said, 'Yes.'

"'Tell him I want a car. He can meet us, but I want a car, and we'll drive it ourselves.'

"Well, when he got in contact with my mother, he said, 'I'll do the driving for the boys. I'll show them around.'

"The next time I talked to my mother in San Francisco I asked, 'Would you phone Dan London?' Dan London was the general manager of the Saint Francis Hotel. He knew us well because of her job there.

"She calls him and says, 'José's coming in. Is it possible that they could get a suite? They don't need to sleep, but they need a room where they can clean up and dress and such.'

"He said, 'For José, no problem.'

"So, we came down from Sacramento on the train, and we were met by Paul in a huge, shiny boat of a convertible. He was all dressed up like a chauffeur. We cleaned up at the hotel and then piled into the car, and he drove us all over San Francisco, up and down the hills. We went to a nice restaurant, and he picked up the bill. Of course none of the boys knew he was my lover. He acted like my servant; he clicked his heels and opened our doors. You should have seen the looks on their faces! Oh my dear!"

None of the young men had ever seen a town quite as sophisticated and worldly as San Francisco. Their bravado melted into wide-eyed wonder. The streets of buildings rising at impossible angles, the ships docked at the wharf or plowing through the waters of the huge bay ringed by rolling mountains, the cries of seagulls and sea lions, the cable cars, the teeming crowds of people from every corner of the world, the palatial hotels and world-class restaurants, the endless sounds of exotic lives: this was José's world, and they were the astounded bumpkins.

As the sun dipped below Twin Peaks and the city lights started to click on one by one, Paul turned the car south to drive the weary visitors toward Redwood City. He dropped half of the boys at José's sister Josephine's house in Woodside, a small town just south of Redwood City. She and her husband, Cushman Riddock, lived in a Swiss chalet-style house outside of town, surrounded by rolling hills and open fields. Today their chalet is just another house on a crowded suburban street. Paul took José and the rest of the Texans to the farm in Redwood City. Despite the recent loss of her husband, Jesserina made every effort to make the young men feel comfortable and welcome. In fact, she enjoyed the distraction of having a full house.

The "boys from Texas," as José called them, had had a taste of the big city. Now José would have a chance to show them gracious California country living. He hoped they wouldn't grow bored after the excitement of the city. He needn't have worried. Cushman made a suggestion that made boredom unlikely.

"That weekend there was the burning of the fields up around Woodside to prevent grass fires, and my brother-in-law was a volunteer fireman. That is still done in many places in California since the winter rain makes the grass grow thick and then the summers are so damn hot and dry. So he asked, 'Why don't you boys come on up and help us?' These Texan kids thought it sounded like a lot of fun.

"So after we had gotten up and the family had all eaten we all went over to my sister's home, and we got the fire trucks out and we burned the fields, and oooohhhh we had a wonderful time! We were all very young, and our mannerisms were all very . . . limp. A lot of culture, a lot of refinement there. Do you understand? And yet, when we worked, we were really very rough and tough. We got pictures of the fields burning, of us hanging onto the trucks. And we've got pictures of us driving the truck, putting the fires out, and oh, we had so much fun! The boys had a gas! We stayed there until my sister rang for us all to come in.

"Afterward Paul, my sisters, and I took all the boys up to Skyline Boulevard and all the bars up there. We drank and had a wild time. We danced and talked and sang. My godmother cooked dinners for all of us the rest of the weekend. We had a ball! I mean, they were shown carte blanche!"

On the day José and the Texans were to return to their assignment, they were gathered at the house in Redwood City with the family. No one wanted to speak of their leaving. They talked and ate and tried to make the time stretch. Finally it was time to leave to catch the train back to the great central valley and the river town of Sacramento. As the young men rose to gather their things, Jesserina turned to her daughter and asked, "Couldn't you get these boys on a plane so they can stay later?" Teresa worked in the air cargo division of United Airlines. She said she would try.

"So she did! She arranged to get us all onto United Airlines. I think it cost us only the tax. Five dollars and a few cents altogether. She got us on a plane that left much later and wouldn't interfere with dinner.

We could eat and have wine, and then they could take us to the airport, and we would get to the camp on time.

"When we got to the camp, they could not tell the rest of the men enough about what a good time we had. 'My God, you just don't know! José's family is so sweet! And his sisters, why they are the 'drinkingest' girls you ever did see! We danced! We drank! We stayed at the Saint Francis Hotel! We had this gentleman who clicked his heels and drove the car! We drove around in a huge convertible!'

"They made this great thing about me and carried on. But then they said that they wanted to pay me. I said, 'No. I don't want your money. Not all Latin people are what you think we are.'

"That embarrassed them a little. 'Oh no no no no no!' they said.

"Well, they did find a way to thank me. One of them, Alanzo was his name, had influence with a U.S. senator from Texas, Senator Gonzales. He made me an honorary citizen of Texas. Alanzo and I became bosom buddies. After we left the Signal Corps, we went to Corvallis where we went through the Army Specialist Training Program together. It turns out that the senator's daughter, Beatrice Gonzales, was one of the language teachers I studied with there. We finished our studies there, and then they called us to active duty. From there we went to Fort Leonard Wood.

"But the boys were fantastic! We are good buddies to this day. One of the boys inherited from his father the Coca-Cola distributors in Hope, Arkansas. His name was Luke Holleman. We still write to one another. He is very, very sick but we still maintain close ties. None of them ever found out that I was gay. They were all very shy about personal things."

José's escapades with the boys from Texas were not to be the last time he worked to build bridges of understanding between groups of people who distrusted and misunderstood each other. Not the last by a long shot!

You're in the Army Now

From the time of José's enlistment, it seemed that the Army intended to take great care with his training. His fluency in foreign languages, including German, was a strong asset in that time of world warfare. He was not put into basic training with the regular infantry, but rather with the Signal Corps. Once his basic training was completed, the Army assigned José to Intelligence School. Because Army Intelligence involved work with sensitive and often classified information, acceptance into that service required a stringent security clearance. Once José was enrolled in the school, the Army began its routine background check on him and the other new students. Agents were sent to San Francisco to interview friends, neighbors, and family about José's character, abilities, social interactions, and morals.

"One day I was told that I was not going to be in that program anymore. It didn't dawn on me why. I didn't put the events together; I thought I just didn't qualify. But I did that same work when I was in the war—interpreting—so I know I was qualified. But it came to me later that, after they put you in the program, and you begin your training, they go to your home to investigate your morals and your character. They must have learned something. I mean I had no lisp, but I wasn't the most masculine guy in town. Anyone could have said something. So I think that they figured that I was a little bit gay. They just made some excuse at the time. I was still in the Signal Corps, just not that part of it. They said, 'We don't think you can handle it,' or something like that. I didn't put one and one together, because, you see, I've never really lived a double life. It's not that I tell everybody, but people know; you're not fooling anybody. The neighbors knew that I was a little different."

The United States military had a policy at that time of discharging any man or woman found to be homosexual. Those discharges continue to this day, even under the so-called "don't ask, don't tell" policy of the Clinton Administration. Yet there have been periods in which the military has tolerated the presence of gay men and lesbians in its ranks: wartime. The military is much less anxious to purge the ranks of gays when it is in need of bodies. In all of America's recent wars, even up to the Persian Gulf War, many gay and lesbian soldiers served with distinction, only to be asked to leave the service once the war was over. Thus many highly decorated soldiers have been, and still are, told that they are unfit for military service. Whether or not this would have been the case with José is a matter of speculation. He did not intend to make the Army his career, and his service ended voluntarily soon after the war was won.

However, the Army was not to trust José with anything as sensitive and fragile as Army Intelligence. (No, dearest reader, the author is not choosing words like "fragile intelligence" out of a bias born of having grown up in an Army family. Okay, well, maybe a little. I'll see my therapist about it.) The Army would not give top security clearance to a gay soldier because it considered a gay soldier too vulnerable to blackmail by foreign powers, because, of course, he could be discharged if his sexuality were found out. (If the logic here seems a little circular, don't blame me. Ask the Pentagon.) And so the Army put José into an area of work that its very straight mentality considered appropriate for him. He was ordered to Cooks and Bakers School.

Being a man who aspired to a degree in home economics, José did very well in cooking school. He loved cooking, and he became a star pupil, though he complained a little of the lack of imagination in military cuisine. The head chef, whom José says once cooked for the Pope at the Vatican, took a liking to José and gave him special privileges. Since José already knew how to cook well, the chef concentrated on teaching him to bake. He often gave José day passes to buy ingredients off the base. Most soldiers rarely were allowed such passes.

When word got out that José was often allowed off base, several soldiers approached him about buying liquor for them on one of his trips into the civilian world. He agreed, and they gave him money and requests for whiskey, scotch, bourbon, vodka, and gin. Because Sacramento had five military bases at the time, liquor stores were plentiful. José soon found out, however, that the stores were more plentiful than the liquor. A combination of high demand and wartime shortages made the shopping trip frustrating. None of the stores he checked had the drink he had been asked to buy. Finally, one store said it had a good supply of sloe gin.

"Well, my dear, I didn't know the difference between sloe gin and fast gin, so I said, 'I'll buy it.' When I got back to the place in the fence where I was supposed to hand the booze to one of the guys, he complained that I had bought the wrong thing. He said sloe gin was like a liqueur, and needed other ingredients for mixing into drinks. I asked what kind of ingredients. He said they'd need fruit juice and things. I told him to have the guys come to the bakery later that night. I was working there alone, and I could get the things they needed. Then I went around to the front gate and went in."

That night José was preparing cherry pie for the next day and doughnuts for the morning. The pies were in the oven and the doughnut dough was rising on the counter when the guys showed up with the bottles of sloe gin. José immediately began playing bartender, taking their directions for ingredients and mixing their drinks. They began drinking and enjoying their own private, illicit party.

"Oh, honey, we had a ball. We got ripped to the tits! Somehow a cherry pie ended up on the roof. In the morning, we were all passed out all over the kitchen."

When the chef arrived early that morning, the doughnut dough was still rising on the counters, overflowing onto the floor in some places. The cherry pies had boiled over, and sticky red filling was smoking on the bottom of the oven. There was flour and spilled fruit juice on the floors and counters. The empty sloe gin bottles scattered about and the snoring, drunken soldiers sprawled on the floor and draped on chairs left little doubt about the cause of the mess.

"No one got any baked goods that day. We were all put under 'arrest of quarters,' like house arrest. We weren't allowed to go anywhere except to our training. I fell out of favor with the chef, of course. I think he would have strangled me if he could. Needless to say, I was no longer allowed off the base much."

José eventually graduated from the Cooks and Bakers School, still officially a member of the Signal Corps. Soon after José's completion of cooking school, the men in Signal Corps began to receive their orders for overseas. They were going into combat. Because José was underage, regulations forbid sending him to battle. Instead, he was sent to the Army Specialist Training Program, ASTP. He went with his friend Alanzo, who had arranged for him to receive honorary Texas citizenship after the R&R in San Francisco.

"We called it 'the flaming pisspot unit' because its insignia was an Aladdin's lamp with a flame coming out of the tip. Soon after that the army needed more infantry because they were planning the Bulge. They closed the school to send us to Europe. They emptied the ASTP and we went into the infantry—that's how I got out of the Signal Corps.

"In the infantry they tried to train me for lead scout, which was the worst. They are the first ones to go over the hill, and I figured that out very quickly. This was one queen who was not going to be the first queen over the hill. So I screwed up on purpose. I did everything contrary. They signaled forward; I went backward. They signaled right; I went left. I was a failure as a scout."

When it became apparent that José was an abject failure as a foot soldier, the Army looked around for the most logical placement for him, a place where his talents in languages and the culinary arts could best serve the Army. They transferred him to the motor pool.

He spent the next month learning to work on greasy trucks and jeeps. (There was no olive oil on this assignment, just a lot of olive green.)

"They sent me to motor school so that I could work the motor pool. Well, I am *not* very mechanically inclined, but I hoped that being in the motor pool would give me a chance to drive a vehicle. I think that's much better than leading a company over a hill. So they sent me to school to learn to drive and do maintenance. Oh, my dear, I passed! There were two hundred and forty people in the class, and I graduated two hundred and thirty-nine. I knew how to keep the machines clean, but I never drove. I was the world's worst driver, so they wouldn't let me drive. I would stay on the base polishing the goddamn jeeps all day."

One warm day, José was out on the blacktop washing one of the trucks. The motor pool was quiet because all of the usual drivers were either out on assignment or off duty. The soldiers manning the desk were lounging around, shooting the breeze. Unexpectedly, the phone rang. One of the soldiers answered in the polite, efficient manner expected of soldiers on the phone: he identified the motor pool and identified himself by name and rank. There was a pause as he listened to the voice on the line. "Yes sir. Certainly sir," he finally said. He hung up the phone, looked at his companions, and groaned.

The executive officer, Major Mataxis, had been the voice on the other end of the call. He wanted a jeep and a driver for the afternoon. He had asked that they send someone to pick him up immediately. There were no drivers available except José.

"He was a very well-liked officer. They didn't want anything to happen to him, and yet I was the only driver there. One of them said to me, 'You've got to go out. You've got to drive for him, but you have to promise that you won't kill him. Good officers are hard to come by.'"

José drove up to the BOQ (bachelor officers' quarters), having avoided any major accidents on the way over. To José's mild surprise, the man who strode casually up to the jeep was very young, only a few years older than José himself. José had expected someone older, though attaining rank at an early age is not an uncommon phenomenon in wartime. José opened the passenger door and saluted. Major Mataxis saluted back, smiled, and hopped into the seat saying, "Let's go, soldier." José hurried around the front of the jeep, whispering a silent prayer that he would not drive them off the road or hit anything.

As the two men drove between Major Mataxis's appointments, they talked casually about their homes, their families, their college studies. The major had studied history. They learned that they had a love of music in common. They began to test each other's knowledge of music; one of them would hum a song and the other would have to name the song, the composer, and what performer made it famous. By the end of the day they were laughing and joking like old friends. As they drove up to the BOQ, they fell back into their formal roles as officer and driver as Army etiquette and regulations demand. José opened the major's door and saluted smartly. The major returned the salute and thanked José for a job well done. José climbed back into the driver's seat, realizing that he had been so at ease in the major's company that he had not even given any thought to his driving. Without the tense worry, his driving had been very good.

The next day José was at his usual job of cleaning vehicles. The phone rang in the office. Several of the drivers stopped to listen and find out which of them would be sent out. The soldier on the phone said little but "Yes sir" until he hung up. He turned to the other men a little dumbfounded. "That was a special request for a driver . . . for José."

José and Major Mataxis spent another day driving from duty to duty, playing word games and quizzing each other on music and movies and celebrities. For the rest of the month, whenever the major called the motor pool, it was understood that José would be driving. At the end of the month, José received his orders for Fort Leonard Wood, Missouri. The soldiers in the ASTP were being called out to active infantry. At Fort Leonard Wood they would be trained in more difficult terrain to prepare them for the rigors of the Bulge campaign, though of course the soldiers knew nothing of the plan at the time. From Missouri they would travel to Boston to ship out for Europe. When José talked to the major about the new orders, Mataxis told him that he too would be going to Leonard Wood, and he had a request of José.

"So the major said to me, 'How would you like to be my personal boy, my orderly?' He offered to pay me fifty dollars a month extra. I would be relieved of certain duties, and I was responsible to him only. So I thought that was fabulous. So I said, 'Okay.' We went to Leonard Wood, then to Boston where we shipped out to Europe.

"When we arrived overseas—we landed in Marseilles—I took care of him, saw that his clothes got laundered and his weapons got cleaned, and I wrote letters to his wife for him because he was so busy he couldn't do that. I would sit down and write a letter for him, and she was always very pleased with each one. I knew him very well by then, so writing the letters was easy."

In addition to driving the major wherever he needed to go, José was expected to cook his meals. Mataxis was regularly amazed and pleased with José's culinary skill, even under lean circumstances, but José felt as if his talents were not being used as they should be. One evening after the major had complimented him yet again on an extraordinary meal, José suggested that he could cook for other officers in the battalion without spending very much more time and without detracting from his other duties. He explained that cooking for many was easier than cooking for one. His boss agreed to share his orderly's talent with his fellow officers, and José began cooking regularly for about ten officers. He became a valued member of the battalion. There were a few, however, who spoke of him with less than affection.

"The men I worked with in the military knew I was different. Nobody ever questioned me. A couple of times we went out drinking, and someone said something about 'that queer sergeant,' and there was a fight. The other guys would defend me. We cleaned out a bar one time. When you first met me, did you think I was gay? You had to. I was that different. I must have given you some vibrations."

(Well, that, and the fact that you grinned mischievously and told me you could take your teeth out.)

"I feel that I've done this all my life. I mean, these kids that go around thinking that nobody knows that they're gay . . . bullshit!

"Later, we were in Limburg on the Lahn—the Lahn River in Germany—something was said.

"Some of the officers did not like the fact that I had the privileges that I had. Number one, I did not pull guard duty. I did not pull regular kitchen duty. But they did not say anything because I was the colonel's boy." (By then, Mataxis had been promoted.) "Now I also had my own vehicle. I had people that I dealt with on the Rhine that I had befriended that worked for the wineries and would supply me with wine. So from Limburg on the Lahn I would send a two-and-a-half-ton truck and load it up. It would come back, and I would negotiate to make a nice profit. I would sell. This is what I did very nicely.

"Once the colonel had to go to Frankfurt without me. I thought, 'Okay, I'll go and get a shipment. My weekend will go faster.' So I picked up a two-and-a-half-ton truck and went to pick up a load. On the way back, I transferred some of the cases into the colonel's car, which was my car also. I went up to the camp, and I sold to whoever had the money. There were no questions, and everybody kept their mouths shut. Well everything went fine. I finished my selling, came back, and went to bed.

"Now, I did not realize that there was one boy in the prison who bribed the guards to buy some liquor. They bought four cases of wine, and they had a party with the guards and the prisoners. Somehow a fire started, and they burnt the guardhouse to the ground. Three people were very seriously injured. And of course, the place was loaded with bottles. The building was demolished.

"The next morning I heard that the guardhouse burnt down, and there were bottles all over. They had had a ball! It came out that the colonel's car had been seen in the area. They asked the guard detail. Finally, they came and asked me did I use the colonel's car.

"I said, 'Yes.'

" 'Where did you go?'

" 'I went out to the guardhouse. I was doing some business.'

"And then it came out that some prisoners had bought the liquor. So I was being held for selling liquor to prisoners, which caused the fire and caused three men to be disfigured for life and to almost die. Somebody had to pay for what happened.

"You see, the prison was not regulation. It was old. It was a firetrap. They had to cover up the fact that the prison was a shack. It was not an authorized building suitable for a jail. I was put under arrest by a captain whose father was an admiral at Pearl Harbor, who became a kind of a scapegoat for what happened there. The captain had a hard time living that down, being the son of this man. And he was one of the officers who never liked the fact that I had the privileges that I had. He was an old-style army man, but he never could say anything before.

"He put me on guard detail when Mataxis, who by then was a colonel, was away, and then he forgot me, left me out in the middle of the wilds all night. But I was a good soldier, and I didn't complain until I was relieved. Then I went over and got him in hot water. On the guard detail you were supposed to be on guard for four hours and then off two. I was on six hours because they forgot me. But I never left my post.

"So the officers were eating breakfast after the guardhouse burned, and I came into the room. The captain didn't know. He turned to another officer and said, 'Well, now we've got the colonel's boy! That's going to break up that bed partnership! I've been after him for some time.'

"Then Colonel Mataxis came in, and I told him what I had heard, the captain insinuating that he and I were bed partners. The colonel was very upset. He went to the captain and asked if he had made the statement to that effect, and he couldn't deny it because there were other officers who said that he did. The next day, he was shipped out. And the colonel went back to Frankfurt and struck a deal with the general. Someone had to be punished for the guardhouse, but no one admitted anything. No one pointed a finger. So they were going to put it on me. The colonel struck a bargain that said, 'If the men die—they were very badly burned—you can take him and have a general court martial. Otherwise, take him out of the company for a while. Send him someplace.'

"Well, the men did not die, thank goodness! They decided to send me back to school. And then after everything cooled down, I could come back. That is why I went to school at American University.

"At that same time, the first team of American plastic surgeons arrived in Europe because there was now such a need. The three victims were their first patients. They came out handsomer than when they went in. I stayed in school for almost a year, and then I came back to my same unit, and we marched into Berlin. The unit had changed, so nobody knew me. Now, because nobody confessed to letting the prisoners out, the guards were all given six months and two thirds. That's six months in prison and two thirds of their pay. Nobody ever confessed. The colonel thought that was very apropos."

The Battle of the Bulge ended in January, 1945, and in the spring, on May 7, Germany surrendered. As the war continued in the Pacific, José returned from school to his division just before it marched into Berlin to relieve the first American troops that had marched into the city as the war ended. They were to become a part of the occupation forces in Berlin under General Clay while the Allied powers negotiated the fate of the defeated nation. By then José had been promoted to staff sergeant.

"Now that was a permanent rank. Many were given a temporary rank during the war. A permanent rank at the same level outranked a temporary rank. So, I really outranked a lot of officers."

In Berlin, José was put in charge of running the confiscated mansion that became the officers' dining hall. Though his official duties were limited to the mansion, José soon gained a reputation for other work among the wives of the married officers. They learned that when they wanted something nice for the house that was unavailable in the postwar austerity, José could get it for them through his "connections." If they wanted fine dresses, they went to José and his staff at the officers' mess hall. José's black market wheeling and dealing kept the officers' wives happy, which kept the officers happy.

"So, you see, in the military, I drove, cooked, got some officers in trouble, and shopped."

André and the Girls

"On our way to Berlin, near the Rhine river, we came upon a concentration camp. We were assigned the liberation of the camp. It was very sad and very happy at the same time. In the camp were three girls from Russia. Their names were Luba, Vera, and Vala. They spoke only Russian and a little bit of German. They had been taken out of the Ukraine for labor. The colonel took them on and said to me, 'This is going to be your squad. You are responsible for them. No hanky-panky. They will work for you, and you will train them.' The colonel thought it was not befitting that the Germans see me doing laundry and serving and cooking. We were the conquerors and had to keep up that appearance. We had to show our 'superiority.'

"It was very difficult at first with the girls because they spoke broken German and no English, but I spoke a little German, and we managed. They would speak the Russian amongst themselves. God only knows what they said. I gave each of them a notebook, and every time I used a phrase in English, they would write it in phonetics, and I would write it in German. In a very short time we were communicating in English.

"When we entered Berlin, the officers were sleeping wherever they could. The war was technically over, but there was still some shooting in the streets, so the general wanted all the officers together where they would be easier to reach in an emergency. In one area of Berlin there were only three or four houses to a block. They were big mansions. We commandeered homes in that area. One mansion belonged to the Gillette family at 18 Pauline Strasse. It had an elegant entry with two Nubian figures beside the outside stairs holding lamps. It served as the officers' dining room and housed me and my squad of three girls; we were assigned to set up an officers' mess hall, dining hall, there.

"I trained Vala for cooking. She was a homespun simple type of a girl. Vera was the 'showgirl.' She loved talking to people and flirting and making everyone feel welcome. And Luba was a very sensible, practical girl. They were almost like the three Golden Girls from television. Vera and Luba became the waitresses, Luba being the head waitress because she was so efficient.

"I trained these young girls to do the laundry and things of that nature as well. I still did most of the cooking myself, although Vala was my assistant cook.

"After we established this beautiful mess hall, I made an officers' club out of it. Receptions and parties were held there. Sometimes during the day the officers' wives would come by, and I would take them shopping.

"As the officers' club grew, I looked for some other people to hire to work for me. There was an office set up where Germans who were screened and those who spoke English were given employment. We needed lots of help. Through this office I got a young lady who was my secretary and did all my writing. I also needed a man who knew the city. They sent me an older man named Hannes Langbein. He had been the president of a bank, and one day when he was out at lunch, we bombed and destroyed his bank. He was a very educated man who just happened to be gay. He became my right-hand man. He knew a lot of people in Berlin. He knew the artistic community.

"Eventually, I had fifty or sixty German employees: furnace man, cooks, maids, waiters, waitresses—we had our own barber. We had a pianist. Bartenders. We were a city complete. And I was the queen. Absolutely fine!

"We hired two more cooks. One was a thin wiry man, Ludwig. Then there was a big heavyset one, Helmut. He weighed three hundred pounds. He was a very, very good cook. He had no teeth, and he refused to put his false teeth in his mouth. He loved mashed potatoes. He would mix everything up in the mashed potatoes so he could eat it. At dinner one night, he mixed this chicken we were serving into his mashed potatoes, and in there, in fact, was a chicken bone which he did not see. He mixed it all up and ate it. Somehow the bone went all the way through without doing any damage until it got wedged in his lower bowels, and when he went to the lavatory, it ripped his butt.

"At four-thirty in the morning, some of the staff woke me up and said, 'The chef is bleeding to death! He's on the toilet and he's bleeding to death!' Oh, it was a mess. So I had to come down and see that he was taken to a hospital. I had to put a towel up his butt because there was so much blood. We rushed him to the hospital, and I had to go in and cook breakfast for the officers. At the hospital they found out it was a bone that had caused the bleeding. They had to do what I call a 'cork and seal.' We roared about that, but he never thought it was so funny. I used to tease him all the time."

Under the occupation of the Allied forces, the people of Berlin began to pick up the remnants of their war-tattered lives. With the tense peace came an attempt at a type of normalcy. Many citizens went to work for their former enemies, and the job at hand was the rebuilding of their city. As the infrastructure of Berlin was slowly revived, there were days for José when the war itself seemed distant, such as the day he met André.

"One day Hannes and I were on a streetcar, and this handsome man got on wearing a fur coat. Everyone seemed to acknowledge him. He was very gracious. Very, very nice-looking. Very sophisticated.

"I said, 'Hannes, who is that man?'

"He said, 'Oh, he is very well known. He is an Austrian from a famous old dressmaking family. His name is André Ehlers. His mother made the dresses for the empress and his grandfather made the uniforms for Franz Joseph. He came to Berlin prior to the war, and he was making costumes for the opera. He also designed windows for the best stores. When the war broke out, he couldn't get back to Austria. He does cabaret shows and calls himself the Merry Widow.'

"I said, 'I would like to meet him.'

"Hannes said, 'He used to come to the bank. He gives a lot of parties. I might be able to get an invitation to one of his parties.'

"After a while, Hannes came in and said that he had received an invitation to an afternoon soirée at André's home. He said it would be a rather smart thing with a lot of people from the theater.

"I got all dressed up and brought a little gift. To the party I went. Well, my lord! This was like going to New York and meeting all the big stars from Broadway. There were actors, singers, dancers, comedians. I met the famous director Max Reinhart. Oh, my dear, I was in heaven! They all took to me. I spoke German. They got a big kick out of my German. It was not, shall we say, the most correct German. I befriended many people.

"Finally, it was getting to be time for us to leave. Parties there ended at a certain time, and then you left. At about seven o'clock, I said, 'Hannes, we have to go now.'

"He said, 'Oh no, you are to stay. You are having dinner with André.'

"I asked him if he was staying too.

"He said, 'No. You are staying alone. He will see that you get home.' There were no taxis yet or anything like that at the time. I wondered how I would get home.

"At the set time, everybody left, and André and I had supper together, served by his secretary, Erica, who had been a performer before the war. She was a dancer and a singer, and she had been performing when a curtain sandbag fell and crippled her for life, leaving her with a bad limp. André had made costumes in that production, and he befriended her. They became very good friends, and he took her under his wing. She was a very sweet woman. We had a wonderful supper, and I asked André how I was getting home. He said he had arranged for someone to drive me home . . . in the morning.

"That night began a relationship with André that lasted until I left Berlin, over two years later. We had great fun, and I socialized with some of the greatest talents in Germany. On my birthday, I think it was my twenty-third, all of the new friends I made performed for me as a gift. They sang. They danced. It was a wonderful birthday. On paper, my birthday is December 12, 1923.

"I was going to stay in Berlin with André, but there was no way I could explain to the colonel or to the Army that I needed to stay. I couldn't bring him home. And I missed my family. And, of course, there was Paul Kolish. The colonel talked me out of staying in Europe. He didn't know about André. Nobody knew.

"Eventually I decided I wanted to come home. I still had some time, and the colonel wanted to go to the East to help the cleanup in Japan. He asked if I wanted to go, and I said, 'Oh no! I've survived this European theater; I'll never survive the other one.' I very upset trying to decide what to do. I developed diarrhea and nervous splotches, and I was a mess. I guess I had to come home. I was in pain. I had put enough time in that I could get out.

"As for my girls, we worked very hard to get all three of them out of Germany, because they couldn't go back to Russia. With a lot of bullshit, we got all three of them out. Vala ended up befriending a sergeant of B Company, and they married and came to the United States, to Georgia, where she raised three boys. Vera and I were to be married so that she could come to the States, but my family objected because she was Russian. We had a lot of fun together. There was never any sexual relationship. We were more like brother and sister. We did manage to get her out of Germany. She went to Canada and entered a nunnery; she became a nun. The colonel sponsored Luba and sent her back to Washington State where his family took care of her until he got back. I believe she married a gentleman there.

"I requested to be returned home. They found a relief for me, and I came back to The United States and landed at Fort Dix. I still had six or seven months to go before my anniversary. They could not reduce me in rank, so they had to get me a job comparable to my rank. It was very difficult because there was no officer or general who needed an orderly. They looked over my past record of service, and I was put in charge of the Post Motor Pool for Fort Dix because I had gone to driving school. I had ninety military personnel under me and two hundred civilians. I was in charge, but, oh God, the men were old enough to be my father.

"The place was really a mess. I arranged the jeeps first. The area was flat, and nothing grows there. There were no trees, and the wind blew all the time, so the dust was terrible. I got some paint, and I painted the house. I took some sheets and made Priscilla curtains. I scrounged furniture and rugs so the men could come in and sit while they were waiting for their assignments.

"I got the jeeps and trucks in order; I had someone check their motors and tires and everything. We had all of the vehicles in tip-top shape. The men liked me. They didn't dare say anything about me. I earned their respect. They thought the world of me. I worked for them, and they worked with me. My motor pool was absolutely the tops. Everybody worked with no problem. Visiting generals were always brought out to the motor pool. They'd walk in and see that the equipment was in order and the books were in order. It was very impressive.

"They knew I was going to leave soon, so they offered me another stripe, but that would have been temporary, not permanent like the rank I already held. I was making more money as it was. So I finished my tour at Fort Dix, they discharged me there, and I came home. I had to stay in the Reserves until I was thirty-five or thirty-six. But they liked me very much. I'd love to go back to where I served."

Corsets in the Wind

José's homecoming from the war was a happy time for him and for his family. They gathered in Redwood City for food and to hear José tell stories from the war. Paul and Jonathan joined them, and the family felt complete again except for the absence of José's godfather Charles. José and Paul spent quiet evenings together, enjoying their closeness after the long time apart.

One evening when the family was together, José announced that he intended to keep the promise he made before he left for war. He would take his mother Dolores and his godmother Jesserina on a trip to Mexico. He joked that as far as he could surmise, he had indeed come back in one piece, though maybe a little worse for the wear, and the bargain had been that he would take them on the trip if he came back in one piece. Jesserina had never been to the interior of Mexico, and she longed to visit her old friend and former upstairs neighbor from Noe Street, Chavalita Ávila. She had maintained a friendship with Mrs. Ávila over the years through letters and phone calls. The three decided that they would take the trip at the beginning of the summer.

That winter was not a happy one. It was during that Christmas that Paul and his son Jonathan died in the car accident with a drunk driver. Once again the family mourned. The sadness of those long winter days and the recent memories of the war weighed heavy on José, and he threw himself into planning the Mexico vacation. His mother also seemed to be planning in advance for the trip.

As summer approached, José noticed that his mother was spending a good part of her spare time sewing and embroidering pillows. José asked her why she was making pillows. She responded matter-of-factly, "I am making pillows so that I can sit comfortable in the back seat of the car on our trip."

"But Mama," José responded, "We have plenty of pillows. We have more than enough pillows to cushion the entire back seat. You don't have to be making pillows."

"I want to make pillows," she replied adamantly. "If I want to make pillows why shouldn't I make pillows?

"Fine," José responded in exasperation, "make pillows! Make lots of pillows!"

That is exactly what she did. José knew his mother well enough to know when it was fruitless to argue with her. He would have preferred that she relax and let him make the arrangements for the trip, but if she felt the need to be involved that way, he was not going to try to stop her. As far as his own preparations, José used the money he had saved during his time in the Army and bought a new car. What money was left would pay their expenses. He gathered maps and planned their route.

"I had planned the trip. We were going to go from San Francisco to Los Angeles, cut over at Los Angeles and go to El Paso, Texas, cross over the border and go down to Chihuahua by the center route all the way to Guadalajara. I had saved my money. It was going to be my treat."

After his return from Europe, José's sister Teresa had helped him find a position at the San Francisco airport. His boss was very good to the young veteran and was impressed with José's desire to treat his mother and godmother to a special trip after all their wartime worries. He gave José the time off he needed and promised to have José's job waiting for him when he returned.

It was mild coastal summer day when José loaded his new car with clothes and personal necessities for a month's trip. He packed a little food for the trip and some water. Dolores arranged her new pillows in the back seat and settled herself comfortably among them. Jesserina sat in the front passenger's seat and gave José a smile of excited anticipation. José ran through his mental checklist one more time, and then started the car.

"So I loaded up the girls, and off we went. Well, everything was all right, except that every time we passed a vegetable stand we had to stop . . . to buy vegetables. Whenever we saw a place that sold fresh fruit and fruit juices, we had to stop. We made separate stops for gas. We would fill up with gas, and everyone would remain quiet. As soon as we pulled away from the gas station, they had to go to the restroom. By the time we left Redwood City and had traveled to the outskirts of

San Fernando, I was already three hundred dollars in the hole, and we had stopped nineteen hundred times.

"So I laid the law down: 'When we gas, we piss, and that's the end of that! And we do not need fresh fruit, nor fresh juices. We will eat three meals a day: breakfast, lunch, and dinner, and maybe a little snack in between.' Otherwise, we would have never made it out of the States. Well, we traveled like that, and it was very nice. They adjusted to my rules, and we went our way.

"Well, my dear, we got to the border of Mexico, and the Mexican border guards wanted money to let us take the car in. They wanted what they call *la mordida:* a little money on the side, and all of this nonsense. I wasn't about to give it to them. It's a bribe. So here we are stopped at the border. You see, you get to the border, and you go fifty kilometers in, and that's the main check. There they check the license and the car motor, everything, so you can't sell the car and come back without a car. Since we wouldn't pay the extra money, they decided to check us very thoroughly. They asked us to step out of the car. I got out. My godmother got out. My mother did not get out.

"Well, they said to my mother, who was sitting in the back seat, 'Would you please get out of the car?'

"My mother said, 'I'm not getting out of the car! You want to see the car? Here it is. What are you looking for?'

"My mother, you must remember, is Spanish, not Mexican. And they knew right away by her accent that they were not talking to a native, and they addressed her very politely. They asked her again to please step out of the car.

"My mother said, 'Here's the car. The motor is up there in front. The numbers are on the motor. You don't have nothing to look at in the back seat except an old woman. There's nothing in the back seat.'

"They saw that they were not going to win, so they didn't insist. She stayed in the car. My godmother and I were standing outside of the car; and they looked under our seat. There was nothing. They opened up the luggage and were making a big display about it. I had to get angry with them and tell them that this was not a sideshow, and I didn't appreciate it. I asked to talk to their leader. All the while, my mother sat calmly in the back seat.

"Well, we finally got out of there, and I turned to my mother and said, 'Why in the hell did you make it more difficult? Why didn't you get out of the back seat of the car?'

"She just said, 'Humpf!'"

The weather turned very hot as the trio entered Mexico. In true Victorian style, Dolores and Jesserina had dressed in travel clothes each day of the trip, and since their travel clothes were only partly for comfort, the other part being style and tradition, the women's garb included corsets. Jesserina, having anticipated the weather in Mexico, had left her corset off the day they crossed the border. Dolores, on the other hand, had worn hers as usual.

The three travelers had rolled their windows down as they drove through the desert landscape. Now and then they would pass through a small, ramshackle town or pass a cluster of small houses out in what seemed to be nowhere at all. As the day progressed, José began to notice that in populated areas people would often stop and watch their car pass. They would smile or even laugh and wave at the three with wide grins on their faces. José found the behavior of the natives baffling, and he commented on it.

Jesserina replied, "Oh, they're very friendly here!" Later, after driving near other cars through one town, she said, "Why, they don't seem to be doing that to anybody else. Maybe it's because you've got two old ladies in the car." Dolores remained quiet in the back seat.

Driving past a small cluster of houses out in the desert, José watched again as a group of people pointed at the car. Finally, another car passed them, and the people inside pointed out the window at José's car and began to laugh. Obviously this was not simply some local custom regarding elderly tourists. They seemed to be pointing toward the back seat, and José looked over his shoulder to see if he could solve the mystery.

"My mother was sitting very calm and collected in the hundred degrees in the back seat. She was so collected. And then I turned around and saw what she had done, and why all these people were looking at us and pointing at us and carrying on. In the heat, she had taken off her corset and her undergarments and had tied them on the outside of the door so that they would dry in the wind as we were driving down the road. There we were driving with her corset and slip flapping in the breeze! I was exactly mortified! How we made it through Mexico, I'm not sure."

Sometime after the "laundry" was dry, José was driving down a small road out in the countryside. Up ahead, near a small settlement, a farmer was leading his burro. José slowed down to pass man and beast on the narrow road. Just as he was passing, the burro sidestepped a bit, and the front bumper of the car hit the animal gently in the rump, pushing it a few feet forward and to the side. The burro kept its balance and stood still for a moment a little dazed. José stopped the car to make sure the creature was unhurt, which seemed to be the case. The burro looked at José, snorted once, and then started to walk again in the direction it had been going.

The farmer was a different case altogether. He jumped in front of his burro to stop its progress and began examining its rump meticulously. José understood that a burro was an economic necessity for many Mexican families, an asset that they valued beyond most of their possessions. He apologized to the farmer and commented that the burro seemed to be fine. The farmer turned to José and began screaming at him in Spanish, "You hit my burro! You have hurt my burro! He will never work again! You stupid man, you crazy tourist driver! My life will be misery! My family will starve!"

José stood stunned. As the man's hysterical rantings continued, the burro began looking for a stray clump of grass to eat. Hearing the commotion, the man's family came running out of a nearby house. The farmer answered their questions with, "This man has injured our burro with his car. He ran him over with his car!"

Apologetically, José interjected, "I'm very sorry. I didn't mean to hit your burro."

The rest of the family joined in with the farmer's wails of despair. The burro would never be able to work and haul lumber again. Their economic future was dire, hopeless. They would have to live on the streets. José watched the display of emotion with a mixture of guilt, indignant frustration, and fascination.

"Oh, my God! I thought the end of the world was coming on! The owner screamed and carried on. The burro never made a sound. He didn't fall down or anything. The family was screaming and screaming and screaming. And what they wanted, they wanted some money.

"I said, 'Please, I didn't mean to hit your burro!'

"'Oh, he'll never be able to carry lumber anymore! It's bad! Oh!'

"I was getting a little angry. I said, 'Well, he hasn't fallen down dead yet!' Then I realized why they were carrying on so. I pulled out my wallet and said, 'Will a hundred dollars satisfy my debt to you?'

"'Oh, yes! The burro will be well!'

"It cost me a hundred dollars, and as we drove away, I told my mother, 'I should have killed the son of a bitch for a hundred dollars. We could have *bought* a burro for seventy-five!'

"The next stop was a real highlight for me. My mother had met Pancho Villa's wife years and years ago. While we were in Chihuahua, we stopped and had lunch with Mrs. Pancho Villa. And she told us how the government was not doing anything for her; after all, Pancho Villa was president at one time. They would not take care of her or provide her with a pension, so she embarrassed the government by taking the car in which he was assassinated, bullet holes and all, on tour, giving lectures for money. The government leaders were embarrassed enough that they finally gave her a pension. We stayed with her for a while and had a very nice visit. I am very history-minded, and so Mrs. Villa spoke to me about her husband and showed me their quarters. It was very, very interesting.

"After our visit to Pancho Villa's widow, we drove to San Luis Potosi and arrived on the day when they bless the animals. That was something new for us. Everybody comes from the country with their chickens and their cows and their goats. I took my mother and my godmother and got them blessed."

José made that last claim with a slight smile on his face. At times it is hard to tell if he is pulling the listener's leg or telling the druid's truth. He has done so many outrageous things that very little of what he claims seems improbable.

José and his mothers continued on to Guadalajara to see the Ávila family. They arrived in the "Paris of Mexico" and followed their directions to the Ávila home. They were greeted with shouts of delight and generous hugs. Mrs. Ávila marveled at how José, whom she remembered as a child, had grown into a man. After the initial expressions of welcome and an invitation to come inside, Dolores went immediately to the back seat of the car and began pulling out the pillows.

José shook his head in consternation. "Those damn pillows again! Mama, just leave the pillows! I'm sure Mrs. Ávila has pillows for us to sleep on! What is it about those pillows of yours?"

"Never you mind!" Dolores replied, unruffled. She gathered up the pillows and walked into the house with José behind her shaking his head.

"Ah, Chavalita, I have so missed our visits in San Francisco!" With that she began to tear at the end of one of the pillows. José was certain that his mother had lost her mind. First she sewed unnecessary pillows, then she treated them like treasured heirlooms, and now here she was setting upon them like a predator on prey. As the pillow spilled open, José finally understood and began to laugh.

"I thought you might have trouble finding some of these things here in Guadalajara," his mother announced to her friend casually.

Out of the pillow fell finely made brassieres and beautiful blouses. Another pillow yielded pantyhose, another panties and stockings.

"She brought in all that loot, and she wasn't going to declare it; she sat on it the whole time! Oh Lordy! She went down loaded! For the family. That's why she wouldn't get out of the car at the checkpoint. Coming home, we had no problems. What we brought back was all right.

"We had a wonderful time in Guadalajara! I hired a mariachi band to play for us during dinnertime. I hired a horse and buggy to take us on a tour of the city. Outside of Guadalajara is a resort called Chapala. It's on a lake. And there we went out for a picnic. And at the next table was a very large family: Mama, Papa, sons, daughters, sons-in-law, daughters-in-law, and amongst them there were a few gay ones—closeted. So naturally, I spotted them right away, and we joined families together, and we had a ball! We all picnicked together, and in the evening we danced. We carried on and had a fabulous time. We saw them one other time; Papa was a very affluent man.

"We traveled to see Mexico City, where we went to the bullfights. Often you see clips of this one famous bullfight where the bull jumps the fence. We were there that day at that bullfight. Whenever I see it I scream, 'I was there! I was there!'

"And we visited all the churches. The main cathedral had sunk down about two feet. It was huge and made of stone. The whole center of the Mexico City is built on an island on a lake: Lake Texcoco. There are lots of bridges connecting the rest of the city to the center part. It's very beautiful.

"We stayed on the Paseo de la Reforma, which goes out in a line directly from Chapultapec Castle. We saw the dressing room where Carlotta dressed, and she could see right straight down the avenue, all the way down to the office. So when Maximilian finished his work in the palace, she knew exactly when he got into the carriage to come home. She was a very jealous woman. The castle still has a lot of the things left by the family. Very pretty.

"We visited the Aztec city of Tenochtitlán, and I climbed one of the pyramids; that's supposed to give me ten or fifteen years on my life. It's such a climb it should either add ten years or take ten off. We toured all over Mexico. We stayed thirty more days before we came back."

Wanting to see as much of Mexico as possible on the trip, José decided to take a different route home. The three travelers looked at a map and chose a road that went to Tijuana. It seemed very direct yet cut through parts of the country they had not seen on the way down. José found the road, turned onto it, and settled in for the long drive north. He drove through two states, but at the border of the third state the nicely paved, wide road suddenly disappeared, and they found themselves on a bumpy dirt road that stretched to the horizon. They had not passed a paved crossroad for hours. José stopped the car, and the three of them discussed their options.

To double back would have used up time and gas that they could not spare. They decided to drive ahead and inquire about the route at the next town, but there they learned that the route on the map was a proposed road that would not be completed for some time. The map had given no indication of that. Although they were nervous about following back roads in empty country, José, Dolores, and Jesserina decided that, since adventure is what they came seeking, adventure they would have. They kept going.

José noticed that the gas gauge was below the half-full mark, so he made a mental note to look for a gas station in the next town. They drove on, marveling at the vast expanse of the land and the subtle colors of the landscape. At the next little village, they looked for gas, but the town had no gas station. They stopped at a tiny cantina for a meal. Several children came out to gawk at the car. The woman who fed them explained that most of the people in the town had never seen an automobile. She asked about their clothes, which were very different from the traditional long, full dresses and rough work pants of the locals. Before they left, José's mother offered the woman one of her stylish hats and a pair of gloves. They enjoyed the woman's delighted reaction; she had never seen anything so fine, much less owned it.

At the next little town José was dismayed to see that there was again no gas station. He began to watch the gas gauge nervously. Finally, when the tank was nearing empty, they rolled into a little village that had a single gas pump. José filled the tank and, in his gratitude, gave the owner a little extra money.

All along the remainder of their largely rural route home, José, Dolores, and Jesserina stopped and ate and talked to people who were living as their families had lived a century before. José's two mothers left many pairs of gloves and most of their hats with grateful women along the way.

"It was very interesting. We ate with the people, and talked to the people. They were very friendly. My mother and godmother gave the women some of their hats and gloves. They never had anything like that. Probably if we went down there now there would be some woman wearing a hat of my mother's. It was all a very good education. We were gone for a good month and a half."

José rolled into San Francisco with a tank of gasoline and fifty cents in his pocket. He phoned his boss at the airport and asked if he could have an advance on his next paycheck. He explained that his mother had no food in her apartment since she lived alone and any food she had left there would have spoiled during the long absence. José's boss instructed him to come by right away and pick up a check, which José did.

"That was the last big trip my mother and my godmother ever took. Not long after the trip, my godmother died. My mother died some years later. But to their last days, they said that was the most memorable and fun trip that we had taken. That trip cost me around nine thousand dollars. It was well worth it though."

PART THREE:
THE BLACK CAT

She Is Like, Out and About:
A Regular USO Show. Mmm-Hmm Honey!
You Hear What I'm Saying?

It took me very little time to grow used to José being recognized everywhere we went in San Francisco. Accompanying José to dinner or to the corner store is not an activity for the sensitive ego. He is, after all, the Empress, and he becomes the center of attention easily. More than once my own diva-wannabe nature grumbled at being just the other person in the room. ("What was your name again?") He does not always choose the lead role. At times in the past, his notoriety even frustrated him. No matter. People will stop to do him honor. These days, he seems content with his lot.

In San Francisco, a few things are predictable and constant: someone dressed in earth tones will ask you for spare change; the air will be cold at night at the lookout point on Twin Peaks no matter what time of year it is; seagulls will try to steal your food at Fisherman's Wharf; the parking space you spot ahead will be taken by the time you drive the one-block distance to it; traffic will creep in Chinatown; the fog will be back; there will be construction work somewhere on Market Street; Haight Street will attract the unconventional; and José will create a sensation wherever he goes.

What I have found astonishing is the number of times talk of José has popped up in the most unlikely places. I took a break from writing one evening and took a walk from my home in midtown Sacramento. I have developed that as a pattern: write at night, walk afterward to relax. Once as a visiting journalist in Washington, DC, I finished a news article at about eleven at night and then left my hotel room to take my usual walk. It was my first (and so far only) experience with being mugged. Actually, it was more an attempted mugging. I did all the wrong things: laugh, refuse to cooperate, engage the mugger in conversation about the ironies in the situation. I didn't my wallet, but I did offer him the fifty cents I had brought for a cup of coffee. He declined. I think he thought I was a little touched. But I digress.

The walk in midtown was considerably safer and saner than the DC escapade. I made my way through the downtown area and into Old Sacramento, the Gold Rush era reconstruction on the river. For some reason the wooden walkways, vintage brick buildings, and musky smell of the river always center me. It's the Tom Sawyer inside me, I guess. I stopped for coffee and a rest in a little bar and cafe on the ground floor of a building on the corner of Second Street and K. I sat at the polished wooden bar, trying hard to look at least a little like Humphrey Bogart, although the coffee mug was a bit of a prop faux pas. Two barstools away was a handsome man who looked to be in his late sixties or early seventies, well-groomed conservatively cut silver hair, nice clothes, a gold wedding ring on his finger. We struck up the mildly inquisitive conversation of two strangers, and he soon learned that I was a writer. When I mentioned José and the Black Cat, he chuckled and stared for a moment at the wall behind the bar.

"You know about the Black Cat?" I asked.

"Oh, indeed I do."

"Have you seen José?"

"That the fellow who sang there?"

"Yes."

"Well, I didn't have a chance to see much of him."

"Sounds like a story."

We'll call him Carl, not because he is a homophobe and fears exposure. Au contraire. He is embarrassed about his own youthful bluster, and fears offending gay people. I wasn't offended, just amused.

With a tone of amused reminiscence, the man told me of his exposure to the Black Cat. He and a buddy left their Navy ship to enjoy a weekend of shore leave in San Francisco just after the big war. They, of course, had reviewed the Navy's list of notorious bars to avoid on pain of stripe stripping, and from that list chose their itinerary for the first night. They had a few drinks at a bar in North Beach, and then decided to check out the rumored nefarious entertainment at the Black Cat.

The two young men entered the Cat quietly and made their way to the bar, finding two stools side by side. My new friend Carl described the two of them as "extremely straight, as only very young men can be." They had no idea that the Black Cat was a gay bar, and they were too naive to pick up any of the clues. They did notice that there seemed to be a dearth of women, but the men in the place looked "normal" enough to them. Some of them even looked like military men. (Many of them, no doubt, were.) On either side of the pair at the bar were strong, strapping men with big arms and rugged faces.

As they waited for the entertainment, watching the patrons push together tables to create a makeshift stage, a man on the other side of Carl's buddy discretely placed his hand on the buddy's leg. Flustered, the sailor ordered the man to take his hand away, muttering something about not being queer. Carl took great delight in his friend's discomfort until the man next to him firmly caressed his own thigh. Carl turned to the man, called him something other than "sir," and cast blue-colored aspersions on the man's sexuality. The man responded in kind. Carl's buddy and his tormentor joined the verbal conflict. Finally Carl asked, "You boys want to take this outside?"

The man at Carl's side responded, "The only thing I like better than fucking is fighting. Let's go."

"We'll teach you goddamn sissies what a real man is," Carl's friend added.

On his way out, Carl noticed a young Latino man on the tables in heeled pumps beginning a comic dialogue with the audience. The sight added to his already growing nervousness about his predicament. The size of his and his buddy's challengers did nothing to ease the feeling. No matter. Time to show the queers what's what.

Out on the street, the men wasted no time. They engaged in fisticuffs. As Carl put it with a laugh, "They kicked the living shit out of us!" Carl remembers being sprawled next to his buddy on the pavement groaning. He looked up and saw his conqueror reaching out a hand to help him up with an amused grin on his face.

"So, you sailors want to join us for a drink?"

Carl looked up at the man and croaked painfully, "No, I think you boys have had enough!"

Neither of the sailors talked much as they staggered back to their ship.

"That pretty much cured me of my stereotypes of gay people," Carl chuckled to me.

San Francisco Chronicle columnist Herb Caen, known more for his one-liners and anecdotes than stories, was no stranger to José. Impressed by a singing performance of José's, he dubbed him in his column "The Nightingale of Montgomery Street." Another time, he wrote about José's annual pilgrimage to the grave of Joshua Norton and noted that the cemetery would provide refreshments. He asked if perhaps they serve a mean planter's punch.

Journalists have seemed to love the flamboyance of stories about José, including the lesbian journalist from *The Bay Area Reporter,* San Francisco's leading gay newspaper, whom I met. Once we identified ourselves as writers, we launched into that delightful kind of exclusive shop talk that people with common professions engage in to the exclusion of the uninitiated. We talked deadlines and editors and metaphors. We shared our respective dreams of the *The New York Times* Best Seller List. And we talked of José.

For the *B.A.R.* issue honoring the fiftieth anniversary of D-Day, Mary Richards had written an article on José, one of the Bay Area's best known and most unconventional World War II veterans. She asked excitedly if José had told me the "German vegetable garden" story. I said he had not. She replied excitedly, "Oh it's my favorite José story!" She began to share the tale.

According to Mary, José was a kind of cook on the run during the march into Berlin. José's Third Infantry regiment was in the right flank of the formation of allied troops that forced its way, like an expanding balloon, into German territory during the Battle of the Bulge. Often, the soldiers had to eat simply K rations for their meals. Whenever he could, however, José tried to prepare hot meals. Often this involved procuring kitchens or other rooms from the people in the towns the battle engulfed.

The Battle of the Bulge ended in January, 1945, and José stayed for a time in a small town along the Lahn river. When the official surrender of Germany was negotiated and signed that spring, José's division received orders to proceed to Berlin to join the occupation forces. The march into Berlin was not some easy, postwar stroll. The land was bleak and war-ravaged. Despite the surrender, there was intermittent fighting still in the countryside. José talks of a concentration camp that they were charged with liberating along the way. And there was the constant danger of engagement with stray stubborn troops still intent on fighting. They marched on alert.

In one town along the way, the troops camped for a brief time. José noticed that there was a field next to the camp that had been someone's vegetable garden. It was untended yet ripe with all sorts of fresh vegetables. Never one to pass up so obvious an opportunity, José made his way into the field. He left his gun behind, and once he was amid the veggies, he took off his helmet to use as a basket to collect the bounty for a nice chicken soup. He had already procured some chickens from townspeople along the way, but what is chicken soup without vegetables? Being a cautious soldier, he kept himself low to the ground on his way out.

It turned out that there was a German platoon that had made camp on the other side of the large field behind a bank of trees. There was José, digging carrots and unearthing potatoes. The Germans noticed him and his American uniform and began shooting. José dropped to the ground.

The first sergeant heard the commotion and looked out at the field. He saw José and exclaimed, "Oh, Jesus!"

The sergeant informed Colonel Mataxis, for whom José worked. "What the hell?"

"Vegetables, apparently, sir."

The colonel ordered his men to return fire. José tucked himself below the exchange and held on tight to his vegetables. Eventually, the Battle of the Vegetables ended, and José was escorted safely back to camp. The colonel demanded to know why José had done what he did.

"I thought it would be nice to fix a hot chicken soup."

"Why the hell didn't you take your gun?"

"I didn't need a weapon to gather vegetables, sir."

The colonel took José's gun and tied it to him with a rope. José had to wear that gun twenty-four hours a day for a week, to bed, during his cooking, while bathing, to the lavatory.

"But it was a good soup!" laughed Mary. "You know, once the general in charge of that part of the Bulge saw José's jeep with its chicken cages and stove strapped on. He ordered the stuff thrown away. He said it looked like Okies on their way to California."

As always, José found a way to work around the system to get what he wanted.

"He found someone to trade a 'deuce and a half' (a two-and-a-half-ton truck) for his jeep. He kept his chickens and stove inside nice and neat. He wasn't about to give up his chickens."

I was discussing José with a good friend of mine in Sacramento one day soon after meeting Mary. Jason said, "I have a good friend in West Sacramento who talks about the Black Cat all the time. I should introduce you."

When Maxwell Gordon and I met, we instantly shared our mutual respect and love for José. "Maxwell Gordon," he told me, "was the name I used when I went to the baths—I mean the health clubs—you know, for inhalation therapy."

Maxwell first saw José during a jaunt to The City from Carmel, where he was living before he moved to San Francisco. He described José's early shows as a kind of cabaret, with popular songs, parodies, impersonations. He remembered José's routine being always fresh and topical. He would poke fun at popular entertainers, especially those who were playing San Francisco at any given time. He would parody movies and songs that were on the tops of the charts, items in Herb Caen's column.

"He did a perfectly awful thing to Jeanette McDonald! He commented on her dentures . . . it was so fun!

"Now the Black Cat was rather long and narrow, and the bar was on the left side. There were small square tables with four bent cane chairs on each. Everybody would be drinking and socializing, and there was music. When it came time for José, all the chairs would be moved around the edge of the room, and the tables would be pushed together to make a stage. His ordinary costume for the Sunday afternoons was tight black slacks, nicely fitted, high heels, patent leather or kidskin, very high, and a pullover, high-necked, long-sleeved, cashmere, black. And always a big, fresh, purple orchid on his shoulder. Full make up. Exotic eyes. Bright red lipstick. Sometimes he'd have a scarf or a Spanish shawl. His drag was not what you would see at Finocchio's or the Jewel Box Review. It was parody drag. I was there pretty regularly.

"If he knew you, and knew that you worked for IBM, he'd say, 'Oh here's Michael from General Electric!' He knew I worked for Frigidaire, so he'd come by my table and he'd say, 'Oh, here's Maxwell from the phone company!' He wouldn't finger you, because very often there were plainclothes police in there. He wouldn't talk blue. He would make suggestive allusions, or he would use gay language that we knew, but he would never be offensive. But he was funny, just a laugh a minute. Even that early, the last thing he would do would be the song, 'God Bless Us Nelly Queens.'"

Maxwell's voice began to quiver a little as he talked of the ending song.

"He'd walk around the room and get everyone to join hands, Hazel would play, and we'd all sing together. For a lot of guys who were so closeted, that was their only outlet."

Maxwell explained that everyone at the time dressed in suits, white shirts, and skinny ties, or at least a sports coat or nice sweater, to go out to dinner or to clubs. A person who was not dressed properly simply was not allowed to enter most establishments. "There were a few beer bars where you could go in with Levis, but most of them were for women. This was before the Castro became a gay center."

Maxwell remembers when José started doing his opera parodies on Sundays. "He would do an opera, and he would play all the parts. I remember once he was doing *Aida,* and he got to one character and said, 'Oh, she's an awful, ugly bitch. Let's skip her!' One time he came out dressed in all these white strips pinned together. He said, 'Do you like it? Do you like it? I don't have a curtain left hanging in my place!' And it was. It was window curtains. He would patter and then sing and then patter and then sing. Of course, he interpreted the operas his own crazy way: 'Now you might think Carmen was just some ugly bitch from the wrong side of the tracks, but actually she is a very pure-hearted girl. Now Don José, he was a son of a bitch!' He made it up as he went along.

"Years ago there was a female impersonator from Finocchio's who made all of his costumes out of crepe paper. He was called The Paper Doll. Once José borrowed one of the dresses, a mustard-yellow Victorian with a bustle. He came out and said, 'Okay, all of you put your lighters away!' When he did Butterfly, my God! He had fans and tassels! It was all very fun and very light."

With a more serious tone, Maxwell continued, "He was very well thought of. He ran for public office—openly. If something would happen, some discrimination, he would be right there. He'd go down either to City Hall or the Board of Supervisors and pitch a fit. He'd tell the newspapers first. He was in the newspapers all the time."

Maxwell spoke enthusiastically about the Tavern Guild's annual Beaux Arts Balls at Halloween, which José always hosted. "Some of these kids from Oakland, some of the black queens, my God! The drag that they would wear! It was fantastic! Peacock's tails and ostrich feathers: I mean, Las Vegas showgirls in *all* their *glory* could not hold a candle to them! Those queens must have stitched over there for months! Sequins and glitter and on and on and on!

"José was always there. One of the last times I spoke to him, he was greeting people. He was dressed as the Widow Norton. I said, 'Oh, it's so nice to see you again. I want to thank you for all the things you've done all these years.'

"He said, 'Oh no, it was just things that had to be done.'

"He didn't take any credit or expect to be treated special because of it. It was just a matter of course. He was so cordial.

"He had postcards printed up of a painting of him as Carmen. He would peddle those as souvenirs. He wouldn't put a price on them; whatever you could pay was okay. He would sometimes go to some cute trick and stuff one in his pants and say, 'Remember me always.'

"I have one story that's kind of naughty. I had a friend from Salt Lake City that I worked with. He decided that he might be gay. He was working in San Francisco, and he had his eyes open. He was a good-looking blond kid. Viking type. He had been on his missions. His parents wanted him to come back and marry and settle down, raise lots of kids, drink milk. He said he would never go back there. I took him to an opera of José's one Sunday.

"Well, José saw my friend and kept coming around. I introduced them. But I said, 'Of course, he's (Maxwell said this with a French accent) Mor*mon*. He's not Catholic like us.' Well that just lit the fuse. He was bound to have him. He ended up taking him home. It was only a one-night stand. I don't know what happened. Maybe they both liked the same things, top or bottom. It wasn't compatible. I once brought a friend of mine from Cuba who had a striking resemblance to a very famous bullfighter, Ava Gardner's paramour. José asked, but I said he wasn't the bullfighter. He was a friend of mine. They began chattering in Spanish, and my friend was very taken with him, with his perfect Castillian Spanish. That's how I learned that José was from Colombia and not Mexico. If he hadn't had to leave to return to New York, José probably would have taken him home too, given him a real Spanish lesson.

"I wouldn't call José promiscuous, but I don't think he ever said no either. He really covered the waterfront. He was very popular. My God, he was popular! I went to dinner once at Jackson's down where the cable cars end on Hyde Street, I think. It was a rather elegant dinner house and bar. I was sitting and eating with friends. Everyone was sort of subdued. There was a piano tinkling. Then José came in with his entourage, and suddenly it was like Ringling Brothers Barnum and Bailey Circus! 'Hello, darlings!' He was kissing everybody and running around the room. Everybody knew him, and he knew everybody there. It was Aunty Mame and Mae West all rolled into one, a big splash. He finally settled down. He was very popular. Very popular."

As I listened to Maxwell Gordon talk of José, I realized that in all the many conversations I have had with all sorts of people about José, no one has ever spoken ill of him. I have heard affection, amusement, reverence, admiration, hilarity, but never ill feelings. What an accomplishment that is in itself.

Jimmy and the Black Cat

"When I came back from the service, my sister was working as a cargo agent . . . no not a cargo agent . . . in those days . . . they used to figure the weight of the cargo and how to balance it on the plane . . . what do you call those people?"

"Scales?" I asked irreverently. José waved his hand in dismissal.

"Anyway, my sister Teresa was the first woman hired for that position. Since she was working at the airport she was able to get me a job in the restaurant, as a dishwasher. I only worked as a dishwasher for about three days. Then I was made soda jerker. That didn't last too long. I was making a soda, and this woman sat in front of me. In those days you made the ice cream soda right there at the counter. You take a little bit of ice cream, a little bit of flavoring, and a little bit of soda. Then you mix it up. After that you put most of the ice cream in, and then you squirt more soda to fill the glass. You have to be careful when you put the soda in, that the soda hits the glass and not the ice cream. If it hits the ice cream, it will fly out. Well, that's exactly what happened! That woman was sitting in front of me, and I hit the ice cream. Soda and ice cream went all over her face and her dress. They removed me from being a soda jerker.

"I was made relief waiter, and then permanent waiter in the main dining room. I was the first male waiter at the San Francisco airport. The group of people that I worked with, waitresses, busboys, and myself, used to come into the city to have a few drinks, and we used to go to the Black Cat and the . . . no not the Paper Doll . . . Coffee Dan's . . . where some of the stars used to hang out. We'd dance there. And Mona's: we'd listen to the piano player and to the people singing. And that place where you went downstairs . . . what's the name of it? . . . in North Beach . . . the Purple Onion! It was very famous; the Kingston Trio was discovered there. We used to go there and other places in North Beach. We'd go someplace to eat. This was about 1947.

"Now, I knew about the Black Cat Cafe. At that time it was not like it was later. It wasn't a gay bar. It didn't get gay until I got there. I made it gay. It's very funny, but it's true. I went to the Cat before the war, but then it was very subtle, not like it was in later years. So when I came back from Europe, it was still there, and it was still kind of wild to go to. Later on I went with my mother and my sister."

The Black Cat Cafe in the North Beach area of San Francisco opened shortly after the 1906 earthquake and had been known for many years as a bohemian hangout where men and women on the fringes of acceptability in society—actors, singers, communists, writers, homosexuals, gangsters, prostitutes, anarchists—could gather for a little food, a few drinks, and some amusingly irreverent entertainment. Writers such as William Saroyan and John Steinbeck often visited the place when they were in the city. According to those who frequented the bar, there were also visits from the likes of Tallulah Bankhead, Johnny Mathis, Bette Davis, Gene Kelly, and a plethora of other celebrities. Sailors whose ships were docked at the port would come in, having discovered the establishment on the list of "notorious places to avoid" handed out by their superiors as they left the ship. The Black Cat's celebration of all things counterculture was subtle before the war, but became more open and flamboyant as the war ended. Anyone willing to share a drink and some good camaraderie was accepted there without judgment and with few questions asked. Among the guests at the Black Cat were also the curiosity seekers, tourists and locals who left their mundane workaday routines behind to rub shoulders with those who were more exciting, more exotic, a little more dangerous maybe, and more fascinating than the folks who peopled their daily lives.

For many of José's co-workers, the nights at the Black Cat Cafe offered lively escape from predictable days. For José it offered more. At the Black Cat, he was not simply the son who was cherished despite his being "different." He was not the colleague whose quirks were tolerated but never spoken of. He was in a place where unique was the norm and conventional was the source of joking tolerance. It was the world in reverse, a place where he was usual, where men and women talked openly of variations in sexuality and where deviation was admired. It was 1947, and as the world began changing its focus from war to peacetime, José too stepped unknowingly into a radically new phase of his life.

There was another reason why José kept returning to the Black Cat in the postwar years: Jimmy Moore.

Just as José was reluctant at first to talk about Baron Paul Kolish and André Ehlers, during the first two years that I knew him he mentioned Jimmy only in passing. I assumed it was his reluctance to talk about the important loves in his life. José can talk about sex in ways that can make a sailor blush, but the intimacy of love remains largely unspoken. I wondered, too, if the story of Jimmy involved a measure of pain and loss, as did the other two love stories, but I decided not to press for information until the time felt right.

Finally, one evening as we sat relaxed in a congenial mood in José's apartment, I asked him to tell me about Jimmy. I remember that night as one of the most fascinating and revealing times that I spent with José, not because of what he said, but because of his dogged, and probably unconscious, efforts to avoid talking about Jimmy.

"The Black Cat, that is where I met Jimmy. With the meeting of Jimmy, I got more involved there. Jimmy was a bar boy and a waiter, and we became lovers. He came to live with me, and when he couldn't make it to work, I would go in and substitute for him. Eventually I took over."

I had known that José bought a house after the war, on Virginia Avenue in Woodside Terrace (he did not have enough of an income to qualify for a veteran's loan, and when the real estate company showed open disdain for "Mexicans" and would not help with financing, José's mother went to the bank and withdrew five thousand dollars), but I had not known that Jimmy came to live with José there. I leaned back in my chair to listen, happy at last to learn about this shadow named Jimmy who had danced across the walls now and then but never took form. José paused, his face a little tense. Sometimes José's face looked like a child's. At other times he looked older than his years and the lines in his face seemed to deepen. This was one of those times. I waited. José smiled, and the temporary somberness left his face. He continued talking, but he did not talk of Jimmy.

"I began as cocktail waiter, but I was more of a hostess, greeting people, and I would sing a song now and then. That was my job: to be . . . what do you want to call it? . . . the social hostess. And I finally worked myself up to being more than the hostess. I started performing more, and I started doing female impersonation. I began my opera parodies. I became very popular. I became the Black Cat. And that's when I quit one time. I told Sol Stoumen, the owner, that I was leaving. The pianist, James Willis McGinnis—we most often called him Hazel after the cartoon character—followed me, and we went to work at 90 Market Street. Sol had no business for one month. Nobody came.

"Sol called me. He said, 'You can never leave the Black Cat. You are the Black Cat. You get your damn ass back here!'"

I listened carefully for some clue that the subject would return to Jimmy. José often took circuitous routes in the telling of his stories, but this seemed different. He had made a huge leap in time, and his talk of the Cat was devoid of Jimmy. This was Jimmy the shadow again, the only Jimmy I knew up to that point. I considered prodding José a bit, but decided to wait and let him get back to Jimmy in his own way. He was, after all, talking about the Black Cat in the early years; he would have to mention Jimmy.

"Sol gave me a raise. He paid me a dollar an hour. That was above the rates at that time. I used to get five dollars a show, but I made tips. Hazel and I both made tips. In the beginning the tips all went to the piano player, until my dresser, Lady Edwina (a.k.a. Ed Farquar) said, 'You know, you are a damn fool! You should share those tips that Hazel gets.' The tips came to hundreds of dollars.

"And so I said, 'Listen, Hazel honey, we're going to share those tips. I'm singing. You're playing.'

"McGinnis said, 'I was waiting for you to say something. If you didn't say something I was going to keep it.'

This storyline was not leading back to Jimmy. I stayed quiet, however.

"So we shared the tips. On a normal weekend we would share maybe three or four hundred dollars in tips. That was a Friday, Saturday, and Sunday opera. He got ninety dollars a week to play the piano, and I got fifty dollars a week as hostess and entertainer. So you see I made good money.

"It was through Jimmy that I became so involved in the Black Cat and our romance lasted nine years. Things didn't always go well. I was too busy being a prima donna and a star."

"Ah, here we go," I said to myself. "Your patience has paid off, and now you will finally hear about Jimmy." I was more curious than ever. I decided to help things along. Aloud I said, "So tell me more about Jimmy."

"That kind of hit me the other day again. David—you met David. He came here and was living with me, then I had to take off and travel. I left him here all by himself, and he went out and got involved with people who had bad habits: smoking, drugs and stuff. And so he got involved with drugs, and I came back. It wasn't very nice."

David? What did David have to do with Jimmy? I would realize the connection later, but at the time David, a short-term roommate and housekeeper, seemed another distraction from the story I wanted to hear. In one sense it was, and it gave José a new direction for his verbal meander.

"Now Miss Beverley Plaza is here."

Beverley is the emcee at Finocchio's female impersonation club in the North Beach area of San Francisco, one of the most famous of such clubs in the world. My frustration increased as José began talking about her. Not that Beverley is not a fabulous person, but I wanted to hear about Jimmy. It was proving very difficult to learn about the lover that José would later call "the great love of my life." Although José would probably dismiss the idea, I came to believe that the story of his relationship with Jimmy was still very painful for him, and he preferred not to revisit it. Instead, he launched into a small gripe session about his current roommate. Fortunately, Beverley calmly handles José's idiosyncrasies better than just about anybody, to say nothing of José's parade of less-than-conventional friends and acquaintances. She also gets away with saying things others might not dare.

(A quick aside to the uninitiated: when you speak of a drag queen while he is dressed in drag or if you use his female "drag name," it is proper to use the feminine pronoun: i.e., she, her. When a drag queen is in "boy clothes," customary male attire, the masculine pronoun is used: he, his. It is a social faux pas to address a queen with his "boy name," his actual legal name, or the masculine pronoun when he is in drag. When a queen dresses somewhere between the genders, say a lace skirt and a leather motorcycle jacket, the rules get muddled and, well, you're on your own. Just smile a lot. Because I know Scott primarily by his drag name, Beverley, I almost always use the feminine pronoun in reference to him although his real gender is never in question.)

Once José pulled out a childhood picture of himself during a discussion of his small stature as a child. He said, "This is 1926. I was four years old. I weighed thirty-five pounds."

Beverley poked her head around the doorway of the kitchen and said, "I guess we've made up for lost time since, haven't we?"

José just laughed. Beverley is good for José, despite the grumbling from the Empress. I let José go on about the home front rather than force the issue about Jimmy. Forcing the issue rarely works with José, anyway. Better to bide my time and try to gently return to the subject later, although it was becoming hard to mask my impatience.

"As you can see, she is a very moody person in the morning, but it drives me up the wall. I pussyfoot around. One day I will explode, because I'm a prisoner in my own house. I don't turn on the lights in the kitchen, and I don't go in there and talk, and I don't bang the pots because she lives an inverted life."

I chuckled to myself, remembering that "invert" was used as a pseudomedical term for homosexuals back in the bad old days when we were considered sick.

"This I can understand. However, she gets off work at 1:00 A.M., the bars are open until 2:00 A.M., and she doesn't come traipsing home until 3:00. That's her business. And then she's a little bit wired, so she's up until 4:00 or 5:00, then she goes to sleep. Well, naturally she doesn't want to be disturbed in the morning. I would be the same way: disturbed, but I don't live that type of a life—nocturnal. I did, but even when I worked until 2:00 A.M., I was in bed early and got up in the morning and ate breakfast. She doesn't even eat breakfast."

An oft-quoted line from Hamlet kept coming to mind: "The lady doth protest too much, methinks." José worked himself into a dither over Beverley, but the emotions were obviously coming from some other source. As I was composing this book, I told Beverley about José's minor tirade that evening, and asked if it would be okay if I included it. She simply smiled with understanding and said, "Just spell my name correctly."

"All of these people are around and I'm wired for sound. Sometimes they get up early. They have to be awake in five hours, before they even think of a cup of coffee. I mean, to me, that's a lot of bullshit. You get up in the morning, and the normal thing to do—and it's neither straight nor gay—is to have breakfast or something. The Europeans call it a continental breakfast: a piece of bread, a little jelly, and something to drink. Then you have your lunch. Then you have a break for four o'clock tea, and then you have your dinner. That's the way I live my life. Always."

My therapist calls this "avoidance." I remember thinking that as I listened to José talk. I suppose he has earned the right to avoid what he doesn't want to think about. Besides, his ethics and his methods of coping predate the age of "my therapist . . ." Ya do what ya gotta do.

"I'm getting older, and I'm getting heavier, so I cut out something."

I began to try to project my thoughts psychically. "José . . . tell me about Jimmy. Jimmy . . . Jimmy . . . Jimmy . . ."

"So I don't always eat breakfast since I get up so early to go to work. But I have coffee, and the girls at work share a doughnut with me. Then I work all day with nothing to eat other than that, and then I come home, and I'm wired from what goes on at work. And then she'll make me some tea, and we'll sit down at tea, and I'll talk about what I've done, unwind, and then think about dinner. And that will be my meal for the day. Not eating too much in the meanwhile, my stomach has shrunk a little bit, and I've lost a little bit of weight. And if I watch what I eat, all vegetables and fruit, less fried foods, chicken, fish, no red meats, and automatically I went down. Because I weighed two hundred and twenty-seven pounds. So now I weigh a hundred and eighty-five pounds. So it's all right, I'm doing it, and I can't afford to be heavy."

There was a pause in José's dietary commentary. It was as if at some level he knew that I was not going to let him off the hook, but he was running out of unrelated things to talk about. I opted to take advantage of the silence with a straightforward approach. I became the journalist and asked, "So you started at the Black Cat because of Jimmy?" Jose looked at me a little quizzically, as if I had spoken out of context, a look I had seen before during interviews when I missed the timing on my question. He looked down at his lap briefly as if considering whether to acknowledge the question, and then began speaking as if his digression had never happened.

"I worked at the Black Cat from just after the war until it lost it's liquor license at the end of 1963 and finally closed in 1964. Jimmy's father was very high up in the labor movement under Harry Bridges—big labor man who went to jail for the 1917 big bombing to-do that happened at the waterfront. Maybe it was 1916. Jimmy's father was second in command to Harry Bridges, so he was pretty high up. Jimmy had a drinking habit because he was fifteen years old when he left school and became a merchant seaman during the war. He was young kid dealing with older men. He left in junior high, but he was educated because he read. He was educated because he traveled. He was educated because he could talk and carry on a good conversation with educated people. But he had a drinking habit.

"After being out at sea for long periods with the merchant seaman with no place to spend any of his money, he would come into town with ten or fifteen thousand dollars, and it would be gone in two days. They all did the same thing. He got a part-time job at the Black Cat, as a cocktail waiter, between ships.

"Well, after the war there were no ships. There was no cargo or anything, and there was no good money. Typical Irishman, he made good money, and he spent it."

José smiled at me, checking to see if I caught the teasing tweak at my Irish heritage.

"So okay, I went to the Cat and saw this very attractive boy, and he made good tips. We began seeing each other. His family liked us together. After a while, he moved in and lived with me. For the family I was like another son. His mother made me some kitchen towels. I still have one.

"And so it got to be that he was drinking pretty heavily. He was drinking pretty heavy."

José's voice grew soft as he repeated that statement. He stood up and walked into the other room. I wondered if that was all I would hear about Jimmy. In a moment, José returned. He had retrieved a couple of photographs from the other room.

"This is him when I met him, and this is him when he was older."

There was another pause as I looked at the pictures. I took my time, commented on how handsome Jimmy was. I thought about how the earlier photo had the same ragged white border as some of the family photos of me in the 1950s. I figured that José needed another moment to collect his thoughts. Don't tell him I said so, though. I stared at the last photo and waited. When he began again, his voice was subdued—unusual for José.

"I was too busy being a star. I had to devote myself to making a career. What else was I going to do with my life? As you know, I had been arrested. I couldn't just sit around and cry, and it was a secret that I had to keep, because nobody knew about it. Nobody knew why I had to work so hard to find a career. I had to come up with what I was going to do pretty damn fast, because I had no income coming in other than a little rental from the house.

"So I was very busy, and he was drinking. He would take off from me for two or three days. He would take the car, and I had to walk to work.

"So I said, 'Jimmy, you're going to get out of the bar business.'

"I went to his father and said, 'Can you get him a job?'

"Jimmy didn't want to accept his father's help finding a job in the warehouses.

"I said, 'You're going to do it whether you like it or not. You're not going to live in the bars!'

"So the father pulled strings and got him working in a warehouse, which was pretty good money. He got a check for thirty-five dollars per week. He was in the warehouseman's union. He worked like that, and he liked it.

"Monday through Friday was work for Jimmy. Saturday and Sunday we had off together. However, Saturday and Sunday nights were my big nights at the Black Cat, as well as Sunday afternoon. Sunday afternoon we'd get something to eat; he didn't eat much. His body was like you see it in the picture."

I looked again at the picture. Jimmy was slim, handsome, nicely built. There is always so much that a picture doesn't reveal. Sometimes words are just as inadequate.

"Jimmy felt left out of my life at the Cat. And we could never be by ourselves. No matter where we went, someone knew me. We would go to a restaurant or whatever, and someone always picked up the tab for us. And they would always say, 'There's someone I want you to meet.'

"Jimmy would say, 'Let's go somewhere where they don't know you. I don't know where that would be—in heaven I guess.'

"I would say, 'Try to make the best of it.'

"Because I spent so much of the time making a career, Jimmy would never come to see me at the Cat. He knew my act was an act that I did, not me. Just like everybody that's on the stage, you have an act, and sometimes people can get jealous of it too, as if it's for real. The opera *Pagliacci* is based on that, the clown act with the tears underneath."

I thought again about how rarely José talked of the tragedies in his life. Sometimes the masks we wear, onstage or off, are our salvation. And sometimes not.

"And so, Jimmy met a handsome young man who really played him for a sucker. This person needed somebody to take care of him, pay his rent, and help him with his schooling until he got out of school. I saw this right away. But Jimmy didn't. So I said, 'Fine!' We talked about breaking up."

In José's personal lexicon, "Fine!" means that he has conceded that something is as it is, and that he can do nothing to change it. He may not like the situation, but his exclamation expresses his decision to let it be and not waste his energy in a fruitless attempt to force a change.

"We were the ideal couple. We each had an income of our own. We were entertaining often. But I, being very proud, didn't want a scandal, so I said, 'Fine. Monday, Tuesday, Wednesday, Thursday you are at home with me. Friday, Saturday, and Sunday you can go out.'

"So he lived in two places. Nobody suspected, but it finally got to the point where he said, 'I can't take it.'

"So I said, 'Fine,' and he left. The day the boy graduated and became a hairdresser, he said thank you and see you later. He lives here today—never left the city.

"Now the year was 1964, and I was going to New York. We always remained friends, and so before New York he says, 'I want to see you, José.' He said, 'You were right that we all have to live with things as they are, but you were wrong that you didn't give me the time that I needed.'

"I realized that I was too busy being a star, and now I'd be a lonely old man in my old age. I said, 'This is not necessary, let's get back together.' I said, 'I'm going to go now and work at the World's Fair. I'll be able to come back with a lot of money. We will get ourselves a nice little place. You're working for a good company. You get good money. We'll have nothing to worry about.

"Before I left for the World's Fair, Eddie Paulson, who used to work at the Cat with me and was there before I came there and who now is dead, Eddie said, 'José, why don't you fix lunch for Jimmy and have a nice rendezvous before you leave?' I was leaving the next day, for New York City, for the World's Fair. I did what Eddie said. I made lunch, and we had a *wonderful* afternoon, and we made plans about what we were going to do and everything and all, and we partied. It was nice. The next day I went to New York. I got one or two letters, I think. I probably have them somewhere."

José paused as if he were going to go search out the letters. Like a kid at a movie, I found myself rooting for a happy ending to the story. The writer in me, however, found it hard to ignore the foreshadowing that said otherwise. I found myself hoping José would leave the room to find the letters, prolong the story. He didn't.

"Now Jimmy had been drinking heavily once in a while, and he had been stopped by the police a couple times. In those days they would stop you on the street for public drunkenness and take you to the drunk tank. They don't do that today. You can sleep on the streets, you can piss on the streets, and you can be drunk on the streets, and nobody picks you up. Nobody does anything. And so that's what happened. He got arrested. Now, the last time he was arrested for drunkenness, the judge said, 'The next time they arrest you, I'm going to lock you up and throw away the key. It's ridiculous, a young man like you drinking so much!'

"He had gone to a party south of Market, you see. The jail had just been built. He was coming home past the jail because he lived on this side of Market Street, and he was kind of high. He sat on the steps of the new jail to catch his breath. It was the changing of the guard, midnight, and a young, rookie cop coming in saw him sitting on the steps a little bit high and took him in for drunk. The cop put him in the drunk tank with five other men. It was not necessary. If they had just left him alone, he would have walked home. Well, I think the words of the judge preyed on him, and being with the other people in there.

"Nobody deigned to contact me at first. Eventually they told me. Jimmy had hung himself in the jail.

"It was a disaster. I couldn't come back from the exposition; it was toward the end of the thing. I debated whether I should come back. I had to bring the exposition to an end. It was 1964. We were going to be open again in 1965. That was two years, the years that the New York exposition existed. Pierre said, 'Well, do what you wish, but please stay,' and so I stayed.

"I came back at the end of the summer. I saw Jimmy's father right away. We had a long talk. I couldn't understand how a person could be so suicidal and nothing was done about it. If I had been there, I would have fought. There would have been a big investigation. It was a drunk tank! They don't take anything in with them. How could he hang himself?

"Anyway, he was dead, and we laid him to rest. I've got to find somebody to take me out to put flowers on his grave. I haven't been out there since he died.

"His father wanted to know what happened, why we broke up. I was the best thing that ever happened to Jimmy, according to him, and I was considered his son.

"I said, 'Well, it's one of those things.' All this time, you see, I had to be very careful, because we never talked about it, about being gay. I couldn't discuss the truth. He kind of blamed me for not being there.

"You and other people, all of us, we all think that ours are the worst problems in the world, and they aren't. We've all had some kind of problems. Some of us maybe are stronger than others, or we just are very rational and we figure that we have to do certain things because this is the way our life is going to be.

"Jimmy's father and I confided in one another as much as we could. We talked about the relationship in roundabout ways. He said, 'I know you loved my son.'

"And I said, 'More than you'll ever know.'

"Never was 'homosexual' mentioned. But the father knew. Now the mother is dead. The father is dead, and he had a brother that died. There is only a sister. I didn't know her until after his death.

"And so, that ended my big romance. The great love of my life. It carried on for nine years. I have a ring. I have some things that he gave me: lavender ashtrays that are on the end tables there, and a pair of cufflinks."

One of the clocks in José's apartment chimed deeply. I thought of death knells. José looked tired.

"With him not working, I came to a point that moved me, a point when I had to decide how to make a living. I became the star of my act. I was that until the day he died. The star of my show."

Again a weary pause.

"The reason the bar got closed was because of the apathy about the way the city was trying to stop the bar from running. Nobody helped us. People realized, I guess, that we could fight as long as we wanted to, but we had to surrender our license."

Good night, Jimmy boy. Thanks for loving this incredible man the best you knew how.

"Well, shit! Why are you going to fight for something when you can't make it right?

"Fighting costs money, thousands and thousands of dollars. You shouldn't lose your license for no reason. But they took it. You had to surrender it. How are you going to make a living? We could have made it with food, I guess, but that wasn't enough. Eventually nobody came back.

"Fine!"

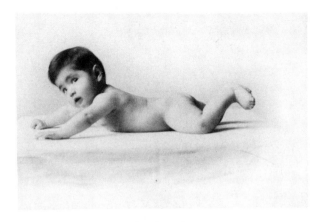

José before drag.

José's father, Julio Sarria, just before returning to Nicaragua.

José at age one with his godmother and godfather Jesserina
and Charles Millen in San Francisco.

José at age seven with his mother, Delores, on Easter Sunday.

The Boys from Texas.

José with his "squad" of Russian women
who were liberated from the camps on the march.

José home from the war, March 1947.

José at the Black Cat with (l to r) "Hazel," his accompanist, "Norma Jean Honey," a waiter at the Cat, and Eddie Paulson, the Cat's head waiter.

José and his great love, Jimmy Moore, in Golden Gate Park.

The coronation of Empress José I at the 1965 Tavern Guild Halloween Ball.
José is seated before his "ladies" in waiting.

My Platform is Completely and Eloquently Engraved for All Time on the Facade of San Francisco's New **HALL OF JUSTICE** TO THE FAITHFUL AND IMPARTIAL ENFORCEMENT OF THE LAWS ★ WITH EQUAL AND EXACT JUSTICE TO ALL ★ OF WHATEVER STATE OR PERSUASION ★ THIS BUILDING IS DEDICATED BY THE PEOPLE OF THE CITY AND COUNTY OF SAN FRANCISCO

JOSÉ JULIO SARRIA, Candidate for Supervisor
City and County of San Francisco
November 7, 1961

A campaign card handed out during José's historic run for political office.

José's winning costume at one of the last Tavern Guild Halloween Balls in 1978.

The grave site of the Widow Norton's dearly departed husband, Emperor Norton.

José as Grand Marshall of the 1989 San Francisco Gay Freedom Parade.

José in his apartment with the painting of him as Carmen at the Black Cat.
(Photo Credit: Brian Ashby. Used by permission.)

The Arrest

José first worked at the Black Cat Cafe as a substitute for Jimmy when Jimmy could not make it to work because he was sick or, more often, because he was drunk. José found himself enjoying the patrons as much as they enjoyed him. He would serve drinks, flirt with and tease everyone, and he would sing. Revelers began coming to the Cat just to see José. Sol Stoumen noticed the business increasing at his establishment, and he offered José a steady job.

At the same time, José had returned to school on the GI Bill. He was working toward a teaching credential and continuing his studies in language and music. Because he had to work to support himself, his schooling was taking longer than the traditional four years, but he was determined to finish and settle into the life of a teacher. It would be the perfect career to combine his love of learning and his love of people.

Jimmy found it increasingly difficult to find and keep a job after the ending of the war forced him out of the merchant marine. Jimmy continued to work occasionally at the Black Cat, but as José's popularity there increased, he found himself in the background. More and more Jimmy disappeared for days at a time on alcoholic binges. José would come home from the ribald gaiety of the bar to a silent, empty house. The tension between the lovers escalated. Finally, in his frustrated anger, José decided to do what he now says is very bad form; he would do what Jimmy did. He would go out on the town alone to party.

"I figured, you know, whatever he could do I could do. Which, of course, is a very, very bad philosophy. Never, never, never do it."

In the 1990s there are multitudinous bars, restaurants, motels, bed and breakfasts, clubs, and recreational facilities that cater very openly to a primarily gay clientele. In the early 1950s there were none. There were, however, places that were frequented by gay men, but social interaction was very discreet and cautious and filled with secret clues and signals known only to other gay men. Finding a place to safely share intimacy was even more problematic. Being caught meant loss of job, family, and reputation. Many of these closeted men resorted to quick, anonymous sexual encounters in restrooms and parks, and such "cruising places" were also known within gay circles, and sometimes to the police who often raided them.

When José decided to "give Jimmy a taste of his own medicine," he dressed up one evening and headed to the bar at the Saint Francis Hotel, a place where gay men knew they could discreetly meet other gay men, in particular, gay men of the upper classes. Often younger gay men would go to the Saint Francis bar to meet older men. What José did not know is that the men's restroom near the bar had become a cruise spot, and many patrons had begun to complain about stumbling upon sexual encounters there.

José sat in the Saint Francis bar and let his eyes roam the room. He made eye contact with a few men and exchanged smiles. He assessed his chances of meeting someone and wondered which of the men might continue to cast glances his way in order to express an interest. He pondered the secret clue phrases he might use should he decide to approach one of them: "I think we've met before . . . *aren't you a friend of Aunt Dorothy's?*" Or perhaps he could start off with, "Are you a musician? You seem like you might be musical. *Are you musical?*" He could look for the subtle clues in dress as well.

Before making any serious attempts to make contact, José figured he'd better first relieve the pressure in his bladder. He stood up and made his way to the men's room. There were three other men in the restroom when he entered, but he took little notice of them. He stood at one of the urinals and did what he came to do. As he finished, the man at the urinal next to him reached over and touched him in a decidedly sexual way. Although José was not interested in a bathroom tryst, he was also not particularly offended. He knew firsthand the fear and secrecy involved in attempting to find connections to other gay men, and he felt a twinge of compassion for the man. He smiled in what he thought was a gently dismissive way and prepared to zip up and return to the bar. Suddenly a strong hand gripped his wrist roughly.

"Police. You are under arrest!"

José's arms were pulled behind his back, and he felt the cold metal of the handcuffs and heard the clicking as they were tightened around his wrists. The man next to him was cuffed as well, and the two of them were led out of the restroom to face the humiliation of being escorted out of the bar and into police cars.

"At that time, the sex squad, I mean the vice squad, consisted of two men, Murphy and Gallagher. It was Murphy who came over and grabbed my wrist, and he knew me. He knew me. But they had to make an example of somebody because of the complaints. I was in the wrong place at the wrong time."

Telling about the arrest at the Saint Francis Hotel that so drastically changed his life, José remembered another brush with the law which angered him and left him frustrated and a little more cynical about what he sees as the influence of image and politics and prejudice over safety and justice in our system of law enforcement.

"A similar thing happened with Social Security in the 1970s, when I was collecting unemployment and disability, and working. People were screwing with the Social Security, so they needed to make an example. You see, I was chosen as an example. And yet people collect Social Security for years with the names of people who are dead, or they use phony baloney names. I had two jobs, and I got tired of two jobs. So I got myself fired from one of them. Then I went down and applied for unemployment, because it takes two jobs to live in the manner to which I had become accustomed.

"I was very honest about still having one job. The son of a bitch at the unemployment office said, 'Oh yes, you can claim unemployment against the job that you left.' So I collected unemployment under one job, and meanwhile I was still working the other job. That is when I developed hepatitis, and I ended up in the hospital, almost dead.

"I'm in the hospital, and the doctor fills out the Social Security forms for disability. So now I'm getting unemployment, working, and collecting disability from the Social Security Administration, all under one name. They put my name in the computer and it blew up.

"Here I was dying, and they sent a federal officer out there to arrest me. My doctor told him to get the hell out of the hospital. He told the officer that I wasn't about to go anyplace. He said, 'If God is not on his side, then you can pick up the body at the cemetery, because that's what's going to happen to him.'

"Then they were going to put an officer outside my door, and my doctor said, 'No, you will *not* put anybody in this hospital! When he's finished, he'll see you.'

"Meanwhile, with the few checks that I had gotten, they charged me with embezzlement. Well, I wasn't an embezzler. I did exactly what they told me to do. It was not my fault. I paid that money back, but the police were still looking to charge me even though they did not have anything to charge me with. I'll never forget that officer; his name was De Rosa. He said, 'Well, we have to make an example of you.' So he says, 'You paid back the money, so we'll give you three years suspended sentence, during which time you cannot apply for any federal money or receive a pension.'

"So there were three years when I could not touch disability or unemployment. And I did it. At the end of three years, I quit my job and applied for it."

The effects of José's first brush with the law were more extensive and longer-lasting than the later case it brought to his mind. Although the police in San Francisco frequently raided known gay hangouts and made arrests on morals charges, the city at least handled the trials of the men discreetly, unlike most American jurisdictions at the time, which made a point of exposing arrested gay men, often before their court hearings, to the community at large, a mean–spirited and punitive action that often led to devastating losses and even suicides. José was not exposed to wide public censure, but the fine that resulted from his arrest at the Saint Francis was very large. He had to sell a piece of property to pay it. And he had to rethink his career plans.

"Contrary to what people say, your name never appeared here in the papers in San Francisco when you were arrested on a morals charge. In Los Angeles I know they did, and they did it on the peninsula. But here you could be arrested, and you could tell your boss you had a dental appointment when you went to court. Nobody would ever know as long as you didn't go to jail. So anyway that was secret, so that's what I had to do. After the arrest, I couldn't get my teaching credential. The opera wouldn't take me."

In the middle part of this century in this country, a teacher who was found to be gay would have his or her credential to teach revoked. Any sex offense, no matter how minor, was also cause for revoking of a teaching credential. José knew that his dream of teaching school was over. He left school without completing a degree. He considered joining the opera, but, although companies were well aware of the gay people among them, they did not want to risk their reputations on *known* gay people. The closet, at least in terms of the public at large, was a prerequisite for a chance in professional opera. José was too well known for his performances at the Black Cat Cafe.

José found his options falling away one by one. He went through a period of depression and bitterness, but those feelings slowly turned to defiant anger.

"My entertainment career began because I had nothing else to do, and I had a lot of talent. I began entertaining because I needed something to be doing, and I was very, very bitter. I was bitter for a long, long time, but I've gotten over it because it doesn't pay. But at the time I said to myself, 'You sons of bitches! Fine! You named me a homosexual. You think I'm going to carry a card? You think I'm going to register? You think I'm going to do all those things? You are crazy! You are going to pay, and pay very, very dearly! You! You label me a queen? Then I'll be the best goddamn queen that ever was! And one day you will pay to see me!'

"I borrowed money from my mother, and used her charge account, and I went to an amateur hour. That's how my career started. My performing became my job. Then the notoriety began, and more notoriety than fame because of the things that I do. The arrest happened in the early fifties. Nobody knew anything about this arrest until I ran for public office. They dug it up during the campaign.

"So, you see, I didn't start performing to be famous. I just did it because people were going to support me in the manner I wanted to live and that I was used to. That's why I insist on the butter dish, and I insist on silver. I was brought up to live that way, and until the day I die I will live that way. And I certainly didn't do things for the betterment of human nature. I did it for my own benefit. But it happened to get twisted and work out to a cause. But I didn't begin for that cause. I had my own cause. I've been gay all my life and I don't care—I've managed to live with it, and I've been adjusted to it. So I didn't have to fight for laws. I didn't give a good goddamn. They could pass any laws they wanted to, and I could still live my way."

Pierre

It is a beautiful Sunday afternoon in midsummer. The World's Fair in Seattle had been open officially since early spring and traffic to and from Seattle was rolling in the four directions of the compass. More than a few tourists that summer included a stop in San Francisco on their West Coast vacation itineraries. Those among the summer nomads who were gay or just adventuresome often made their way to the Black Cat Cafe, which by then had a considerable reputation that included one outrageous female impersonator named José Julio Sarria.

José could always recognize newcomers to the Cat, and he often included them in the verbal banter that had become a regular part of his act. The fourth wall was a decidedly temporary concept in José's stage life. The audience never knew when he would break character and turn to engage some member of the crowd in conversation, usually embarrassing conversation. The unpredictability of his acts and the spontaneity of his teasing asides made his shows unique and extravagantly delightful each time. His opera *Carmen* would not be the same *Carmen* twice, nor would *Aïda*, nor *Faust,* and each performance could be enjoyed equally by virgin viewers or experienced regulars.

The Black Cat was full that afternoon, and the crowd was in a jovial mood. Conversation was raucous and the drinks flowed liberally. As had become the case since José became the cafe's headliner, a large percentage of the patrons were gay, but there was a considerable representation of straight singles and couples and those in between. The air of camaraderie and festivity that was usual to the Cat seemed heightened on that day. José anticipated a fun and responsive audience for the forty-five minute opera parody he planned to perform. He, of course, would play all of the parts, unless he decided to pull some unsuspecting audience member into a supporting role.

Tables were pulled together into a makeshift stage, and José made his entrance to the dramatic piano accompaniment from Hazel. He was wearing a fitted gown and a tiara, and, of course, his signature red-heeled pumps. José launched into a dramatic opening song, arms raised in a larger-than-life opera pose. As the music rose to a crescendo and José's voice swelled toward a dramatic high note, he abruptly stopped and began talking in a matter-of-fact voice to a man at a front table. The jolt of his impeccable comic timing sent a wave of exasperated laughter through the room. He began explaining the story in a soft voice to the man he had first addressed, punctuating his narrative with comments like, "Now pay attention you handsome man. This is very sophisticated stuff. You should learn this. You won't always be beautiful, you know. You'll need something to talk about when the plumbing gets rusted . . ." Leaning close to the man and drawing the audience into the intimacy of the exchange, José suddenly burst back into song, hitting the anticipated high note in a booming voice, and startling the man into almost tumbling backwards in his chair, much to the delight of the rest of the room.

Back on stage, José continued singing in his impressively trained but always campy style. The show went well, and when José announced the second act, the listeners were in his control. The applause and laughter increased as the people gave themselves over to the experience. It was one of those days when José could feel a connection to his audience that was almost flawless. Drawing energy from them as they drew it from him, he seemed to perform seamlessly. The notes were clear and precise, his timing was perfect, his wit was sharp; it was one of those rare stage-to-house interactions that performers hope for and cherish.

"To be honest, I can't remember which opera it really was, except that I know that when I was in the middle of a beautiful aria, and I had taken a deep breath, ready to reach one of my unusual and very rare high Cs, my immortal high Cs, when all of a sudden at the door appeared a young man. He stood in the doorway with the light beaming through and around him, this image, this god, this well-formed man carrying a giant 'revolver' in his pants. I did not believe what I saw!"

The debonair young man was dressed in white Levis, a white shirt, and white sneakers, which added to his backlit heavenly appearance in the doorway. José assumed the man was gay since the attire was typical of what a gay man would wear in San Francisco in 1962.

"Yes, even in 1962 we had dress codes for upstanding, righteous queens. There was a uniform."

The man took a step into the room. José stopped, frozen in his puffed-up posture, and stared. Hazel paused in the accompaniment. The crowd fell silent in anticipation. In a voice slightly strained with too much air behind it, José demanded firmly, "Young man! Do you have a license to carry that hidden weapon?" He released the rest of his breath loudly.

"Of course, everyone turned around, and all you could hear was '(Gasp!) My God!'

"And there he stood with the most innocent look on his face. I could tell immediately that he did not speak English and that he did not understand. He just did not know what was happening, although he must have suspected. Right away I said, 'Do you speak English?' and I had even a dumber look returned to me. So I said, 'Do you speak German? *Sprechen Sie Deutsch? Parlez-vous Français? Habla Español?*'"

The patrons moved their focus from the stage to the man who had entered. No one thought the change odd. When they came to see José they knew they had to expect the unexpected. They chuckled good-naturedly at the young man's discomfort, trusting José to know when to tease and when to back off. They could simply enjoy the spectacle.

"Finally he recovered his composure enough to say, *'Oui, je parle Français.'* Then in French he said, 'And if you embarrass me any more, I will leave.'

"I thought to myself, 'He could be dinner tonight; I better not insult him.'

"So I said, 'No, no, no, no. But that is absolutely formidable! What you are carrying there? It can't be real!' We were speaking in French.

"He said, *'Oh, mais oui! C'est vrai. C'est vrai.'*

"And now, of course everyone in the Black Cat sets up a hum of conversation. You'd think there was a nest of bees the way they were buzzing. Then we stopped talking French, and everybody waited for a translation. I had asked him while we were talking where he was from. He said he was from the Seattle World's Fair. He was going to Carmel where he had owned a restaurant. He sold it, but the new owners defaulted, so he was going down to repossess it."

Knowing that much more interaction in French would lose him his audience, José turned from the young god and addressed the expectant patrons. He explained that the new arrival was down from the World's Fair in Seattle and had stopped by on his way to a restaurant he owned in Carmel.

"And his name is . . ." José gestured to the young visitor and waited.

The man apparently understood enough to respond cautiously, "Pierre."

José continued, ". . . Pierre. And he says that if I insult him anymore, he will leave."

The crowd protested good-naturedly and waved Pierre into the room with expressions of welcome. Someone offered him a chair and ordered him a drink. It was the reaction José had anticipated. He smiled and continued the show, occasionally flirting, sometimes in and sometimes out of character, with Pierre.

"This gentleman turned out to be Lucky Pierre, the famous restaurateur. His restaurant and his reputation were very well known in New York and around the United States. You had to make reservations six or seven months in advance to go to Lucky Pierre's to eat. It was *the* in place in New York. He also had a little restaurant in Carmel, which was also called Lucky Pierre's. Believe it or not, he did not have a stove in the restaurant. He served luncheons, and he cooked on a hot plate. The little dowagers of that area would come down there to see this character who would come out stirring the pot and saying, 'I cook for you.' He would make fancy luncheons on that little hot plate.

"He served a very fabulous French bread that was made next door to his restaurant, and he had tied the bakers up with a contract for twenty-five years in which they could not sell the bread within a radius of fifty miles. So Pierre had exclusivity on the French bread. People would come to Pierre, buy the bread, and ship it back to Chicago or New York, or wherever."

After his performance, José took a break, ordering a drink and then asking Pierre if he could join him at his table. Pierre welcomed a chance to converse in his native language since his English was very rough. They enjoyed each other's company, and spent as much time together as they could that day. From that afternoon on, whenever Pierre came to San Francisco, he and José would meet for lunch or spend the day together. Although José had initially been very attracted to Pierre, they soon developed a strong and trusting friendship that was clearly not romantic in nature.

"Sometimes we would visit some friends of his here in San Francisco, several doctors and lawyers. Through him I met some very rich and very nelly gay people here.

"When I met him he was connected with the World's Fair. He was helping out two French girls; they were both lesbians. They had met the future commissioner of World's Fairs for the United States back in Paris. He met one of them and was madly taken with her, not realizing that she was a lesbian, and that she had a 'wife.' He thought he was going to make out like a lion. Well, he never got anything. When it was time for him to leave France, he said, 'Well, when you come to America, you look me up. I'm the new commissioner of World's Fairs that the United States is going to become a part of through the French World's Fair Association. That's why I'm here.'

"So the girls, hearing about the Seattle World's Fair, packed their bags, came over to Seattle, went to his office, and said, '*Nous sommes ici!* Where can we put up our shop?'

"They had brought hundreds of dolls that they were going to sell at the fair. Well, in the World's Fair, only one person could sell one thing. Two people cannot sell the same thing. There was this Italian lady who had the concession for dolls. The commissioner said, 'I'm very, very busy. You go set up anyplace you want. But you cannot sell dolls.'"

Initially the two French women were unsure what to do. They could not sell their dolls, and they had no money to invest in a new inventory. The only thing they had was the permission of the fair's commissioner to set up and sell . . . something. Checking a map to see how far away the town of Carmel, California was, they decided to call an old friend, Pierre Parker.

Pierre was delighted to hear from the couple, and he listened intently to their plight. When they were done recounting their troubles, Pierre assured them that there was nothing to worry about. He suggested that they investigate the menus of the food outlets already approved for the fair and pick a type of fare not yet claimed by another vendor. The initial investment would be minimal, and he would help them with that. He offered to come to Seattle to help them run their operation, claiming that selling food at the World's Fair sounded like an adventure he would like very much. Besides, the timing was perfect since he was just winding up the sale of Lucky Pierre's in Carmel. The women asked about the expense of kitchen equipment. Pierre just chuckled, thinking about his hot plate, and told them not to worry.

When the restaurant sale was finalized, Pierre set out for Seattle. In the meantime, the women had decided to sell French onion soup and soufflé. Their next task was to find a place to set up their booth at the fair site. Because they knew their resources would be limited, they chose an area below the stadium that could provide partial protection from the elements. At that point they were stumped. They had no materials to build a booth, let alone a small eatery. By the time Pierre arrived, they were deeply discouraged.

Pierre's natural buoyance lifted their spirits when he arrived. He congratulated them on their simple but elegant choice of menu. He talked as if the greatest hurdles had already been leaped. He asked to see the site. They showed him the stark area below the stadium that provided shelter from rain and wind but little else. The area was about fifteen feet by fifteen feet. There was no running water, no walls, no tables, no chairs. The women stood a little embarrassed, but Pierre was energized by the challenge. He mumbled something to himself and began exploring the surrounding area.

"Ah, voilá!"

The women hurried over to where Pierre was bending over. He pointed to a single metal faucet. "We have water. A hose will be no expense at all!"

They found a store where they could buy a hose, a saw, hammers, nails, a few washtubs, and other assorted hardware. Back at the fairgrounds, Pierre explained his plan. With a renewed enthusiasm, the women joined him in searching the grounds for discarded crates and boards, railings, whatever they could find. The design of their French cafe evolved with each new discovery. Like Paris ragpickers, they scoured the area for treasures that others did not recognize as such. The cafe began to take shape as Pierre reassured his partners that presentation is everything, and the illusion can be inexpensive.

Thanks to Pierre's slightly crazy sense of whimsy, the cafe started to include stairways that led to nowhere and doors that opened into nothing, but from the inside it all looked fabulous. The kitchen was primitive with metal tubs for water and ice, some wooden tables, a tiny electric stove attached to one of the several extension cords they had run from a distant outlet, and, of course, the hose. All of this was hidden behind the scenes. With some quickly sewn curtains and table-cloths to hide some of the rough edges and a bit of paint, the appearance of the dining area blossomed into something impressive. They were ready for the opening of the fair.

"Well, they were not very much businesswomen. They kept no books. It was a hanky-panky operation. If they saw you, and they thought you had money, the soup was ten dollars a bowl. If they saw you, and they thought you were very sweet, the soup was two dollars a bowl. They did everything contrary. If they were to be open at five, they opened at ten. They had no cash register. The money was kept in their bras, and all the papers and receipts were kept in a duffel bag. The government didn't know they existed at first. When the federal government did find out that they existed, they wanted to see the register receipts. They didn't have a register. They dragged this duf-fel bag out. 'We have all the receipts here. You can find them.' Well, my dear, it was a three-ring circus. At the end of a day, Pierre, the two girls, and a waitress, when they had one, would sit down on the floor and they'd divide the take. 'One dollar for you. One dollar for you. Three dollars for me . . .' every night. They paid no taxes. At the end of the fair the women kissed the commissioner, went back to France, and established a trucking company in Bordeaux, where the two girls lived and retired very nicely. Their one truck gave birth to a fleet of trucks. They were one of the biggest cargo carriers in southern France.

"That fair is where Pierre got his little nest egg to pay for going to all the other world's fairs. The Seattle World's Fair was very success-ful, and that's how Pierre got his start. There he met two lawyers. One was named Mr. Taggert. He saw the operation of these kids, and said, 'Let me invest what little money you make for yourself here, Pierre, and we'll make it grow.'

"So Pierre said, 'Fine.' He handed them ten thousand dollars on the side. They invested that money well and it grew. Pierre used that money to finance the New York World's Fair, the San Antonio World's Fair, all the world's fairs where he worked. The two lawyers grew into an incorporation of seventy-eight lawyers, and they owned the Washington Building in Seattle. That was where Pierre's office was. He was on the thirteenth floor. He went there once a year to sign the contracts that he had to sign.

"Pierre did very, very well. He retired, and the money went to Switzerland. He gets a check every month for doing nothing to this day. He owns condos in Paris and a home in Carmel. It all began with a measly little ten thousand dollars from that crazy soufflé stand at the World's Fair. From little acorns, big oaks grow."

Pierre so enjoyed his time at the World's Fair that he decided to apply to the Bureau of Fairs to be a food vendor at all future fairs. As his capital increased, so did the elegance of his temporary cafes, but he always kept the operations as simple as he could so that the profits compounded with each event, and his lawyers continued to expand the funds with wise and lucrative investments. He was well established in that circuit the year the city of San Francisco finally closed the notorious Black Cat Cafe. The city and the State Alcoholic Beverage Control Department revoked Sol Stoumen's liquor license on Halloween, 1963 for serving homosexuals. The Cat limped along into the new year serving food and nonalcoholic drinks, but it finally had to close at the end of February 1964. It was the same year that José's mother died and just two years since he lost his bid for a seat on the San Francisco Board of Supervisors.

"Pierre and I were like brothers. When the Black Cat closed, he offered me a job, because it was quite a disaster for me. My life fell apart, more or less. The Cat closed. My mother passed away. I lost the election. Nothing was going right."

José was first declared the Empress of San Francisco in 1964, but that milestone Halloween ball was yet to come.

"Pierre said, 'You know, I'm going to be in New York. I finally got a little space at the World's Fair. We're calling it The Luxembourg. I've given the grand duchess there forty thousand dollars to use the name. I'm in the international restaurants section of the fair. I bought a name and *voilá!* I'm Luxembourg.' I agreed to go."

José's entrance into world's fair food service was not an easy one. The world's fairs have everything to do with image. The countries featured want to show their best faces, and the host city wants the world to remember it as a stylish, worldly, and hospitable place. Consequently, the vendors at the fairs are screened carefully and thoroughly. Each vendor is allowed to bring one or two key people, and the rest of the workforce has to be hired from the local population. Pierre submitted José's name to the Bureau of Fairs. Since José was to be Pierre's key person and primary assistant, he had to be scrutinized as carefully as his friend and boss. The investigation reminded José of the military intelligence scrutiny during the war, except that this time he had an arrest on his record.

José was called before a board of officials to discuss his suitability to work at the fair coming up in New York. Their approval meant that he would be cleared to work at any future fair as well. José remembers that fair hearing as one of the few times he ever saw Pierre wearing a suit and tie. The board openly discussed José's military record, his education, his performing career, and the arrest. It was the first time Pierre had heard of his friend's troubles with the law, but the revelation was not a problem for the Frenchman. He was well aware of the precarious place that gay men held in society, and such arrests were not new to him. The board of review questioned both José and Pierre about José's abilities and views and intentions. In the end, they decided that José's assets far outweighed any trouble from his past, and he was given certification to work.

José remembers that afternoon as a time of deepening friendship between the two men. The revelation that had such potential for division was not an issue for his friend, and so his trust in Pierre grew stronger as a result. Pierre was privy to José's most difficult secret, and he felt privileged. He also became very protective of his new partner.

"That afternoon made our friendship solid. That's when we became like brothers. After the whole thing was over, we sat and we talked. We started discussing plans for the fair. He told me that he was going to repossess his restaurant again. See, people would buy his restaurant because they saw it was always packed. They did not realize that the restaurant was built on his personality. People would pay the price he asked for the restaurant because they thought they were going to make a fortune. Well, the minute he wasn't there, they made no fortune, they fell behind in the payments, and he repossessed again. He repossessed three times. He was going back and forth between Seattle or New York and Carmel. Each time he would come back, and I'd say, 'Oh, not again!'

"And he'd say, 'Oh, these people are very stupid! But if they want to give me that kind of money, fine. Now I own it again. Now I will build it up again.' Finally, the last time he sold it, they put a stove in, and that helped the new owners a little bit. It's been sold ever since. It still operates, but not as the famous place that it was."

The New York World's Fair was held in the summer months for one hundred and eighty days. It ran for two consecutive years, 1964 and 1965. José's leaving for the fair in the spring of 1964 was not the end of the tragedies for him that year. It was toward the end of that first year's run of the fair that Jimmy killed himself. Yet as he and Pierre began planning and decorating their temporary tribute to the food of Luxembourg, the world seemed a lighter and less somber place.

Because Luxembourg had no international reputation for its cuisine, José and Pierre felt that they were safe in taking liberties with the menu in New York. They prepared an onion soup recipe and several other dishes, their main criterion in selecting them being low overhead costs and readily available ingredients. When the fair opened it took little time for the cafe called The Luxembourg to gain a reputation and become very popular. The food was basic but good, and the two proprietors were personable and very charming. According to José, there was another, almost subliminal source of the cafe's popularity, one that he was not above exploiting.

"Pierre was very charming, and that special part of him that I noticed when he first came to the Black Cat, I used to call his 'money maker.' When we went to New York, our restaurant only seated twenty people. Twenty was a packed house. We would have twenty people, feed them, then out! He would say, *"Mangez, payez, et sortie!"* Eat, pay, and get the hell out! He made three quarters of a million dollars in that space, after expenses, in a hundred and eighty days.

"Some days I would say, 'God, we're not going to get anybody today!' There would be maybe a hundred and fifty-five thousand, a hundred and seventy-five thousand, two hundred and sixty-five thousand people at the fair: that was the attendance count. You needed good attendance like that to get a good house in the restaurants. But some days it seemed like nobody would come in. So I'd say, 'Pierre, come on. Fluff it up and go stand in the doorway.' We had two doorways: one that you go out, and one that you come in. So he would stand there very innocently, and sure enough, the customers would come. The first ones that would notice him were the queens. I would stand in the window and look out, and I'd say, 'Ah-ah! *Voilà!* We got some! Put the bait out and we got a bite! We got a bite! Here they come!'

"We made a small fortune. I think my bonus the first year was five thousand dollars.

"He built a reputation with both men and women, straight and gay. He spoke very, very broken English, and made himself even dumber to add to his charm, but he was a 'smart frog' as he would say. But you always got more than you paid for with Pierre. You paid a dollar, you got a dollar and a half back. He used to say, 'A good laugh is worth a steak.' If you could sit down in a restaurant and have a good time, and enjoy yourself, no matter what you paid, it was worth it. People would keep coming back.

"He would tell me stories about what happened in Seattle, and I wouldn't believe him. I'll be a son of a gun if those people didn't come to New York, or to Montreal, or to Spokane, Washington, or to San Antonio, Texas, and say, 'Do you remember me? You charged me twenty-five dollars for a bowl of soup! You still selling that same soup?'

"I'd say, 'I don't believe it!'

"He'd say, 'Yup. She looked like she had money, so we charged her twenty-five dollars,' or 'She gave us a bad time, so we charged her twenty-five dollars.' But it was true. People would come back."

As Pierre's resources increased, he and José started making more elaborate plans for decorating the fair's restaurants. They took trips to Europe together to search at flea markets and estate sales for lamps, tables, sewing machine stands, pews, paintings, and antiques of all kinds. They would bring their eclectic haul back to the fair and use it all to decorate the current restaurant. Of course, the pair was too conscious of expenses to make such extravagant purchases merely for aesthetics. Everything in the restaurant was always for sale. They did all of the decorating work themselves, spending weeks with saws and hammers and screwdrivers. They both enjoyed these blue-collar days immensely. They would cover the walls with material to create a plush effect that enhanced the salability of the antiques.

Pierre had learned through his lawyers to keep careful books. The antique sales were recorded in a large master book along with their original cost, the tax for importation, and a projected cost necessary to make a profit. José was a good salesman and often sold items for much more than the amount needed to show a decent profit. For him, salesmanship was just another kind of performance. A woman during the second summer of the New York fair expressed an interest in an ornate brass lamp. José looked at her stunned.

"Oh madam, no, not that lamp. I'm so sorry, but I could not sell that lamp. Not that we do not need the money right now, but that lamp used to sit on my grandmother's nightstand."

When the woman offered more money, José looked torn.

"Grandmother did always tell me never to let sentiment interfere with my chance to make it in the world. But, no, I just could not sell that lamp. May my grandmother forgive me."

After reassurances that the lamp would be well taken care of and honored, and after a considerable inflation of the original price, José relented with a tear in his eye.

When José told Pierre about the sale, Pierre responded, "*Oh, mon Dieu!* Not again! It must have been a very large nightstand to fit so many lamps! Your poor grandmother is going to turn over in her grave!"

José sold a chandelier to a couple in New York. It was disassembled at the time. He had seen pictures of the chandelier when it was whole, but he had received no guarantee when he bought it that all of the pieces were accounted for. Still he managed to sell it, and years later, when he and Pierre were working at the fair in Montreal, the couple returned and mentioned that they had not been able to assemble the chandelier. They asked José, "Are you certain all of the parts are there?"

"*Oh, mais oui! Mais oui!*"

They eventually had some missing parts manufactured; almost ten years after the original purchase they finally had their chandelier, but they never spoke ill of the charming men who sold it to them.

"After the New York World's Fair, Pierre took a vacation to Mexico. Before he left he said, 'I will send you a little gift as a memento of our friendship.' He sent me a beautiful hand-blown horse. And I still have it in my curio case."

After that first fair as The Luxembourg, Pierre incorporated and became Pierre's Interlude. He and José began developing all of their future establishments as French restaurants. To keep the atmosphere consistent, Pierre changed José's name. He told José that his name was not very French-sounding in a French restaurant. José became "Carpentier," after a famous boxer who was the husband of Edith Piaf, a woman Pierre knew very well.

"His family made some of the simple, black, princess-cut dresses that Edith wore. The first dress that she ever wore in a concert came from a secondhand thrift store. That was her style after she became famous: the same cut and color, but more expensive materials. Many were made by the Maison Royale, which was the dressmaking shop in Paris that Pierre's family owned. It was on La Rue de Faubourg St. Denis, the dressmaking street in Paris. They were also known for the beautiful white silk men's shirts that they made. They made unique accessories, covered buttons popular in the twenties and thirties. Every once in a while you come across a bag of buttons labeled La Maison Royale. Those are very valuable. Coco Chanel would get her buttons from them when she started. They won many, many awards. And Pierre, as a young man, would deliver the dresses and accessories that Edith Piaf would wear. The shop does not exist today; the last of the aunts died, and it went out of business."

In Canada, at the Montreal World's Fair, Pierre's Interlude had a garden patio that seated two hundred and fifty people. Pierre had come a long way from the metal tubs and hose. The menu included onion soup again, French onion soup this time, coq au vin, and escargot, genuine French cuisine with their own touches added. José wound up on Canadian television one day cooking escargot. The restaurant served wine from Pierre's grandmother's chateau in France.

After the opening of the Montreal fair, José and Pierre noticed that their sophisticated menu, most suitable for afternoon or evening dining, left them at a disadvantage in the mornings. Schedules at the fairs were very precise. The fairs lasted exactly one hundred and eighty days, food service began at 10:30 A.M. on the nose, and the fair closed at midnight. As José expressed their dilemma, "Who the hell is going to eat French onion soup at that hour of the morning?" Evening hours could not be extended because of the strict closing time. Only private parties were allowed on the grounds after twelve.

Ever resourceful in his willingness to work within the system . . . sort of . . . José made a suggestion that became a tradition for the restaurant. It was closing in on midnight one evening, and Pierre's Interlude was still crowded, with a line of potential customers waiting for tables. José offered his solution, and Pierre, shaking his head in amusement, gave his blessing. José went into the back and found the pens and white cardboard signs used for announcing specials. He made up a sign, carried it to the front entrance of the restaurant, and propped it on a simple tripod. It read, "Private Party—Invitation Only." He looked at the bemused customers waiting there and said, "Welcome, my friends! May I extend my warmest invitation? Come on in." The "private party" lasted until 3:00 A.M., and each new "close friend" to arrive received a personal invitation at the door.

During their time in Canada, José and Pierre began a tradition of inventing dishes and desserts to fit the climate of the host city. In Montreal they offered hot teas and cocoa drinks and hot fudge desserts in the evenings. Later, in San Antonio for instance, they concocted cool fruit salads with cottage cheese or ice cream and always had iced teas available. One dessert that José dreamed up in Montreal earned him the nickname Carpentier le Flambé.

"One day it was so quiet in the restaurant. Everybody was eating, and they were enjoying it, but there was no excitement. There was no energy to make the waiters work faster. It was just a restaurant, you understand. So I said, 'I'm going to put some life into this place.'

"Pierre said, 'Okay. We will show them that we can create excitement.'

"I said, 'We should invent some kind of a dessert.'

"He said, 'I know what. Peach and some black cherries . . . and we'll burn 'em!'

"I said, 'Yes, I like that!'

"He had some alcohol, one hundred and ninety proof eatable alcohol. 'Well, that will set the house on fire,' I told him. So we made a sauce for the cherries and peaches; he made it with Cointreau. We put this cube of sugar soaked in the alcohol in the middle. I had a bell which I picked up. We lit the dessert, and I grabbed it and ran from the kitchen, screaming at the top of my lungs in French, *'Flambé! Flambé! Attention! Je vais un tout sucré le flambé!'* The whole place looked up when they heard me shouting. They all saw the flaming tray as I ran around the tables. I just caused such excitement. I ran to the table that had ordered dessert. The people jumped up and the dessert landed in front of the person who had ordered. They were embarrassed. They were excited. They loved it. It became our most popular dessert. And they would pay two dollars and fifty cents for this bullshit. I became very famous for this. I was Carpentier le Flambé. In fact, I became so famous that in Texas, I almost ended up in jail charged with attempted assassination of the President of the United States and his family."

It was 1968, and the restaurant Pierre's Interlude was in a converted Victorian home at the site of the San Antonio World's Fair. Guests entered into a formal entryway with a high ceiling and delicately carved wainscoting along the walls. A step down to the right led to the front dining room. An archway in the rear wall led to another room behind it, and a third archway led to yet a third dining room in the rear of the building.

Since Montreal, Pierre's Interlude had been designated a VIP restaurant. Important visitors to the fairs would be directed there for an outstanding meal. Other than the prestige and the chance to serve the rich and famous, there was no added compensation for the restaurant. As José put it, "That meant you served important people and got no money for it."

Occasionally, when security demanded, the back dining room would be reserved exclusively for some famous personage and the accompanying entourage. More often, however, guests preferred to sit in the front dining room. The fair's street entertainers made a point of stopping in front of VIP establishments, and the front room was the best place to listen and watch through the windows the performances of the Folklorico Mexicano or the Scottish Dancers. Many patrons came to eat while being serenaded, and they were willing to wait for the front tables. José met quite a number of celebrities in San Antonio. Now and then one of them would mention having seen him perform at the Black Cat.

On a particularly memorable day at the fair, Pierre's Interlude made special arrangements for a rather large party of guests. The Secret Service had visited earlier to inform them that President Lyndon Johnson would be having lunch at the restaurant. The third dining room was reserved for the president and his family, and the middle room was set aside for the accompanying Secret Service agents and a few members of the Federal Bureau of Investigation, the FBI. Pierre and José had decided to provide all of the meals on the house. The meal was quiet and uneventful, and the president's family seemed to be relaxed and enjoying the food. Many of the regular patrons in the front room spoke in excited but hushed tones and a few tried to strain their necks to catch a glimpse of the first family.

José cleared the family's dishes as they finished their lunches, and then went to the kitchen to prepare the desserts. With the help of Pierre, José spooned out the peach slices and cherries in their sweet liqueur. They placed the alcohol-soaked sugar cubes on top of the chilled fruit. As Pierre prepared to light the desserts, José donned his white top hat and grabbed his bell. He balanced the tray, and Pierre lit the cubes and held open the door to the front dining room.

José flew out of the kitchen ringing his bell and screaming in mock alarm, *"Flambé! Flambé! Attention! Flambé!"* The diners in the front room reacted with their usual amused delight as the crazy pseudo-Frenchman ran frantically around the tables. At the archway he spun and lurched into the middle dining room, *"Flambé!"* Suddenly his voice caught in his throat and he stumbled to a halt. The metallic clicking sounds settled into silence as he stood there with the flaming tray of desserts in one hand and his bell in the other frozen in midclap. Facing him from three sides around the room was a veritable army of gun barrels, each pointed at some crucial section of his anatomy.

The stillness seemed to linger timelessly until it was broken by the frantic voice of a Frenchman. "Oh, no, no, no, no, no! Please. It is dessert, monsieurs, dessert!" A few of the guns rotated in Pierre's direction.

Stunned, José slowly lowered the dessert tray and showed the agents the flaming fruit. "Dessert for the president's family . . ."

The men slowly lowered their guns, a few of them chuckling. José walked cautiously into the third dining room to serve cherries and peaches to a president struggling to conceal his amusement.

"They thought I was going to run in and set the president on fire! The story appeared in the *San Antonio News:* 'FLAMING FLAMBÉ BRINGS OUT THE FBI! BELL RINGER SETS PRESIDENT ON FIRE!' It was a cute caption. I gained some notoriety for that. They came back again to eat at our place, not the president, Lady Bird with the little birds."

José's work with Pierre at the World's Fairs led to a lifelong friendship between the men.

"Pierre was a very, very close friend. We were never lovers. We slept in the same bed once, but he made me sleep on the boxsprings while he slept on the mattress. We've done such crazy things. We were like brothers. When I retired at the age of sixty-two, he promised me an easy life. He asked me to come live with him as his roommate."

(That's *real* roommate, a platonic sharing of a household. José doesn't much traffic in euphemisms. He has little patience for the facial distortions and sing-song inflections people go through to change the word "friend" to the euphemistic *friend*. He's more interested in people saying what they mean.)

"I had a choice of either going to Carmel, Florida, or Phoenix. I chose Phoenix. In the meanwhile, Pierre met a young man, got engaged and then married, not legally of course. I was the mother-in-law. After three years, I decided that it was time that the mother-in-law move out and let the lovebirds have their own home. After traveling to Russia and Bermuda and other places, they bought a condo in Fort Lauderdale. They were living there when the young man passed away of AIDS on a trip to Paris. He's buried there in a very celebrated cemetery where the composer Hector Berlioz is buried. I came back to San Francisco from Phoenix, and my life resumed."

God Save Us Nelly Queens

"The pep talks and singing 'God Save Us Nelly Queens,' oh, that started right away. You see, I already had a problem, but I was coping with it. And I saw these queens. These silly men! At the Cat they were one thing, and outside they were something else. And I thought, 'How could these people do this? How could they lead these double lives? How could they be killing themselves? So I started to talk to them about it. I had no problem that made me hide. I had no problems like that, like you've had."

José and I have talked about the differences in the way we grew up. I come from a conservative, military, strict Catholic, male-dominated, competitive, sports-oriented, heterosexist, white family that rejected me cruelly when I came out of the closet. As a child, I was also sexually abused by my mother. Add to that family mix alcoholism, drug addiction, gang affiliation, teenage abortion . . . but that's all fodder for a different book. When we first discussed these things, José did not want to accept that such families exist. They are so foreign to his own experience. In many ways I envied his patchwork family when we first met. Today I have my own family of choice.

"I did not have a family. I had to make a family. You had a family, and it's all fucked up, but I had no family. I had to manufacture one. I called them my brothers and my sisters. It was just a matter of technicality that they weren't, you understand? They changed my diapers when I was four months old. It was just a matter of technicality that I was not their little baby brother. But that made no difference for me or them.

"When I found out that I was illegitimate, that was a big shock. But I managed to get along with even that. I threw it up to my mother one time. That was a very, very sad thing, and I regret it to this day because it was painful for her, and it was senseless, and I was angry. My mother paid her whole life for my birth. She could have married some very big millionaires here in San Francisco, but she never married. She never married for fear that they would mistreat me because of my illegitimacy. She would say, 'No one's going to punish you but me.' She could have been well off. Now today it's common; who cares? I regret that I did that, because my mother was a good mother and she paid for it. She paid a bigger price than I ever did.

"Through it all, I never had any reason to hide. I did not know why the men who came to the Cat felt they had to. Also, the city was trying to close the Cat down, you see. They would make all these rulings and laws and fights, and this all tied in and became a part of the same issue. We didn't have a say in these laws because we had all these queens coming in here to buy a beer, and then when it was time to vote, they were nowhere around. If they kept sitting on their asses, there wouldn't *be* a place to come have a beer with their boyfriends. I became a bitch, and I started to scream. We didn't need these queens to go out and get sick, and when it came time to get a shot in the ass for syphilis and gonorrhea so it wouldn't keep spreading, they weren't around. And I notice now that syphilis and gonorrhea and herpes are growing again because everybody thinks it doesn't exist. And that's why I began to scream. I'd end my performances with a talk about how things had to change, starting with us.

"They were afraid to go to the Health Department for fear of being found out. I was already found out, so I went down there and showed them that it was not a matter that everybody knew. You were a number. They didn't know who 50278 was. They didn't know that it was Joe Blow. And I got a lot of commendations from the Health Department because I started the queens going. We ended up buying the chairs for the department. We put a gate on the door to protect them from people shitting and pissing and sleeping in the doorway.

"I sang the song as a kind of anthem, to get them realizing that we had to work together, that we were responsible for our lives. We could change the laws if we weren't always hiding. God save us nelly queens, that's what you are, be proud of it and get off your butt and do something about it. It was a silly song, but serious too. I'd tell them to stand up and hold hands.

"All those things that I did just tied in, and without me realizing it, I became a kind of champion. Without me realizing it, I became the queen bee of the San Francisco gay community, and it took me a hell of a long time to even come to cope with this situation. Even worse was to be stopped on the street and be told, 'Thank you for what you've done!'

"And I would think, 'Thank me for what? For bitching at you? You could have done it yourself if you'd gotten up off your ass!'

"Now though, it's not difficult for me to stand and be praised. It's not difficult for me to be in a crowd and talked about. I laugh now when I'm in a crowd and they talk about the 1950s and the 1960s, and then they turn to me, and I go back to the 1940s, and they look at me and wonder, 'How is that possible?' Most of them didn't even come to The City until the 1950s. But you see, I was here before all that."

Nervous Queens in the Temple

"It was the dedication of the Chinese Buddhist temple in San Francisco, on Washington Street off Laguna. It was near Mamie Pleasanton's place. She was a black madam. She was very notorious. She had the dirt on everybody. She caused a lot of people to die or be killed. The temple was near her home, which stood across the street from the Green Eye Hospital, which doesn't exist anymore. What exists still are the eucalyptus trees that were in front of her home. On the corner was the temple.

"Now, in the audience of the Black Cat one night, I noticed these Chinese men. They enjoyed my show very, very much. They would applaud and laugh. They came in to see my show that evening, and then to my Sunday show. Finally one of them approached me and said that they would like to have me come to the dedication of their Buddhist temple and do an opera.

"I said, 'But mine are gay!'

"He said, 'Oh yes. We would like to see *Carmen*. Can you do it?'

"So Hazel wrote a script in which I had other people join me as characters. I got the other people all lined up. We went and did *Carmen*.

"Now, traditional Chinese people are, as you know, not a demonstrative people. They don't hooray and ah and laugh loudly. I wanted to find ways to make the audience feel comfortable. So the curtain went up, and I always figured from past experiences that if you try to talk in the foreign language of wherever you're at, and try to assimilate and not be American it works better. So I had written out a phonetic Chinese list of things like 'hello' and 'how do you do,' basic things like that so I could carry on a conversation.

"So the opera begins, and I get up and sing, and Don José sings. Finally the first act comes to an end . . . and there's no reaction. I thought, 'Oh my God, we've laid down a bomb. They don't know what we're talking about. They don't know what we're talking about.'

And they didn't have a friendly look. I said, 'Those people will stone us!'

"I tell the others, 'The next act, Carmen comes out, she dies, and immediately we pack our bags and leave out the back door!'

"But the man in charge comes back and says, 'It is very, very good. Everybody likes it.'

"I said, 'But there's no applause.'

"He said, 'Never you mind. It's not the custom. You continue.'

"I said, 'Well, we're leaving. She's dying and we're leaving. We're finished.'

"'No, no, no, no, no. They know the story of *Carmen;* you can't do that.'

"So we went through the second act as written. We were singing and acting and, my dear, doing magnificently! Never had I worked with other people in the operas, but we had studied. We had rehearsed. We were wonderful!

"Same reaction. No reaction. When the curtain came down on act two, no reaction.

"I said, 'Mary Louise! I don't give a good goddamn what that man says, we are leaving! Goodbye!'

"The man came back again and said, 'No, no, no, no. Carmen dies next act. You do fantastic! Fantastic! You see. You will see. I'm right.'

"The others in the cast said, 'Well, we better stay, José.'

"I said, 'We are going to be stoned!'

"Well. Carmen comes in and the music swells, the 'Toreador's Song.' The drama increases to the final scene between Don José and myself. I throw the ring back to him and we sing, and he stabs me, and I die. Oh! It was just not to be believed! Well, I hit the ground, and of course I had to bounce back up a few more times before I actually die. They think I'm dead, and then I pop up and sing some more. And of course the opera ends as the piano comes down with a crash, boom, bang. I am lying there on the floor as Don José is crying, 'My Carmen! My Carmen!' Hazel is just moved by this whole thing. It was absolutely fantastic! The piano crescendos, and then silence.

"All of a sudden, the auditorium comes alive. The audience is standing up, and they are applauding. And they are saying a word that sounded to me like 'Hic!' and they are bowing to us.

"And I said, 'Come on, my dears! Let's hic 'em back.' So we are hicing them, and they are hicing us and we are bowing back and forth. Hicing and hicing. Everybody was in on the excitement!

"The man who had talked to us before comes back and says, 'You see, they loved you.'

"I said, 'Yes, but why didn't they applaud before?'

"He said, 'Never mind. Just bow.'

"Finally everybody was quiet, and I said in phonetic Chinese—I had it all written out—who had played all the different parts. And they laughed! I went through Pinkerton and Suzuki, the piano player, and I tried very, very hard to pronounce it all in Chinese. They applauded. They got a big charge out of my trying to talk Chinese.

"The host got up and wrapped it up, talking in Chinese. Then he said to us, 'Now you are all invited to participate in the banquet.'

"I said, 'Oh fine. That would be very, very nice. We'll just go and change our clothes and . . .'

"He said, 'Oh no, no, no, no! You got to go down in your costumes. And you will sit at our tables. The people here already have chosen certain characters that they want to sit at their tables.'

"So the whole cast sat at various tables. We all got a prayer cloth. And we each got a souvenir of the evening. I still have mine. And that was my experience. I got also a beautiful set of imperial jade cufflinks which I want to have set in a ring, because I don't wear cufflinks.

"That was our big presentation. I am very proud of that. We dedicated the Buddhist temple on its birthday. That was a real excitement for me to perform there. But to perform in a room that was almost completely silent was very unnerving. It reminded me of my performance at the first International Deaf Mute Conference, another wonderful experience, but unnerving at first."

Singing into the Silence

Among his countless performances at the Black Cat Cafe there are a few that José remembers vividly and with considerable fondness. One such performance occurred the week that San Francisco hosted the first International Deaf Mute Conference. After a long day of lectures and panels and classes, the men and women in attendance wanted to relax and spend an entertaining evening in their beautiful host city. One of the evening events offered was a show at the outrageous and notorious Black Cat Cafe. A large group excitedly piled onto a bus for their sojourn into West Coast bohemia.

One of the entertainment hosts from the conference called the Cat to let the management know about the coming guests. José was called to the phone, and the host explained. Always one to make "playing to the audience" a priority in his shows, José grew a little nervous. He had never performed for a deaf audience before. How could he improvise and interact with a group whose lives were so unfamiliar to him?

He asked the host, "How will I know what to say? How will they know what we are saying?"

The host reassured him by saying, "Don't you worry about that. Just make sure we can all sit together; we are bringing our interpreters to translate the show into sign language. Just do the show the way you would any other night. Just be yourself. That's what they want to see."

José had the usual makeshift stage set up early, and he went on to announce the special guests to the other patrons. "Now you've all read in the paper that the first International Deaf Mute Conference is being held here in the city. Well, my dears, tonight we are going to be the entertainment. So I am asking everyone here in the center to give up their seats so that our guests can be seated together and can see their interpreters. You can stand around the back or sit on the bars . . . or the bartenders."

The bus pulled up to 710 Montgomery Street just before the show was to begin. The patrons in front of the stage stood with their drinks and made their way to the perimeter of the floor. A few made jokingly suggestive remarks to the bartenders about providing seating. The special guests began making their way into the bar. There were men and women of widely varied ages. Most of the patrons had not been around large groups of hearing-impaired people before, so to them the animated silence of the conference folk as they entered was strange and fascinating. It was obvious that spirited conversations were flying back and forth, conversations they were not privy to because they were carried out with very little sound.

As everyone settled into their seats and the interpreters took their places near the stage, Hazel's piano began its introduction, and onto the tables that doubled as a stage stepped the red high heels of the infamous José Sarria.

"I sang my opening number and then welcomed them with a song I often did:

> Hello, hello everybody
> We're glad that you are here
> We'll sing and dance and entertain you
> And bring you lots of cheer
> For all of us are a dandy
> On that of course you can rely
> So hello, hello everybody
> We all welcome you
> The Black Cat welcomes you
> We are glad that you're here.

"The interpreters signed, and they applauded very generously. They were a very nice audience. I continued the show. I sang my songs and said my punch lines. It was very emotional for me. I would say things that were very risqué, and when they were translated, many of them would cover their mouths in embarrassment. But then they would laugh, some silently, some very quietly, and hold their stomachs. They were a delight. The rest of the audience watched them as much as the show. It was quite an evening. They carried on so after the show. It was very late when they left.

"Years later, this year, 1996, about six months ago, a person came up to me. He was deaf, you could tell, but he spoke pretty well. He said, 'I first saw you at the first International Deaf Mute Conference. I enjoyed your show. I remember you well. Thank you for that.'"

I remember José's voice turning pensive as he spoke of encounters on the street with people who remembered the days of the Cat.

"That was kinda nice. Every once in a while, people come up and talk to me about seeing me at one time or another. A lot of people say, 'Oh, I remember the Black Cat,' and they're not old enough to have been there. You have to remember, the Cat closed in 1963. Actually the doors didn't shut until 1964, because we stayed open as a restaurant until there was no longer anyone who came in for lunch. Before that we would have two or three hundred people for lunch, but with no license for liquor, and with the stigma that the newspaper reports had created, nobody was about to come down, where before, everybody came for lunch because the food was sold by the ounce: five cents an ounce. So there was no reason not to come down; the price was right. So we stayed open almost until March, until the end of February of the following year actually, at which time we liquidated and sold the bar and all of the furniture and things.

"So the bar is already closed thirty-two years, and if they are only forty years old, they couldn't remember the Black Cat, although there were younger people that we would get into the bar, not that many and not *that* young. So you have to be at least fifty or sixty years old to remember the Black Cat.

"There are people who say there were crystal chandeliers, and my dear . . . they just want to be a part of an era which they will never be a part of. They can only be a part of it by listening to the stories of the people who were actually there, or by seeing pictures. Like the Stonewall Inn in Greenwich Village. It was just a nice little neighborhood bar. People tell such stories. They want to be a part of it. They can be a part of it in a way if they listen to us old farts."

The American Legion Performance

"I can't tell you the year, but I have the letter in which I was invited to perform for the American Legion. It was on an anniversary of some sort. And the letter came to me signed by the general. It said that they wanted me to participate in a program in which the leading entertainers of the city would be performing. I thought to myself, 'My God, the American Legion! A gay performance at the American Legion!' Right away I phoned Walter Hart at Finnochio's and asked, 'Did you get an invite?'

"He said, 'No.'

"Then I said, 'Well, it's supposed to be the leading entertainers of the city.'

"He said, 'No, we didn't.'

" 'The Kingston Trio is going to be there. You know, all the big people of The City. I got one.'

"He said, 'Well, you're lucky!'

"I got on the phone and I talked to the general, and I said, 'I received this invitation. . . .'

"And he said, 'Yes, I know.'

"I asked, 'Do you know what my act is?'

" 'Yes, we know. The Black Cat.'

"I said, 'Well, I'm not a family entertainment.'

"He said, 'Yes, but we feel that you will add to the show, and we want you there.'

"So I said, 'Fine.'"

Soon after his popularity at the Black Cat Cafe began to burgeon, José made an agreement with owner Sol Stoumen that he would not perform anyplace but the Black Cat, with the exception of charity events. If he did perform for charities, something José always loved doing, he would make sure that the people attending knew he was "José Sarria of the Black Cat Cafe."

"I never worked anyplace other than the Black Cat. No place. You wanted to see José, you came to the Black Cat."

Because the American Legion is a nonprofit organization, and because the performance had the potential to provide the Black Cat with some very positive publicity with people who might not otherwise go there, José agreed to be a part of the entertainment.

José arrived at the Commerce High School Auditorium on Hayes Street very early in order to have time to execute his gender transformation with costume, makeup, padding, accessories, and wig. Other performers were arriving to dress, tune their instruments, check for sound and lighting, and do all of many detailed backstage tasks necessary for creating the illusions that captivate an audience. A volunteer from the American Legion met the entertainers near the door and directed them to their dressing rooms: men to the right and women to the left. José smiled briefly when given those directions. He decided not to comment, however. He walked right.

There was to be a quick rehearsal with the band after everyone was in costume and makeup. José learned that the conductor was a friend of his from the local musician's union. From time to time José hired members of the union for special events and shows. Knowing that he was not completely among strangers did little to stem his nervousness, however. He entered the dressing room with some trepidation. He found a free table over in one corner of the room and quietly set his bags down.

"We were going to have a small, fast rehearsal, and I had to be ready. I sat down at my table and started to put on my makeup. The other men were just putting on their basic subtle makeup, and I thought, 'Oh, Lord, what am I going to do? I have to get undressed. Oh, my God, I have to put on a bra and a dress. And my makeup . . . oh, screw it!'"

As unobtrusively as possible, José began applying his makeup. He had his back turned to the room, and despite the flamboyant colors of his eye shadow and the size of his false eyelashes, the men in the room took no notice. When his makeup was done, he reached into his bag and pulled out the girdle-bra combination garment that would transform his figure. He took off his pants and shirt and bent down to step into the undergarment. Some sixth sense told him that a change had come over the room. He raised his head to look. The other men in the room stood staring. José smiled.

One of the men chuckled, raised and eyebrow, and asked, "*Well,* and what kind of act do you have?"

"I'm from the Black Cat. I'm José. I'm a female impersonator."

"Ohhhh, yeah! We know about you. Nice to meet you. God, we're in good company tonight!"

José smiled again and continued dressing. Though they were done with their own preparations, the men stayed to watch. They were fascinated by the magical transformation happening before them.

Just as José was finishing his preparations, the bandleader came into the room to discuss a few details of entrances and such before the rehearsal. He was delighted to see his old friend José, and even more delighted that he would have a chance to perform with him.

"So, José, how did you end up at this party?" he teased with a grin.

"Don't ask me," José replied sardonically from under his rather large wig. "Let's talk about how I'm going to enter."

The bandleader made a few quick comments to the other men, and then turned to José to talk about how the diva would make her entrance.

The show began, and most of the acts were polished and well-received. The few awkward transitions between acts, born of too little rehearsal, did not significantly distract from the fun of the show and the enthusiasm of the performers and audience. The mood was lighthearted and receptive when the lights came down, leaving a single spotlight on the center curtain. The snare drum rolled expectantly and a few seductive notes rose from the band. A curvaceous ankle and shapely foot wearing a shining, red, high-heeled shoe thrust out from the crack in the curtain, pointed, and then came down on the boards with a forceful but feminine slap.

Laughter and whistles and hoots burst from the crowd. The music fell silent. The audience waited. The foot tapped once, eliciting some laughter. The music continued a little more insistently. The foot moved forward gracefully, and a nylon-smoothed calf and knee came into view. Again the music stopped. The whistles grew louder, mixing with humorous catcalls. The leg rotated sensuously in reply. Again the music started up and a rounded, shapely thigh came slowly through the curtain as the leg began bobbing, much to the delight of the crowd. The leg performed to the music and the oohs and aahs and applause of the audience.

The music segued into the introduction for "A Good Man Is Hard to Find," and the owner of the leg, a flamboyantly dressed woman, shimmied onto the stage, lifted her microphone, and began to sing in a full, sultry voice. The more savvy members of the crowd knew the score immediately. Others just naively enjoyed the flashy, opulently done-up woman on the stage. Still others wondered. José told two comedic stories after the first song, and then finished his set with "Rose of Washington Square." The audience applauded and cheered boisterously.

José bent in a delicate bow and then thanked the audience, explaining that he had to go. It was early evening, he explained, and he still had a show to do at the Black Cat Cafe. A few heads nodded in recognition.

José retired to the dressing room, pleased that his act had been so well received. He removed his makeup and his woman's clothing and dressed in his street clothes. It was intermission by the time he was able to gather his bags and leave. The audience was milling about enjoying refreshments and discussing the first half of the show. He caught a few snippets of conversation as he wended his way through the auditorium.

"And that one with the red shoes. I could have sworn that was a man!"

"What is the Black Cat?"

"Really? She wasn't a woman? Well, for goodness sake!"

"That was just so crazy. Was that a woman or a man or a boy? I swear I didn't know if I was coming or going."

Now and then as he passed, someone would catch José's eye and nod politely or say hello. One or two of them looked quizzically at the bags he carried. No one, though, recognized him as the woman in red high-heeled pumps.

"Who is that? He looks like a performer."

"Probably someone in the second half."

"Why would he be walking out that way?"

"I don't know."

It was a memorable show for José despite the brevity of his part in it. He always seems to cherish most dearly those performances that gave him a chance to break down the barriers between his world and the mainstream culture. His humor and vocal talent made bridging the gaps a painless experience for most of those who came to see him, but that never diminished the courage that always underpinned his willingness to go where no drag queen had gone before. And like so many Sarrias before him, he enjoyed the struggle.

"It was fun and exciting. I got a nice thank you letter from the American Legion which I still have with my memoirs."

I Am a Boy

Unlike many contemporary civil rights activists, José did not directly defy unjust laws. He always had a strong respect for law. Neither did he bow to such laws. Instead, he often looked for ways to circumvent the laws legally. In San Francisco in the early years, as in many places, there was a law forbidding men to dress in women's clothing. The City made an exception one night a year, on Halloween; however, any man caught in drag one minute after midnight on November 1, would be hauled off to jail.

Since the bars did not close until 2 a.m. then as now, it was common for the Halloween revelers to end up leaving a bar after midnight. The police would traditionally roll up with the paddy wagons outside the Black Cat at the stroke of midnight and wait for the queens to emerge. Every year, wagons full of men would be arrested.

A few weeks before one Halloween, José decided to try to find a way to protect the patrons of the Black Cat from the yearly harassment from the city. He procured a copy of the offending law. It read that a man shall not dress in women's clothing "with the intent to deceive." José thought hard about the wording of the law, and finally came up with a plan.

Next to the Black Cat was the law office of a young, very bright lawyer named Melvin Belli. José presented his idea to Melvin and asked if he thought it would stand up in court. According to José, Belli said he would love to take on a case based on José's idea. That was enough for José. He proceeded to enact his plot.

Back at the Cat, José took black and white felt, glue, safety pins, a pen, and scissors. He set to work. A week or so before Halloween, José began handing out his handiwork.

October rolled toward its close and the gay high holy day of Halloween came. As usual, hundreds of men dressed in their best high drag and made their way to the parties at the clubs. At the stroke of midnight, the paddy wagons rumbled up like cattle trucks. Instead of racing out of sight, scores of queens began sashaying out of the Black Cat and other bars in seemingly open defiance of the waiting cops. Almost by rote, an officer trudged up to one queen and demanded that he/she come along.

"What is the charge, officer?"

"You're a man in girl's clothes. That's a violation of code."

"But officer, the law clearly states that it is unlawful to dress with intent to deceive. Looky here."

She pointed to the tag pinned neatly to the collar of her dress. It was made of black felt material cut in the shape of a cat's head. In the center of the head was glued a strip of white cloth with clear lettering that said, "I am a boy."

"There is no intent to deceive, officer. I am stating my sex clearly for all to see."

There was quite a bit of blue uniformed huddling that night. Very few queens were arrested—none of the ones who wore the tags. The police knew a potential lawsuit when they saw one. That was the beginning of the end of the Halloween raids. And nobody had to break the law.

The Feud

"James Willis McGinnis was a piano player. He came to try out for the job at the Black Cat and stayed for fifteen years. He was a very accomplished musician. He had been in a band that played a concert for Roosevelt at the White House. That is, Eleanor Roosevelt, not what's his name . . . Edith . . . you know . . . not Frank Roosevelt . . . or Theodore. He was a graduate of the Juilliard School of Music."

McGinnis, affectionately known as Hazel, was a bit of a prima donna, and he enjoyed his premiere position as entertainer for the Black Cat Cafe. He only grudgingly shared the spotlight with anyone. If he was asked to accompany a singer he particularly did not like, he would often switch keys unexpectedly or otherwise change the music so that the singer was unable to follow. He was subtle enough that most would assume the singer had erred when the song went out of key. Sometimes he would simply modulate to a higher key in a dramatic flourish, and keep modulating until he was out of the singer's range. He was smart enough and talented enough to keep himself looking innocent, except to the offended singer. Singers he did not like rarely came back to sing again.

Fortunately for José, James McGinnis took a liking to him. When José sang, he would work to make him look and sound good. They enjoyed each other's company and respected each other as performers. Their rehearsals were vigorous and professional but congenial. At the end of each performance, they would hold hands and bow together to the audience. Their friendship and musical partnership became an important part of the ambiance and lore of the bar.

Though they had become fast friends, José and James did not cease to be temperamental at times, as is common with so many show biz folk. During one particular rehearsal, their temperaments clashed over some detail of the show, and their anger escalated into a heated argument. Neither of them could remember after a few weeks what sparked the feud, but by the time the dust had settled, enough had been said that resentment seethed on both sides. Pride would not allow either one to apologize or otherwise play the role of peacemaker, so there was no resolution.

Being professionals, and knowing the importance of their working relationship for the image of the Black Cat, as well as its importance for bringing in healthy tips, they hid their rift while performing. They would laugh and joke and tease with each other in the spotlight, and refuse to talk to each other once the show was over. Both of them refused to bend. Each considered the other the cause of the antipathy.

The two men were faced with the problem of rehearsing with someone to whom they did not speak. They cut their rehearsal time to a minimum, each rehearsing his part independently as much as possible. They would come together to polish the pieces in a coldly professional practice in which terse conversation was limited to the music and the performance.

"He would write the scripts, and on Sunday after the show, he would hand me the new script for the following week. I would take it home and practice. If I didn't have the record of the arias I was going to sing, he would come over and bring me the record. I would rehearse on Monday, and then on Tuesday, I'd go to his place, ring his doorbell. He would let me in. If I had not picked up the script on Sunday, then it would be on the table in the hallway with the record. I'd go in to the piano, and he'd start to play, and I'd start to sing. Nothing was said, except when I was singing. If I didn't do it right, he'd say, 'You're not doing it right. This is the way you should do it.' And he'd play it over again. We'd go through the whole opera to get a feel for what I was doing, and what the tempo was, and how the words matched. Then I would leave, go home, and rehearse. I'd come back Friday. I'd ring the doorbell. He'd buzz me in. He would be sitting at the piano. I'd walk in. We would go through the music. Now I had practiced, so I knew what I was doing. We went through it once. If I felt that I wasn't sure with an aria, I would ask him to play it over again. I'd sing it over again. If I felt that I needed another rehearsal, I'd come in Saturday for the Sunday performance.

"At the Sunday performance, McGinnis would play the music, and at the end of the show we'd smile at the audience, and take each other's hand, and bow to the audience. Nobody knew we were not speaking to one another. He played the piano, and I sang. We would bow. The money was counted and divided, the tip money."

Their interaction went on this way for six months.

As the new year approached, José tried to remember why he and McGinnis were at odds, but he could not recall the cause. On the Sunday before the Cat's New Year's Eve celebration, José approached McGinnis and offered, "Hazel, we should bury the hatchet. After all, I don't even know why we're mad and not talking to one another. Let's start the new year with a clean slate."

McGinnis replied in character, "You're right. I agree with you. I can't remember why we argued either except that it was your fault."

Half jokingly, José retorted, "Well, with my sweet disposition, I'm sure it was not my fault. I don't know why we argued, but I'm sure it had to be your fault. Sometimes you can be so . . ."

"Careful, Mary! Keep this up and we won't be speaking for another six months!"

The truce went well until the following week when they were rehearsing for the New Year's show. José questioned James's interpretation of one passage, and as soon as the comment cleared his lips he knew he had made a mistake. Though a quick scowl twisted the pianist's face, it subsided just as quickly. José made a mental note to kick himself later for challenging a sensitive artist on his way of seeing a piece.

"It's just like an artist! You just don't say that to these people. You cannot question what they do or why they do it. And me, like a damn fool, I did question him."

Yet James seemed to recover quickly from the unintended slight, and the rehearsal continued. José found himself impressed with the man's new maturity and professionalism in dealing with constructive criticism. Surely McGinnis had seen the error of his ways since their feud. Perhaps the conflict had its positive side after all. José's momentary vision of a renewed feud dissipated, and he relaxed. The rest of the rehearsal went very smoothly, the piano player even seeming to smile more than usual. Only much later did José realize that he clearly underestimated his accompanist's internal sense of justice, equity, and retribution.

Not long after José's verbal misdemeanor, the men were again at their places in the dim, smoky confines of the Black Cat. Hazel's hands descended to the keyboard, and the magic of the operatic overture began. José made his colorful entrance and launched into his first aria. His voice felt tuned and flexible and strong. The song ended with a flair, and José began his comic commentary to fill in the opera's story line between the songs. His timing was on, and the audience fell in with him. He played off their laughter and applause and relaxed into what promised to be a very satisfying show.

As the second musical piece began, José felt his voice straining a bit. He made mental note of his breath support and his vocal technique. Nothing seemed to be amiss. Perhaps it was a temporary frog from the smoke or the night's cold air. He motioned subtly to the bar back to bring him a glass of water. The water appeared in moments, and he took advantage of a short break in the lyrics to take a few sips. The rest of the song went well, but the strain continued. At the end of the song, Hazel whispered reassuringly, "That was very good, José."

The audience never had a hint that José was struggling vocally. He simply redoubled his efforts to make it all look effortless. In one particular aria near the end of the opera, as he approached a section with several particularly high notes, José's confidence faltered for a brief moment. When the intimidating passage came, he drew in a deep breath of air, tightened his abdominal muscles, pressed with as much power as he could muster, and belted out the notes, clear and loud and true. He glanced at Hazel who watched him with a raised eyebrow and then with a nod and smile of reassurance. José finished the opera to rousing applause, whistles, and shouts. It had been a stunning performance, but José was drained.

He stepped down and joined McGinnis for their traditional hand–in–hand bow. Again the pianist, in uncharacteristic effusion, complimented José extravagantly on his performance. José assumed that his friend was trying to compensate for the months of animosity, though he seemed to go a bit overboard.

"When the show was over, we took our bows, and I said to him, 'Oh my goodness, today was a hard show!'

"And he said, 'You did beautifully!' He said, 'You hit every note. I was so surprised how you reached all those notes. You were wonderful!'

"I said, 'Well, I've done this opera before, and I've never had such problems trying to reach some of those notes. Oh, I'm exhausted!'"

After that night, the professional and personal relationship between José and Hazel fell back into its old, comfortable patterns. No one but they knew about their six-month battle. The two remained musical partners and friends for many years following.

More than a decade later, some of the regulars from the Black Cat threw a party in honor of the long Sarria-McGinnis partnership. As they were all reminiscing about their times at the Cat, one man in the group asked "Hazel" James Willis McGinnis if he and José had ever fought in all their years together.

McGinnis replied with a smile, "No, we always got along perfectly . . . except one time when he tried to tell me how to play the piano. And I taught him a lesson. However, it kind of backfired."

José tried to think what incident McGinnis meant. To what retaliatory lesson was the man referring? He listened as intently as the others, trying not to let on that he was as much in the dark as anyone.

McGinnis continued, "He had this question about the way I played an aria, so I said, 'I'll fix her wagon!' We did the opera, and I played it all in a much higher key, knowing that she would fall flat on her face, that she wouldn't be able to reach all of the notes. Well, the damn fool, she hit every goddamn note, and she hit it right on pitch! I was so pleased with her! She did the whole opera half a goddamn octave higher!"

The widow peaks.

Blessings from the Black Cat

One evening during the 1950s as José was starting his performance, the door of the Cat opened, and in walked a handsome man in his fifties. Accompanying him was a young man in his late teens or early twenties. It was obvious to José immediately that the two men were a couple, and he began to tease them as he did so many patrons who braved his shows.

"Oh, well, look! Here comes Winter and Spring in the flesh! And what a pretty little Spring he is. His hair is so well groomed. Don't anybody touch it. God knows what might happen! It could break off in one piece and hurt someone! So, has the boy been nice to Daddy?"

The older half of the couple laughed along with the rest of the listeners, but the young man scowled at José and whispered something to his partner. The older man shook his head no and responded with a smile and a brief comment. He put a hand on his young lover's back to guide him toward the bar. The young man looked disappointed and very displeased. José did not let up.

"It looks like little boy May is a little upset with his December Daddy. Maybe it's just time to change his diapers!"

The older gentleman, Frank, seemed to understand that during José Sarria's cabaret performance at the Black Cat Cafe, anyone was fair game. He was flattered by the attention. The boy, Bob, was less charmed.

"This young kid did not particularly like to come there because I would make fun of him. The older man enjoyed it terrifically because, number one, it put him in the limelight, and everybody likes to be in the limelight. And the young kid, oh he just really hated it! He hated me very, very much."

José likes to emphasize a point by preceding it with "number one." Don't bother looking below for "number two." With this particular rhetorical device he never gets around to a number two or a number three; one of his many charming quirks. Of course, the first time I scoured a rough transcription of a taped conversation looking futilely for number two, I was less than charmed. I got over it.

"They would come in every Sunday for brunch. Well, this one Sunday they came in. It was Easter Sunday, and being a good religious man, the older partner saw to it that everything was new. I know in my family Easter meant new clothes, from underwear to shoes to stockings. Mama put on a brand new dress. Everything had to be new. You went to Mass. It was the day of the Easter Parade. People showed off. Well, this young boy came in with his lover, and he had a brand new gray ensemble suit, and oh, my dear, they had either come from church or were going to church!"

José started his audience banter by teasing the couple about their Easter finery, asking where their Easter bonnets were. He speculated about their church affiliation and said that he could tell by the boy's clothes that it must be a fine, uptown church. As usual, Frank was enjoying the show, and his young partner was seething. José wondered out loud about the holiness of the couple, making comic innuendo and suggestive remarks. He told the crowd that they had to make sure the purity of the boy matched the purity of his clothing. They would bless him.

José swept over to the table where the two were seated and picked up young Bob's water glass. "Well, we have to bless him, on this blessed day of Easter, this religious holiday." As he sprinkled the water over the angry young man, he improvised a song, "By the power invested in me by hurley and gurley, I hereby bless you, my son! *Dominus vobiscum espiritus sanctus nominus patre vermicelli macaroni nabisco! Aaaamen! Aaaah, men!*" The patrons joined in the final amens, and José blithely continued the show while Bob's eyes shot daggers.

"I sprinkled the water, and of course the water dripped on his nice brand new suit. Well, as you know, that will make water marks, which come out, naturally, but they *are* in the suit. Well! The kid was *furious!* Here his brand new suit had sprinkled water all over it! The lover was rolling in the aisles, laughing hysterically. The kid— if he'd had a gun he would have shot me! Oh, I tormented him so! Finally they left.

"This is the way I treated people that came to the Black Cat. We had music on the jukebox that I could sing to, and I'd make up words and prance around. People came there because of this; this is what made the Black Cat, my outrageous behavior. This is probably why I became the Black Cat. This is what they expected. You didn't expect to go to church when you went there. You didn't know what would happen next. And when I did something, it was always with a flair. Because you see, you had to come and pay to see me. And I was really very, very . . . I had a chip on my shoulder. I was going to become somebody that you would have to pay for. I was going to be noticed.

"Even making my deposits on Monday morning in the financial district, that was a three-ring circus. Bobby Newman used to act as my personal gofer. I would ride in a sidecar I bought for his motorcycle. Bobby could always procure anything I needed. I never asked how, but I did offer to pay for things. He would say, 'That's all right, princess.' He never made me pay. He never told me how much things cost. I didn't realize he was something of a kleptomaniac.

"I would ride in the sidecar in my red high-heeled shoes to make my deposit. The doorman opened the American Trust bank on California Street—it's now a Wells Fargo—and I'd walk in with a shopping bag with my tips in it. When I had to go shopping I would announce when I was to go, and the people would congregate—forty to fifty people would congregate to watch me purchase a dress or a pair of shoes on Sunday. It was unheard-of in those days for a man to go in and buy all these shoes, but I did it all with a flair."

As the years passed and Frank and Bob grew older, the younger half of the pair learned to tolerate José, and eventually developed a grudging affection for the lampooning performer. He relaxed enough to note that he was not the only person to be the focus of José's relentless teasing. It was a part of this impersonator's shtick. The men continued to attend the Cat frequently until it closed.

Soon after the city of San Francisco shut down the Black Cat Cafe, Frank died. As his estate was being examined, authorities began to notice irregularities. Through an exhaustive tracing of the paper trails associated with the man's money, they were able to determine that he had been laundering profits, both legal and allegedly illegal, through accounts in his young companion's name. Consequently, he paid very little in taxes through the years. Bob had not known about any of his partner's financial dealings in his name, but after his lover's death he learned he had millions of dollars in accounts and that he was the proprietor of a monopoly on jukeboxes and pinball machines in several states.

José had known that Frank was involved with the Mafia—his father, Frank Sr., worked with Al Capone—but in the world of the Black Cat, each man's life outside the bar was his own business. Because the law viewed gay people with such animosity, many gay men were unwilling to help law enforcement any more than they had to. Any dealings with the police one day could lead to a morals charge the next.

Despite his claims of ignorance, the young man was convicted of tax fraud and sent to prison. He was ordered to pay a substantial fine, and, under a new law designed to splinter commercial monopolies, he had to sell a percentage of the pinball and jukebox business. Bob paid the fines, served his time, and in 1974 was released from prison. He purchased a bar and a cement company and settled into a very comfortable lifestyle.

José went to work for a time in Bob's bar, the Royal Palace, and he made a point of recommending his boss's cement company to any friend or associate who needed masonry work done. He wanted to help make Bob's business successful. Bob never seemed too worried. José laughs now at his naiveté, because the cement company was a front for other activities.

"He was into gambling. I didn't realize it, and I was forever and a day recommending him. If people needed a wall, or cement, or bricks laid, I was forever and a day sending them to this man's company. And he would not say anything, because it was a front, and I was forever and a day [laughter] . . ."

The two men became fast friends and would talk now and then about the early years at the Black Cat. "Oh, how I hated you, José," Bob would laugh. Yet despite their close friendship, there were still things Bob did not understand about José, and his misconceptions led to one very interesting confrontation.

Bob loved to give parties, and he particulary liked surrounding himself with young men, much as his deceased lover Frank had, but he was uncomfortable with any flamboyant display of gay sexuality outside of the bars, especially cross-dressing. When he invited José to one of his parties, he made a clear stipulation. He stated emphatically, "Don't you come in drag!"

(Time to break for a quick cultural lesson. The word "drag" means "in female attire" unless it is preceded by a qualifier (i.e., leather drag, cowboy drag), in which case it simply means "dress-up." There are different kinds of male cross-dressers. There are straight men who dress in women's clothes because it gives them a sexual thrill. These gentle fetishists are called transvestites. Their sexuality is strictly heterosexual. Other individuals grow up believing that their internal gender identification, their true identities, do not match their physical bodies. They are "women trapped in men's bodies." It is these "transsexuals" who sometimes undergo sex-change operations. They may be gay or straight in their identified gender. There are other men who dress in women's clothing for entertainment or to make a political or social statement, or both. These men, usually gay, are called drag queens. They do not want to be women, as some believe, any more than an actor wants to be his character. Closely related to the drag queens are men who transform themselves into women professionally on stage, female impersonators. Unlike many drag queens, who enjoy playing with the disconcerting juxtaposition of male and female, professional female impersonators attempt to create the illusion that they are actually women; they try to be "real" as it is called in drag parlance.)

What Bob failed to understand about José Sarria is that he is not a transvestite who might venture out in women's clothes on a sexual adventure, or a transsexual learning to live daily as the gender with which she identifies, nor is he a drag queen who might mischievously show up in an unlikely setting in order to tweak at society's gender steroetypes. José is a female impersonator, a man who dons a female persona onstage, a gender illusionist. In his daily life he wears conventional male clothing. Bob also failed to understand that José is a man who does not like to be told what he can and cannot do in his personal life.

"Well, my dear, I dress in drag professionally; I don't just dress in women's clothes to go to a party . . . unless you tell me not to."

José assured Bob that he would not dress in drag, but inside he determined to teach his friend a lesson about dictating to José Sarria. He could simply have sat down and explained to Bob the difference between a professional impersonator and other wearers of things feminine, but José has always had a penchant for more creative solutions. He can be what in the gay subculture's dialect is referred to as a "drama queen." Why do subtly what you can do with a trumpet fanfare?

"I said, 'No, no, no. I won't.' And then, Mary and Margaret, I dressed up in drag. I got across the bridge, and I went to the first police officer I could find, and I told him that I wanted to go to so and so address, that I was lost, and, 'Would you please take me there, officer?'"

José took advantage of his ability to create a "real" illusion. He dressed in clothing that a typical middle-aged suburban housewife might wear for a night out on the town. He kept his outfit, makeup, and accessories understated enough to be fully believable. As he did on stage, he "got into character," took on the personality of the illusionary woman he had created. When he talked with the police officer he spoke with polite deference and a bit of distress. He was a lost, middle-aged matron trying to find her way to a social function in an unfamiliar town.

The officer responded with a shy smile of polite deference. This could have been his own mother lost in the big city.

"Yes, ma'am! You just follow me. I'll get you to your dinner safely."

To make that task easier, he sat behind the wheel of his police cruiser and turned on the flashing lights. With the red and blue beams from his roof clearing the traffic and sweeping the surrounding houses, the officer escorted the lost woman to the party. To maximize the effect of Bob's lesson, José had arranged his arrival on "queen's time," that is, late enough to let the party get underway and assure a dramatic entrance with a substantial audience. Needless to say, more than a few of Bob's neighbors noticed the arrival of his latest guest. José parked behind the police car, emerged from his own car, smoothed his dress and adjusted his purse, thanked the nice young police officer for his kindness, and walked to the front door.

Bob, of course, was standing incredulous at the open front door with curious partyers leaning from behind him for a look. He was furious.

"Ohhhhh! I told you no drag, and look at you! Not only are you in drag, but you bring a police escort so the whole neighborhood will see you!"

José just smiled, walked past Bob, and joined the party. José assumed that Bob had learned his lesson, until the next invitation to one of his parties arrived some months later. At the bottom of the invitation, written in Bob's hand, was the request, "No drag." José, as anyone who truly knew him would expect, went in drag.

"I still have the little invitations, and underneath is written, 'No drag, please.' And I would go in drag. And you know, of course I would feel uncomfortable because everybody, about two hundred or three hundred people, were not in drag. I was the only one in drag. So I was an oddball.

"Anyway, we became very good friends. I worked for his bar, the Royal Palace, in 1974, and I made a lot of money, did a lot of shows, and performed very nicely.

"He had a cook working for him who had cooked for his lover Frank's father. She was an old woman. She had befriended him when he and Frank met. Bob had run away from home, and she took over as his mother. She liked me very much. She allowed me to go into her kitchen and exchange recipes, but never would allow Bob into the kitchen.

"She would say to Bob, 'This is my kitchen, stay out! You, José, come on in. We'll talk.' She was a Frenchwoman, and very, very nice. We became very close friends. She passed away just on the eve of her coming to see one of my shows."

José and Bob have remained friends through the years. José teases him often by reminding him that although he was once the pretty young boy being escorted by an older man, now he is the older man bringing the young, pretty boys around.

"Bob Golovich is still around, and for the last fifteen years I have lived in an apartment complex that this gentleman owns. As young men we met at the Cat, and today I rent from him. He is my landlord, and that's why he puts up with a lot of my nonsense. You might say I know where the bodies are buried. And it's a good friendship. He throws an annual Thanksgiving dinner which I will be attending, and I usually act as a hostess. This year, I think I'll go in drag just to upset him."

The Society for Individual Rights Anniversary

In 1897, Doctor Magnus Hirschfeld, a German researcher in Berlin, established the Scientific-Humanitarian Committee, the first known gay rights organization, with three primary goals: normalizing society's understanding of sexuality, particularly homosexuality; motivating gay people to fight for equality; and rescinding Germany's antigay laws. During the first decades of the twentieth century the gay rights movement in Germany experienced substantial success, and gay people began to find more acceptance in the culture.

The budding German movement for "homosexual emancipation" began to spread to other Western countries. In 1924 in Chicago, Illinois, Henry Gerber established what is usually regarded as the first homosexual rights organization in America, the Chicago Society for Human Rights. In 1928, Radclyffe Hall published the landmark lesbian novel *The Well of Loneliness* in England, beginning a strong history of literary activism among lesbians.

When Hitler came to power in Germany, he first exploited the newly open gay community and then turned on it in a bloody purge that began with the "Night of the Long Knives" and ended in the concentration camps. (Gays in the camps were identified by pink triangles sewn to the breasts of their gray prison uniforms and were relegated to the bottom of the camp hierarchy.) Not coincidentally, in 1934 homosexuality was recriminalized in the Soviet Union. In the United States, homosexuality had never been made legal, and with the onset of the Depression and then the war, the small beginnings of gay rights in the States faded, as it did in most Western nations. In fact, when the Allies liberated the Nazi concentration camps, they put any known gay interns back into prison. While other victims of the camps soon began to heal by retelling the horrors they had faced, it wasn't until the 1980s that the men who wore the pink triangle on their camp uniforms and the women who wore the black triangle (lesbians and others) for refusing to bear children for the fatherland felt safe to even begin to tell their stories.

As the war ended and prosperity returned to much of the West, the movement for gay civil rights began to reemerge. Three years after the Japanese surrender, Harry Hay conceived the idea of a gay emancipation organization in Los Angeles. His first male lover had been "brought out," initiated into the gay world, by a member of the Chicago Society for Human Rights. Like José, Harry was open about his sexuality in the 1930s. Hay's organizational ruminations led to the founding of the Mattachine Society, the first modern gay rights organization, in 1950. In 1955, San Franciscans Del Martin and Phyllis Lyon started the Daughters of Bilitis, the first American lesbian rights organization.

These new organizations were subject to police raids and entrapment, and therefore remained very clandestine. The Mattachine Society was originally organized in small secret cells or guilds, and the members of one guild did not know the identities of the members of another. Anonymity was a central concern.

Because of the secretiveness of the Mattachine Society, José believed that it failed to strongly address some of the most pressing problems faced by the gay community: arrest, entrapment, harassment, job loss, political impotence, child custody, familial rejection, registration as sex offenders, gay bashing.

"I saw a need for an organization to educate the straight world, and to help the queens who were being arrested and persecuted. This was in the late fifties. I went to my attorney, Carl, and I told what the purpose was. I said, 'The Mattachine Society is catering to the lawyers and the doctors and the Indian chiefs, and not to the peasants. They are the ones who are getting arrested. They are the ones who don't know the law. They are the ones who don't have the money to buy their way out. I want to talk to the little guy on the street.'"

José and several friends subsequently established the League for Civil Education. It was José's own money that paid for the filing fees and initial costs of nonprofit incorporation. José took on the job of secretary/treasurer of the fledgling organization, partly to ensure that he would eventually be reimbursed for the startup costs of the group. A man named Guy Strait became the first president of the League.

"Everyone thought that Guy Strait was the one who organized it. I let them think that, but I was the one that organized it, who was responsible for it. Guy Strait was not. Guy was called Senator here in the community. My attorney still has all the paperwork for my putting all this together. I should give it to the archives."

The League for Civil Education operated for three years after its inception in 1960, doing what it could to educate people both gay and straight. It provided support for men trapped in the police vice web, and it held regular meetings for the airing of concerns. It provided emergency funds for men facing difficulties due to discrimination. It provided food and clothing and help finding jobs. The League published a newsletter as well, which became both an educational tool and a source of income. Membership grew steadily in this home-grown civil rights organization.

"Then came the rift. An argument developed over what was more important, the publication or the organization's work on the street. Now Guy Strait said, 'We can't operate and we'll have no money if we don't have a publication.' But the organization was not founded for that. It was not based on that. It was based on helping."

José grew more concerned as certain leaders in the group began to put increasing emphasis on the newsletter because of its potential to generate funds. José objected to their focus as too distant from the daily struggles of their members. Although he saw the value of the newsletter, he believed that the group's energies needed to remain centered on concrete activism, or it would simply be a duplication of earlier groups. He suggested that they research other possible sources of funding.

"It was a struggle about what was the most important. Guy said the newsletter. Other people said, 'No, no, no, no, no. What is more important is the business of the group, what the corporation stands for: education, helping, doing.' Guy Strait said, 'No, you cannot operate without the publication, without the money.'

"The others said, 'Fine. We are going to separate. You keep the goddamn publication and print that, and we are going to take the organization.' They sent a letter to me asking me to help them split. With my help they reformed and changed the name. They called the new foundation the Society for Individual Rights (SIR), and that was done in 1963."

Guy Strait continued the publication, becoming the editor of *The News* as it was called. The newspaper gained some respect and was consulted now and then by writers from the mainstream papers on issues concerning gays in the city.

"SIR continued to operate for seventeen years. They raised their money by putting on shows, the 'Celebritycapades," with dinners. I went often and did operas. You know, there's ways to raise money. So they had funds for helping people with legal problems. That was the beginning of the aid within our community, for the young, for the deaf, for the senior citizens. The Daughters of Bilitis didn't come from SIR, but it was a model for them in putting together some of their activities."

José's fundraising activities with SIR foreshadowed the work of the Imperial Court System he would found in a few years. Most of the money the Court raises for charities comes from drag shows organized for that purpose.

"Now in those days, we organized the gay men mostly because the women didn't have the same problems that men did. Women could live together. Women could dress in manly types of clothes. That was the Coco Chanel look. She introduced the freedom of the body. There was no problem there. Yes, the women couldn't get together and do what lesbians do or whatever, but they had no problems being affectionate in public or dressing the way they wanted. Men were going to jail for these things. So the organization was basically there for the men. I tried to incorporate the women, but they wouldn't come in."

In 1965, the year after José declared himself Empress at the Tavern Guild ball, he channeled his energies into the founding of the Court System. The goals he had hoped to pursue in SIR remained constant in his work through the Court. He had more success in including women in the new organization.

"Del Martin and Phyllis Lyon became involved in my part of the movement because they became part of the founding of the Court. They were the ambassadors. They were my first duchesses. That was 1965. They were the first lesbians on my Court. I tried to include everyone. I had people from the leather community, ministers, senators. I had one of the Superior Court judges of the day on my Court. We had publications, but they weren't the focus. We raised money with shows.

"Guy Strait is still alive. He went to prison and spent quite a bit of time in there. He was arrested for pornography along with an heir to a large American company who was able to get out of the country and live in North Africa, while Guy wasn't able to. He stayed here and took the brunt of it. He was finally let out of prison in Illinois.

"SIR collapsed after seventeen years, but there was a celebration of the twentieth anniversary of its founding a few years back. Invitations were sent out inviting people to come and celebrate the years of SIR. I went. Guy Strait went. A lot of early, early people that belonged to the League for Civil Education and later joined SIR went. People were honored. The president was honored, and this and that and the other thing—and they very nicely ignored Guy Strait and myself. That's the way the whole evening went; we were very nicely ignored. SIR appeared. They didn't say how SIR came to pass. SIR appeared because the League appeared first. I guess *Jesus* made the league and three days later SIR appeared. I guess SIR just fell out of the sky!

"After the whole celebration was over, people were just kind of mingling. Hello. How are you? How have you been?

"People said to us, 'Well how come they didn't mention you as the founders?'

"I said, 'Evidently they don't think we had anything to do with it.'

"They said, 'Well, you had everything to do with it.'

"That was true. It was my silverware that they used to feed the poor. I had silverware for a hundred and fifty people. It was all bought in little stores. I paid nothing more than five cents for a fork, knife, or spoon. I had salad forks, dinner forks, knives, spoons, soup spoons, bouillon spoons—a queen never serves soup; she serves bouillon. I had a complete service, and God knows it was all silver plate, and I had enough for a hundred and fifty poor people to sit down and have a correct meal. So it took some nerve to say I was not involved. I was very involved.

"So anyway, that was the thing, and Guy Strait and I said, 'Evidently we were not that important. Fine. But we won't worry about it. We know the truth.' I always thought that was so funny.

"Every once in a while I'll have someone come up to me and say, 'Do you remember that big celebration they had for SIR, and you were there, and they acted like you weren't even born yet?'

"I'd say, 'Yes, their memories are as long as their peters.'"

The Ice Queen

The place of drag in the gay community has always been a source of controversy. Modern activists who believe that the most progress will be made by avoiding anything that might offend the mainstream straight world often wish the drag queens and female impersonators would stay in the closet. Other gay activists call such advocates of mainstream appearances assimilationists who deny the true natures of gay people. Speaking instead in favor of embracing diversity, they point out that homophobes are just as offended by two men in suits showing open affection as they are by men in dresses. In fact, they will often say, it was the drag queens who had the courage to finally confront the bigotry of the police at the onset of the Stonewall Riots in 1969.

In one sense, historically, gay men who do drag have more readily and openly stood up to the forces of bigotry and ignorance. Because they tended to be identified already as gay and somewhat on the fringe, many had less to lose than their closeted brethren. Others were simply more willing to fight the status quo. Because dressing in drag itself is a provocative and defiant act, it attracts those with the courage to be different.

José was not going to be fired from his performance jobs for being gay, because being gay was an integral part of his stage persona, and he was used to taking flak for his unabashed belief in the basic equality of gay people and his willingness to stand up publicly and say so. These things gave him a measure of freedom that other activists did not enjoy. They also tended to open doors of opportunity to be seen and thereby chip away at the secrecy and resulting ignorance surrounding all things gay. Such an opportunity arose when the Ice Follies came to town.

"In 1964, on a weekend after the Tavern Guild Ball in which they made me Queen of the Ball, and I named myself Empress José Norton the First, a Court function was held at the site of the Ice Follies, because, at the time, we couldn't hold it in any hotel, and the price was right. The Ice Follies were beginning the following week. Now the guy that rented the place to us asked, 'Would you open up the Ice Follies for us?'

"And I thought, 'Fine. As the Empress, it will be my first official event.' So at the end of the room he made a booth with a flag and chairs for me and my court. I arrived fifteen minutes late from the time it was supposed to start. They played an anthem, and I made an entrance. I officiated at the opening of that season's Ice Follies. That was my first appearance as the Empress, in drag.

"After that there was no more drag for a while in the public appearances. There was a big fight about it. The community didn't want to be represented by a person in drag—uptight queens!"

The Election

Some of the greatest grassroots movements in our country's history have been started by people who never intended to enter the realm of politics and political lobbying, but found themselves faced with tragedies or injustices that the government was not addressing, or worse, that the government was exacerbating. From the Underground Railroad to Mothers Against Drunk Driving, our history is decorated with regular folks who became leaders simply because they did what they felt they had to do when nobody else seemed willing to stand up to the problem.

José Sarria never set out to become a gay rights activist, nor did he ever plan to run for political office. When his plans for teaching and singing with the opera fell through, politics never made the short list of options he considered. He was simply a man unwilling to acquiesce to the repeated injustices and indignities he faced as an openly gay man, and he was even less willing to run into a closet to avoid them. He was determined to live an honest life, and if that meant pushing back at societal conventions, then so be it.

José's beloved Black Cat Cafe had been the focus of a campaign by the California State Alcoholic Beverage Control department (ABC) to close down gay bars in the state. At the time, in all parts of the United States, homosexuality was not considered a natural orientation, but rather a criminal activity. Establishments that catered to gay men and lesbians were seen as encouraging illegal behavior. Gay bars in the decades before the Stonewall Riots in New York (which provided a catalyst for the modern gay rights movement) had elaborate methods for hiding the sexual orientation of the patrons from the authorities, from secret signals and code words to back rooms and warning bells similar to those employed during Prohibition. The Black Cat was more bold than most. Its door opened on the street. Yet even there caution was essential. If a patron of the Black Cat wanted to flirt with another patron but wanted to avoid inadvertently being trapped by an undercover vice cop or a hustler, he would pull aside an employee and ask if the object of his desire was "okay."

Because of these protective conventions in the gay community, it was difficult for police to implicate the bar in the "immoral" activities of the patrons. As a result, the revocation of an owner's liquor license became the weapon of choice in most antigay campaigns. Liquor laws are among the strictest statutes on the books, and since liquor was the source of income for places like the Black Cat, revoking the license would effectively close the bar.

On August 20, 1956, the ABC issued a liquor license revocation order against Sol Stoumen, the owner of the Black Cat Cafe. The order claimed that "lewd acts" between known homosexuals had been regularly taking place there. (Such lewd acts could include holding hands, touching a leg, hugging, kissing, or putting an arm around a shoulder or waist; these were cause for arrest.) Superior Court Judge Richard M. Simms upheld the order. With the help of his lawyer, Morris Lowenthal, Sol appealed the ruling and managed to receive a stay of the order pending the outcome. The Black Cat was able to stay in business, but under a cloud.

Harassment of the Cat was not always so overt and official. As the appeal worked its way toward the California Supreme Court, José faced other, more homegrown opposition to the Cat. He tells of one incident that helped drive him toward a greater public advocacy of his rights.

"The election came about in a funny way. We had taken over 90 Market Street, and I was running a food concession, cooking and serving there and delivering food to the Cat. It had regular kitchen facilities, very nice, so we cooked there rather than at the Black Cat. This was about 1960, and . . ."

José fell asleep in mid-sentence. At first I couldn't tell if he had closed his eyes to remember, or if he had drifted off to sleep. My lack of financial resources to cover the distance from Sacramento to San Francisco when researching for this book made it critical that we make the most of the time we had together. We often talked late into the night. Sometimes José's spirit was willing but his flesh less so. After about a full minute, he opened his eyes, smiled with mild embarrassment, and asked, "Where was I? What was the last thing I said?"

I replied teasingly, "I think you said, 'I want to fucking go to sleep!'"

He laughed and continued.

"We would prepare the food there for the Black Cat. That's when the Southern Pacific Railway Company announced on their bulletin boards that anyone coming across to eat in my restaurant would be fired. And I mentioned it to some of the kids that used to come over and eat, and they said, 'Yes, it's true!'

"So I went to the manager and said, 'You put a notice up denying the right of the people to eat at my restaurant. That's against the law.'

"They said, 'We've never done any such thing!'

"Well, one of the queens took the notice down and gave it to me. I said, 'You're lying. And here's the notice that was taken off the third-floor wall.'

"So with that as ammunition, I told them that I was going to bring suit against them: defamation of character and this, that, and the other. So they backed down. But the damage had been done. That was one of our very early fights against discrimination. The company later became one of the first to have domestic partner benefits for gay husbands and wives and for straight live-ins without papers."

The struggle to keep the Cat's liquor license and the harassment faced by local entities and businesses helped form José's belief that his push for civil rights for gay people needed to be more overt. Not convinced he could depend on the local chapter of the Mattachine Society, whose members were still using pseudonyms to avoid detection, José decided to start another organization.

"Meanwhile, I had come up with the idea that the only way that we could show some strength was to have a voting power, and some kind of a union. So I decided that I would form a nonprofit corporation. And I wanted to let the City Hall know that I was doing this. So I went and wrote a letter to the mayor, the chief of police, the probation department, the district attorney's office; I wrote letters to all of the very big people. They came to the meeting I called, except the mayor. And I told them what I proposed, and asked if they had any objection to it. They told me, 'No, but you are a fool. You'll never get them to agree. You will never unify them. They are the most diversified, independent group that exists.' Up until that time the gay community was not unified. So many of them were in the closet just protecting their asses.

"I said, 'Watch me.'

"So that was the beginning of the League for Civil Education. That was also the beginning of my plan to run for public office. I wanted to show that we had rights. Up until then, gay people thought that they were second-rate citizens. They were so browbeaten. Insurance companies would cancel you out if they knew you were gay. You couldn't buy a piece of property with a partner. You had to put the money up yourself and buy the house, and then later file a quitclaim deed to put his name on it. You couldn't rent an apartment with another man. You could be fired. I said, 'That's wrong. Nothing in the law says you can't buy property with another man. Nothing in the law says you can't live together. And why do they always say 'dubious character' to deny you insurance?' I had that happen to me, and I was going to prove it wrong. And that's what I did.

"Women could live together, and nobody thought anything of it. Women could buy property together. Men could not. And part of my message was that not all men that want to do these things are gay. Not all men that go to the toilet go there to play with one another. Many of us actually use the toilet for what it was made for.

"As the corporation was being formed, I went down to City Hall and found out what I had to do to run for office. I had to have twenty-five signatures and twenty-five dollars, I think it was. Well, my dear, nobody wanted to sign any paper helping or saying that they were going to back a homosexual. And the only way I was going to run was on an open ticket. The world knew that I was gay, and I was going to run as a gay man.

"How I finally got the people to sign was that I picked people out that were closet queens who had a little dirt on them. I told them, 'You sign the papers or I'll expose you.' That's how I got my signatures. The ones who are living today think it's wonderful that they did that. But at that time it was a matter of life and death for them.

"There were five seats open on the Board of Supervisors. Twelve hours before the filing deadline, there were nine people running. My chances for winning were very, very good. I campaigned in schools and before organizations of all kinds. I went on radio. My mother's name and my name were very well known. I spoke Spanish, so I was capturing the Spanish vote. Many of the queens were behind me. They were divided, as they always are, and if they had stuck together, I would have won.

"Twelve hours before the filing was to close, the people who didn't want me running went out and got almost thirty people to apply for the office. Now the field was large, and they made my position weak. Instead of five openings with nine people running, it was now five positions and thirty-three people running. But that didn't stop me. I still campaigned. I came in ninth in that whole field. I proved my point. From that day, at every election, the politicians in San Francisco have talked to us.

"The whole world knew I was gay and that I had run for office. Willie Brown (former speaker of the California State Assembly and now mayor of San Francisco) at that time was just beginning his political career. The Berkeley Brothers were there. They and a few others said, 'He's crazy, he's a publicity seeker, or he's just got his head up his ass! Nobody would run for public office saying that he was gay!' So they came down to see me at the Black Cat. And I talked to them. And they said, 'This man is sincere.' But they came to me and they said, 'You know, we cannot help you, because the minute we said we would help you, we would lose our jobs.' That's how Willie Brown knows me. They say he has a good memory for people, so I'm sure he remembers me. When he pushed the Consenting Adults legislation for the state, I worked on that campaign here.

"Well, I proved my point. I proved my point. And in time, we had San Francisco as you see it today. In time people got courage and openly came out of the closet all over the United States. But it took some time."

José Sarria was the very first openly gay candidate for political office in United States history. He ran for the San Francisco Board of Supervisors in the election of 1961, over a decade and a half before Harvey Milk followed in his footsteps and won a seat on the board in 1977. Although many see José as a pioneer and a hero, the man himself puts a more personal spin on it: "If I'm not hurting anyone or ripping anyone off or raping anyone, don't tell me what I can and can't do with my own life!" Anyone who does will most certainly face a fight.

Rising to Heaven, or Thereabouts

"I began doing my operas at the Black Cat back in the early fifties, and I'm still doing them today. I've been doing the operas for . . . what's fifty from ninety? I've been doing operas for forty years.

"One of the operas I did at the Cat was *Faust*. And of course Faust makes a contract with the devil giving his soul for eternal youth, and with this eternal youth he violates Marguerite. She has a baby out of wedlock by Faust. In the last act, Marguerite must pay for her sins; she is condemned to die. Well, now Faust is remorseful, and he wants to pay for his sins, but it is too late because his soul has been sold. And so in the last act, Marguerite is at the stake about to be burned, and, in the opera, God forgives Marguerite and opens up the heavens and takes her into heaven.

"I thought, 'Wouldn't it be exciting if I could die singing the last aria of the opera and then ascend and go to heaven? Well, how would you do that?' So I thought awhile, and we talked about it and everything, my dresser Ed Farquar and my prop man Bobby Newman.

"Bobby said, 'Get a ladder, and climb a ladder.'

"'Oh that's a good idea!'

"So in the early days at the Black Cat we climbed a ladder.

"Then Shirley (Shirley's 'boy name' was Tommy Brown, and she later became Empress Shirley of San Francisco), who used to make the costumes said, 'I'm going to make a dress that'll have wings on it. You climb the ladder. You can lie on the ladder horizontally, and the wings will come up, and it will look like you are flying.'

"I said, 'Oh that'll be fabulous!' So I did all of these crazy antics, and this death scene in *Faust* was absolutely gorgeous! I would go up the ladder and then come down, and then go up. It takes a long time to die in opera. I would lie on my stomach, and I'd make my shoulder blades move, and the wings would flap. I would look like I was flying. Well, you know you always want to be spectacular and crazy."

José and Hazel performed their first "camp opera" at the Black Cat in March 1958. The opera they parodied was *Madame Butterfly*, and the response from the audience was so overwhelmingly positive that they decided to extend their highbrow burlesque to other operas in the future. They created a comic version of *Aïda* which became a favorite. Their performances became a popular diversion for the more adventuresome tourists and an entertainment landmark for the locals. In later years, and even today, when journalists write of José, they frequently identify him by mentioning the operas. Even the San Francisco Opera has paid its respect to its leading satirist. When charities ask José to perform, more often than not, they want an opera.

"I remember in the seventies I was working at Bob Golovich's bar down the street, the Royal Palace. And I decided I was going to do the opera *Faust*. I wanted to make the last act even more dramatic. I thought it would be great if I could actually rise into heaven. I looked at the ceiling. I saw where I could cut into the division of the floor of the second story above the stage to make a kind of trapdoor. We had access to the upstairs, and if someone up there could open that very quietly, and if I put my hands up in a gesture, and if I had somebody up there who could *zip* me up, I would die and disappear.

"So I asked Bob if I could cut a hole in his ceiling. He said, 'Hell no! Damn! Don't you dare!'

"Every day he'd come in, and every day he'd look to see if there was a hole.

"And I thought, 'Well, tell me I can't do something, and I'll tell you how it can be done!'

"So I studied that very carefully, and I thought, 'Boy, if I could saw right along this edge of the beam where it won't show, and just let it sit there . . .'

"So that's what I did. When he wasn't around, I cut the section out, and I set it back again. You'd never know. Then on the top I put handles.

"So here comes the Sunday show. Bob is sitting with a group at the bar laughing, 'That old poop! She thinks she's gonna cut hole in my ceiling! I told her she'd better not. I told her she couldn't cut a hole in my goddamn ceiling! I wonder what she's going to do now. She's up to something.'

"So the opera came to the third act, and Marguerite was about to ascend, and it was all absolutely gorgeous. I climbed the ladder, and then I came racing down again. *'Oh mon Dieu! Mon Dieu!'* And I had my costume on with my wings, and I was beginning to flap them and flap them.

"Before I started the act I found these two men, leather guys that were in the audience. I very quietly asked, 'Now, could you go upstairs very quietly and move the trapdoor and stand there so you can't be seen? And when I give my gesture of raising my hands with the *'mon Dieu,'* you grab my wrists, and with one jerk you will jerk me up.' They said okay.

"So there I was up on the ladder in my beautiful gown about to make my last gesture, and down came the last crash, boom, bang from the accompanist, and the *'mon Dieu,'* and the music, and all of this at the same time, and I raised my hands up and *whoop!* I went up!

"Now Bob at the time was serving drinks. He worked the end of the bar. It was one of the longest bars in the city. And he was telling everybody, 'What a bitch! Here in this scene? She wanted to cut a hole in my ceiling for this! She's not going to cut a hole in my ceiling!'

"At the moment that they scooped me up, he was ringing something up on the register. He turned around, and I was gone. He said, 'Did she die?'

"The guys at the bar said, 'Yes, but where the hell did she go to?'

"'What?!'

"Bob was beside himself. He looked around, and everybody was applauding and applauding, and there was no me. I was up above. And then the boys lowered me back down.

"I heard him through the applause, 'That son of a bitch! He cut a hole in my ceiling!'

"I did the same opera at another place, and I had a pair of underpants come floating down after I went to heaven."

Pearls!

During the early part of José's adult life, the closet was still the norm for gay people. Even people who genuinely cared about gay friends counseled them to hide their true selves behind a constant life of lies, half truths, and euphemisms that allowed others to assume a gay person was heterosexual. Lovers became "roommates" or "friends." Older gay men were "confirmed bachelors." Actions too reflected the ruse. Close female friends acted as "rent-a-front" girl-friends for company parties or family dinners. Vacation pictures re-mained hidden in drawers. Many gay men went so far as to marry women and father children, some in the hopes of being "cured," as the conventional wisdom taught was possible. But mostly there was silence, silence about any part of a man's experience, feelings, ideas, dreams, or beliefs that could peg him as different. Gay people them-selves advocated living a double life, some out of fear of the conse-quences of honesty, some because they truly believed that there was something wrong with them, and others because they simply accepted the heterosexist status quo as the way the world was, is, and will be. Sadly, as the twenty-first century approaches, for many gay men in many parts of this country and the world, such deceit is still the norm, a state of affairs that José has never really understood and rarely tolerated.

"We have a lot of queens, a lot of gay people, who work in a straight world and want to be gay and yet want to conform to the straight world, which of course is something that I do not advocate. You cannot be two people, and you cannot please two worlds. That is probably why I would say to people who look in the mirror, 'Accept what you see, and that's it!' I do not find people who are openly gay trying to conform to the straight world. If you are openly gay, you don't have to conform. You are what you are, and that's it. I am what I am, and that's it.

"One of the gay directors here in the city, one of the really, absolutely more talented show people, came from Chicago where he had operated a dinner theater club very successfully. Chuck has always been gay, of course, but his club catered mostly to straight people, understandably since most people love theater. And then he came to San Francisco where things were a little bit different. You could be gay, and you could do things openly, and you didn't have to conform. It wasn't always easy, but you could be different. But down deep he tried to conform.

"He took a job in the Santa Cruz mountains. All these people wanted to put a community theater together, and they picked the gentleman with the most talent, who happened to be gay. They made it clear they did not want him to be openly gay. Chuck thought he was going to live two lives. He put on some of the best productions that they have ever seen. The people, the talent, came from out of the hills of Santa Cruz to sing and dance. They do even to this day. Some of them still perform, all because of Chuck.

"Now Chuck did not turn away his gay friends, people that he knew here in the city. He would invite them down if he thought they could pass very quietly without causing too much ripple, but basically, nobody was fooling anyone.

"Then came the opening of Chuck's production of *The Sound of Music*, and he said, 'José, I want you to come down for this thing, a lot of the kids are coming down and you can ride with them, and having lots of people there from the city will make the opening a big affair.' The play was to be in the Red Barn Theater. We would help it be a big opening. The hills were going to come alive!"

I could not help adding facetiously, "With the sound of music?" José chuckled.

Although Chuck sincerely wanted José to share the grand opening of the musical, he grew nervous about José's ability and willingness to conform, to fit in, to be, as the common expression in the gay world says, "straight acting."

He pleaded with José even before José said a word about the event, "José, please, I'm asking you as a favor, don't wear your diamonds! Don't!"

Don't: that word and José make a volatile mixture. Chuck, apparently, had no experience with José when he's faced with a forced personal prohibition. He would though, and soon.

"Oh, I've had my ears pierced for so long, I can't remember when. Number one, you don't tell me how to behave. I am seventy-plus years old, and I certainly know how to behave. I've been in the company of kings and queens, the real ones, and bums and tramps, and I know how to behave. So when somebody tells me how to behave, well, that's the wrong thing to say.

"So he said, 'Please, would you take your earrings out and promise not to wear diamonds?'

"I said, 'Okay, I'll take these earrings out, and I won't wear any diamonds.' It bugged me to think that he didn't think that I could judge how to dress. So I came home and I thought, 'Well I'm going to go down there, and I'll do what he asks. I will not wear any diamonds.'"

The night of the opening was cold. José laid out a topcoat and hat to add to his planned outfit. Beside them he laid an extremely long scarf, one of what he called his "Isadora Duncan scarves." It could wrap warmly around his neck several times and still drag on the ground behind him. He pulled on a fine pair of black dress slacks and a dark dress shirt, and he put on a warm but stylish pair of shoes with black socks.

Once his basic outfit was in place, José went to his dresser to begin accessorizing—with no diamonds, of course. He removed his diamond stud earrings and placed them carefully in a jewelry case. Then he opened the drawer in his jewelry case where he kept his necklace of seed pearls. He clasped it around his neck and went back for the choker from Japan strung with matching pearls and interspersed with delicate gold balls. Next came the ring with the huge cluster of pearls that looked like a bunch of ripe wine grapes. The pearl earrings he hung from his pierced ears were a carat and a half each and immeasurably larger than the offending diamond studs that he had removed in deference to his closeted friend.

José searched every bin and drawer in every jewelry case he had and found every pearl that he owned. He donned pearl bracelets, pearl pins, and pearl brooches. Every pearl was real, and many were less than subtle. "No phony baloneys," as he put it. With a wry smile to himself in the mirror, he wrapped the Isadora Duncan scarf around his neck with a flair, shrugged into the overcoat, and tapped the hat onto his head. He heard the engines of his escorts out on the street. He grabbed his keys, locked the front door, and went to meet his ride.

Waiting for José out at the curb was a contingent of five or six large, black motorcycles. The riders were dressed from head to heel in black leather: leather caps, leather halters and vests, leather jackets, leather pants, leather bracelets, leather collars, leather chaps, and strong leather boots. Here and there the leather accoutrements were decorated with heavy silver studs and rings. All in all it was a rather butch-looking group of men. José wrapped the scarf a few more times, tucked it securely into his coat, pulled on a pair of gloves, and hopped on a motorcycle behind one of the handsome "rough trade" men. ("Rough trade" refers to masculine, gruff, slightly dangerous, usually blue-collar men, or in some cases, creating the illusion of such a man.) José's biker escorts were not actually toughs from the wrong side of the tracks as they appeared to be. They were gay friends of Chuck's who had also been invited to the party in Santa Cruz. At José's request, they had dressed for the party in their leather drag.

"It had been raining, and it was miserable. As we drove down, I wrapped myself real good with the big, oversized scarf. We arrived at the door, and I was all bundled up—all you could see was just my face. Oh God, were we glad to get there."

When Chuck saw the bundled-up José and his leather men, he pulled José aside and questioned him about the attire of his escorts. José responded with an innocent lilt in his voice, muffled by the layers of scarf, "But Chuck, you didn't say anything to them about not wearing leather. You know how those boys love their leather. I'm sure it won't be a problem."

Chuck gave a resigned huff and led José to the side room where he could check his coat and hat. As he watched, José unwrapped the scarf, and unwrapped and unwrapped. As his ears came into view, so did the pearl earrings. Chuck stood watching with a perplexed expression on his face. José removed his hat and coat and handed them politely and deliberately to the man at the coat check. He turned in all his pearl-bedecked glory, and Chuck's jaw dropped.

"José, my God, what did you *do* to yourself?!"

"What do you mean, Chuck?" José answered with a look of naive innocence.

He blinked his eyes and smiled warmly.

Chuck sputtered, "When I invited you . . . you weren't supp . . . I told you . . ."

"Oh, that!" José replied with mock relief and understanding. "It's perfectly okay, Chuck. You needn't worry. I am not wearing a *single* diamond!"

José left his stunned host standing in the hallway and went in to meet the other guests.

"I thought he was going to die! I went into the main room, and I smiled at everybody. We all sat down to a lovely evening of theater and food and drink. At the reception I had women come up to me and tell me how beautiful my jewelry was. Men just went by and said, "Kind of nice." They were straight men—what else are they going to say?

"But that taught Chuck a lesson. *Never, ever* tell me what to do or how to behave, because it doesn't work, honey! Everybody knew. My good friends and the other guests stood around very comfortably, and I laughed and talked. I was very impressive! (Empressive?)

"Now, Chuck did ask me after that to perform in drag in one of his shows. And I was ready. As an entertainer, I arrived as a man, got dressed as a woman, performed, and then got changed again, and the audience thought it was absolutely wonderful. You see, there is nothing wrong with drag. People make it dirty, but that's not what the beholder sees at a show. What they see is a person out there impersonating a woman and singing and carrying on an act. The audience for Chuck's show enjoyed it. They saw nothing dirty. There was nothing unseemly, no matter what the ABC said. The shows at the Black Cat, my shows, were good entertainment. They were fun."

José was free to perform in Chuck's show in Santa Cruz because he was no longer bound by the agreement with Sol to perform only at the Black Cat. In the fall of 1963 the California State Supreme Court refused to consider an appeal by Sol Stoumen of his liquor license revocation. Attorney Morris Lowenthal's twelve-year battle to keep the Black Cat Cafe open ended. The years of standing up to police harassment, public prejudice, media defamation, and vice squad entrapment were over at the Cat. In a final cruel slap, the agents of the Alcoholic

Beverage Control in Sacramento chose October 31, Halloween, to enter the Cat and pull the license. Halloween has traditionally been the biggest night of celebration in the gay community, and it was the Cat's largest party of the year.

Stoumen, a straight man who had come to embrace the cause of gay equality as his own fight, was determined to have the last word. In defiance, he decided to go ahead with plans for the Halloween night's revelry. He loaded up with soft drinks, fruit juices, punch, lemon tonic, apple cider, and coffee. As the crowd arrived in costume, many of the men in female drag (Halloween was the only time cross-dressing was legal for men), José announced, "We're soft drinking it tonight, everyone!"

Two thousand people showed up at the Cat that night, and the crowd spilled into the street. Hazel played ragtime. José sang and carried on and played hostess to the throng. Twelve police officers patrolled in and around the bar. Mink coats and diamonds mixed with T-shirts, leather chaps, and motorcycle boots. There were tourists and students and businessmen, straight couples and gay couples, all gathered to say goodbye to a San Francisco institution.

As midnight approached, the time when cross-dressing again became illegal, José made his way to the makeshift raised runway and stood to hush the crowd. Everyone turned to listen. José sang a bit and then began his usual banter, occasionally reminiscing about past and present employees of the Cat: "Connie" and "Rocky" the bouncers; big, lovable black jazz musician and pancake cook extraordinaire "Bumble Bee" David Pendleton Thompson; Eddie Walker; diminutive but tough cocktail waitress and queen T. John "La Kish" Darling; Ernie Brandt; pianist supreme and control queen James Willis "Hazel" McGinnis; Jimmy Moore; Eddie Paulson; Michael Tresini; Norman "Norma Jean Honey" Russell; Art Beale; "Toby" Travis Yick; Frank Meilke; "Kit" Kitcherling; "Red" Monahan.

As the final minutes of the Black Cat Cafe's heyday ticked by, José turned serious and spoke to the crowd about believing in themselves and celebrating their individuality. He encouraged them to register to vote and work to change the discriminatory system that made them undeserving outlaws. He assured them that one day, if they stuck together, things would be different. He repeated his often-used admonition, "United we stand. Divided, they will catch us one by one."

Then, as he had done on countless Sundays at the Cat, José told the crowd to stand and hold hands. With a strong voice embellished with a vibrato from training, or perhaps from emotion, or both, he sang. The crowd joined in, some with tears:

> God save us nelly queens
> God save us nelly queens
> God save us queens
> From every mountainside
> Long may we live and die
> God save us nelly queens
> God save us queens!

PART FOUR:
THE IMPERIAL COURT

San Francisco

I love San Francisco. That may sound sappy and cliché (after all, who but the Christian right *doesn't* love San Francisco?), but it's worse. I write that sentence with a tear of emotion in my eye. I won't apologize, however, or even act embarrassed. I love The City unabashedly. San Francisco.

When I was young and feeling like an alien in my macho military family, I used to dream of the City by the Bay and the hippie culture there. It was in the same category as the Emerald City in my mind. Magic. Safe. Different enough that I would surely feel at home there.

"If you're going to San Francisco, be sure to wear some flowers in your hair."

"Sittin' on the dock of the bay, wasting time . . ."

"When the lights go down in the city, and the sun shines on the bay . . ."

"I left my heart . . ."

"California dreamin' on such a winter's day."

I would hug my pillow and gaze out at the snow-blanketed hills of the Appalachian Mountains and dream of sand and sun and Golden Gate Park and people who were as different as I felt, people who hated the war and wore clothes as colorful as my hidden soul, people who would surely love me the way I had always longed to be loved. If I couldn't go to Oz, maybe someday I could go to San Francisco.

We did go there once when I was in junior high school. My father was stationed in the high desert of southern Arizona and soon to retire. We visited one of my brothers in California, a macho, conservative, undercover narcotics cop. He took us to San Francisco's Haight Ashbury to gawk and laugh at the "hippies and weirdos." I vividly remember walking down Haight Street while my family guffawed at the show. I found myself dropping farther and farther behind them, marveling at a man in a toga and sandals playing a flute, a woman in a full, earth-tone peasant dress strumming a guitar, a man and woman dancing in an alleyway. Long flowing hair with cascading flowers, strings of love beads, bell-bottom jeans brightly patched, music, peace signs on walls and skin and necklaces, poetry, leather woven bracelets, unashamed nudity browning in the sun, fluid voices that sounded otherworldly, drums, strange stringed instruments I did not recognize, the sweet smell of marijuana smoke. I remember looking ahead at my family and thinking, "Freaks and weirdos. They're the freaks and weirdos, not these people." It was the closest I ever came to running away from home.

I didn't even know what a gay person was yet; I didn't know that those feelings I had for my best friend actually had a name, that there were millions of others like me, that many of them were moving to San Francisco. I didn't realize that the city was named after my hero Saint Francis, who loved animals and was gentle and took his clothes off in public when he renounced his father's materialism. I didn't know, but my heart raced a little every time I thought of that distant city.

"Make love, not war."

"War is not healthy for children and other living things."

"Peace!"

I was certain that San Francisco was not simply a collection of people living out mundane lives. It was a city of characters, of flamboyant beings who ignored the conventions and lived more fully, more honestly. When I finally came to know San Francisco, I learned that my perception as a child was true. San Francisco is a city of characters: Willie Brown, the O'Farrell brothers, Harvey Milk, Emperor Joshua Norton, Herb Caen, Robin Williams, Phyllis Lyon and Del Martin, Harry Hay—and these are just a few of the famous ones. All over the city are the punkers, hippies, Castro queens, street musicians, street activists, artists, poets, and liberal little old ladies. The place is magic. And not least among the characters is José Sarria.

I have come around the curve in Interstate Highway 80 countless times to be confronted with that most unique skyline across the waters of the bay. The Pyramid, ancient meets contemporary. That wonderful collection of green-arched windows my son Mack calls the Oz Building. Coit Tower, built by a little old lady in honor of the city's firemen and modeled after the nozzles of their hoses. (Hmm.) The Embarcadero Clock Tower. Alcatraz. The Golden Gate Bridge. The canyons of the Financial District. City Hall. The streets that rise toward the sky everywhere. And when all of this is lit up at night, it is a truly mystic thing to see, whether from the shore across the bay or from the heights of Twin Peaks.

I love driving to see José.

When I first came to interview José, my son Mack was eleven, and he accompanied me. José had given us directions to his apartment building near the top of Nob Hill on Bush Street. He had said, "Turn right off Leavenworth onto Bush, then have the boy roll down the window, look up to the sky, and ask Joshua for a parking place, because that's the only way you will ever find one." I told Mack what José had said, and sure enough, when we rolled onto Bush Street, he rolled down the window, put his head out, looked at the sky, and said, "Josh! Please find us a parking space." I chuckled. We found a space half a block from José's. Mack was not surprised. He has absolute faith in the benevolence of San Francisco and its characters, living or dead. I've never had to park more than a couple blocks away from José's whenever Mack is with me.

Once my son, my lover, and I brought a friend from southern California to San Francisco. Down at Fisherman's Wharf Danielle had a street artist do a pastel of her. She was so impressed that she asked if he could do a matching picture of her beloved cocker spaniel. She had a picture in her purse. He agreed, though explaining that he usually only works with live models. When he finished the second portrait, she took the rolled papers and moved on with a smile as bright as the silver flashes of sunlight on the capering waters of the bay. Next stop: Chinatown.

The line for the cable cars was too long and too slow, so we took the handsome black man's offer of a ride in his personal limousine at the same fare as the cable cars. We piled into the limo along with a couple who wanted a ride to South San Francisco, miles beyond our destination. At the corner of Broadway and Grant, we tumbled back out. The black chariot disappeared into the city traffic, and we prepared to stroll the narrow canyon of Grant Street with its fruit stands and paper fans and silk dragon jackets and ceramic Buddhas.

Suddenly Danielle cried out, "My portraits! I left them in the back of the limousine!" Her mood settled quickly into a melancholy resignation. My son, who was about ten at the time, stepped toward her and said, "Don't worry, Danielle. He may see them and bring them back."

She puffed sarcastically and replied, "Yeah, right! He had to take those people to the other side of the city. Like some limo driver is going to come all the way back across the city to look for us to return some sketches! No way!"

Mack retorted, "I think he will. You don't know this city. San Francisco is a magic place."

With a decidedly depressed friend, we began to slowly explore the shops of Chinatown. Danielle had little enthusiasm for the multitude of Chinese imports. Her sense of adventure had leaked out with her earlier joy. Finally, we were in a large curio shop about halfway up the length of the street. Mack quietly slipped surreptitiously out of the big glass front doors and onto the sidewalk with a knowing smile. In a few moments he stood in the doorway facing those of us within, red and gold Chinese lettering behind him from the store across the street, and said in an exaggeratedly modulated voice, "Oh Danielle! Come here!" We all hurried out onto the sidewalk and looked south down Grant Avenue. There, very slowly making its way down the narrow thoroughfare, was a small black limousine. We could see the driver's head swinging side to side, looking into each of the shops he passed. With an I-told-you-so smile, Mack glanced at Danielle's astonished face, and then hailed the driver, who broke out into a wide grin. Once she found her voice again, our previously jaded friend giggled something about magic. Between profuse expressions of delighted gratitude, she told the driver she couldn't believe he had come back. He smiled and said gently, "You're in San Francisco, girl."

"If you're going to San Francisco, be sure to wear some flowers in your hair . . ."

As Mack and I walked from the car parked safely in our Emperor Norton-appointed parking place, we passed little corner markets and little hole-in-the-wall stores all shoulder to shoulder with multistoried apartment buildings. At the wrought-iron gate of José's building, we rang the number on the intercom, and José's sweet, tenor, slightly gravely voice answered, "Yes?"

"José, it's Michael and Mack."

"Well, my dears, come in." The door buzzed, and we entered. After spending time in José's Victorian, knickknack-cluttered, grand piano-dominated, doily-protected sanctuary, and after watching José sweep around the place in a flowing caftan, Mack later remarked that visiting José was like visiting a grandmother and a grandfather all in one person. José, of course, thought Mack was the handsomest, smartest, cleverest young man he had ever met, and he said so profusely. Being Irish, Mack recognized the touch of blarney, but he loved the praise nonetheless. Maybe more so because it was overdone. That's what grandparents are for.

That and being keepers of the magic.

The Victorian Chapter

The first time I walked into José's Bush Street apartment some two years ago, immediately after my virgin experience with the annual Norton memorial service, I thought, "Someone needs to describe this place. It's incredible!" But his apartment is so visually rich that I worried it would require one of those long, boring, descriptive chapters like the ones you have to suffer through in Victorian novels. But then, José was born not too long after the Victorian era, and my first great writing hero was Charles Dickens, and he always had long, boring, descriptive passages, which I liked even if I had to wait two chapters for anything to happen. I always wanted to write one of those upholstered chapters in C. D.'s honor. So here it is. If you don't like long, boring, descriptive passages, I suppose you could skip this one, although you will be missing the depth of character for which José's apartment is a deep and profound metaphor. (Okay, so skip it, but I'm writing it anyway!) Here's to you, Charles Dickens and José Sarria!

The building itself has little to make it stand out from the surrounding buildings. Its front is tall and narrow with a terra-cotta–colored brick. Up the center is a series of dark gray metal fire escape ladders and balconies. On either side, are three-sided bay windows stacked up five levels. The small tiled porch is enclosed by a heavy wrought iron gate, obviously tacked on in recent years in deference to more dangerous times. The gold spikes at the top of the gate add some color but little in the way of decorative distinction. Visitors have to call up through the intercom (be sure to hit the pound key first) to be buzzed in. The first time I entered the building, however, I was with José. I had only known him a very short time by then. As he slid his key into the gate with a metallic scrape and click, he glanced back at me over his shoulder, smiled seductively, and said, "You know, I can take my teeth out."

He chuckled at my embarrassed blush.

We stepped across the white marble tile steps and porch and entered the inner hallway through the original reddish-brown, wooden double doors of the building, each holding the ubiquitous rectangle of glass in its center. Beverley Plaza tells me that the left-hand door of the pair only opens for moving large pieces of furniture in or out. Inside we made our way down the main, rather plain hallway, passing the stairs to the basement (where José keeps his archives) and a couple of apartment doors painted the same off-white as the walls and the high ceiling. Over the mailboxes on the right-hand wall was a partially completed mural being created by one of José's tenants. (It has been a work in progress since I've known José.)

At the end of the hallway, we keyed ourselves into José's apartment. The contrast between the rather nondescript hallway and the apartment of the Widow Norton is immense, much as José's flamboyance contrasts with the conventional world he must live in. (See, I told you there would be deep metaphor involved here!)

One of the first things I noticed entering the hallway was the sound. Above the gentle, soothing purr of the small koi-filled aquarium in the corner was the constant and subtle ticking of the clocks, many, many clocks. José's clocks create a never-ending fairy drum symphony, constantly varied in its contrapuntal rhythms: the tick of this clock and then the tock of that clock, seeming to synchronize and then passing each other. Clicks, ticks, tocks: the place was alive with the sound of clocks.

I love José's clocks. Sometimes during my visits I just sit and listen meditatively. Sometimes when I am working, I hardly notice them. That's when one or another chimes, indignant that I have ignored them. There are wooden clocks and ceramic clocks and metal clocks. There are mantle clocks, wall clocks, wind-up clocks, a Bavarian cuckoo clock with a bird and a line of moving Bavarian dancers, and clocks in the bellies of things. To avoid an absolute cacophony of chimes on the hour, José has his clocks all set at different times. Not a practical solution in any conventional sense, but perfectly rational in José's world. Periodically during the hour, the rhythmic ticking is interrupted by bells, the Big Ben chimes, a music-box tinny version of "Ave Maria," a wooden-sounding cuckoo backed up by the musical strains of "The Happy Wanderer," a hiking song we used to sing on Boy Scout hikes, and all sorts of bells, bells, bells, bells, bells, bells.

The high ceilings hover above the clocks with elaborate molding where wall and ceiling meet. In the dining room, the first room off the entryway, a knickknack shelf runs around the walls about seven feet up. All along the shelf, like saints perched on a medieval cathedral, stand ceramic dancers, Hummel children, seventeenth-century dandies in white wigs, a little backpacker in lederhosen and suspenders, a carved ivory Catholic monk that looks suspiciously like a dildo, beautiful dolls dressed in gingham and lace, naked Greek wrestlers with penises unashamedly dangling, a shy, white-faced geisha girl, a golden mock Oscar statuette, a metal plate in golds and reds with the logo of the "Gay Cock Peaches," Kewpie dolls in overalls or diapers, cut crystal decanters reflecting the soft room lighting into subtle rainbows, and strong, square whiskey bottles. A cookie jar in the shape of a fat boy with a baseball uniform stands shoulder to shoulder with a pair of gracefully embracing lovers in lace collars and cuffs on a park bench. A yellow feathered bird sits frozen on its plain wooden perch in a gilded cage. (Another allusion. Impressed yet?) Grinning clowns are dressed in floppy jumpsuits and oversized red shoes, and open-mouthed singers and soulful black blues musicians and iridescent ducks and big-eyed owls, and muscled, macho leather daddies, porcelain dragons, ceramic cows, graceful silver coffee urns, blue and green and copper colored glass bonsai trees, tall, graceful wine decanters, Saint Francis of Assisi in his austere brown robes and partially shaved head and Betty Boop. There is a small brass scale with opposing hanging pans like the ones used to measure gold during the Gold Rush. Balance . . . and diversity: this is José's life. (Okay, I'll ease up on the overt commentary!)

Every foot of wall space in all of the rooms, as well as the entryway, is covered with photographs, fine oil paintings of European cafes or Mexican cantinas, certificates of award, letters from civic leaders, Tom of Finland erotic prints of bulging male bodies, old family photographs, snapshots of friends and fellow performers, posters from past performances, and pictures of black cats, given by friends in honor of José's long tenure as a performer at the Black Cat Cafe.

It is a musical, magical place, one part social criticism and one part comfortable grandmother's place. It is José's life in high relief.

The wooden floors are warmly covered by Oriental-style carpets, blue and gold in the entryway and thick cream color with pastel highlights in the main room. Standing along the walls like a miniature city skyline are wooden bookshelves, credenzas, china cabinets, a free-standing wood-frame mirror, tables, chests, curio cabinets, and plant stands. Most of the furniture is fine, highly polished, and quite old. Below the crystal and brass chandelier in the dining room is an elegant wooden table, the hand-embroidered tablecloth most often obscured by José's voluminous correspondence from around the world; but the ceramic swan in the center of the table always has fresh flowers.

Through an archway from the dining room is the less cluttered, but still warmly filled living room. The thing that struck me most as I first entered that room was the soft, yellow-white sunlight filtering in from the large bay windows in the wall behind the black, baby grand piano with its fringed Tiffany table lamp. José has hung the windows with gossamer white curtains that catch the light and glow, bordered of course by royal red velvet side drapes tied back with gold cord. Lined up below the windows is a miniature hedge of houseplants. And beyond them, through the lace curtains' soft focus, are the green shadows of the trees and bushes growing, like ghost images, on the rear terrace, one of those mystical hidden places between the towering buildings that you can sometimes find in the older cities. José's private Eden.

The piano is adorned, in addition to the lamp, with a large lace doily that protects the instrument's glossy finish from the lamp, the standing photos of family and friends, and vases that rest atop it. The photos are numerous, a kind of photographic Stonehenge.

The couch in this room is a hide-a-bed. José is very generous with his home. The tables are covered with handmade lace doilies and embroidered squares of cloth, and there are antimacassars on the backs of the chairs, though few visitors remember Macasser's Oil, much less worry about staining the furniture with a careless resting of oiled hair on a chair back. There is a thick, fluffy feather tick for the bed when it is open for guests. On the cream-painted walls behind the couch are two very large, elaborately framed oil paintings of José during his Black Cat days. One shows him dressed in an opulently red *Carmen* costume smoking a cigar. The other painting is in shades of dark blue, green, and black, and is a rather sensual portrait of José as a young man, his large, lushly lashed black eyes gazing out from his smooth, round, young, Latino face. His look is distant and almost sad. He is draped in an androgynous, velvety green cape, his elbow resting on a wooden pillar subtly adorned with a tan phoenix rising. José has been wounded in the battles of a life open and unpretentious, the artist obviously knew, but the phoenix in José is indomitable.

José's bathroom too, is lined with memorabilia of his long years in entertainment. The old claw-foot tub has been supplemented with a shower head that rises like a swan neck from the faucet, and an oval metal hoop suspended from the ceiling to hold a shower curtain. A window behind the big porcelain toilet opens into a narrow breezeway shared by surrounding apartments and providing an opening for the cool bay air. Never having lived in a large city, I always found myself rather smitten with the romantic secrecy of such inner passageways for the sky. They are so much more connected to reality than central air conditioning systems with their little aluminum tubes to nowhere. Towels rest on shelves above the toilet's little nook at the end of the tub, easily reachable over the white porcelain throne from the shower head end of the tub-cum-shower. A towel rack below the shelf holds the towels currently in use, an eclectic collection of pastel fluffiness.

The bathroom has a rather contemporary, cabinet-top sink, though the surface is marble and the fixtures are brass and ceramic levers rather than the too-common round plastic knobs most mortals live with these days. The medicine cabinet has four-part folding mirrored doors reminiscent of a Japanese screen. The counter next to the sink holds an assortment of pink cut-glass bowls, cream jars, atomizers, and dishes for the magical creams and potions that transform José and Scott into the Widow Norton and Beverley Plaza. There is an occasional eyebrow pencil, powder puff, or tin of eye liner, though the room is usually kept meticulously neat and clean. The little room is one part dressing room, one part museum, and one part grandmother's water closet. It is difficult to leave the room in very short order.

At the north end of the apartment, off the dining room, is the small kitchen. There is a large white sink with drawers beside, a stove and oven combination, a counter along one wall, a small, round 1950s-style breakfast table with shelves above of course, and two walls topped with cabinets. The single window opens east into another breezeway and has an outdoor shelf for a few flowering plants and a basket of onions. At the opposite end from the window is the pantry, which holds the refrigerator, the microwave oven, an abundance of shelves, and one wall displaying a three-dimensional mural of hanging pots, pans, and utensils. I never stop wondering at the volume of produce and tools that can be squirreled into such a modest space. Considering the meals that emerge from there, I often wonder if one of the drawers or the back of a shelf might hold a magic wand as well.

Off the kitchen to the north are the narrow double doors to Beverley's room. It is his private sanctuary against the silly diurnal world that actually works and rumbles noisily during daylight hours, so I have never spent enough time there to have absorbed its adornments, a fact that I teasingly lament in front of the delicately beautiful Beverley.

The hallway between the entryway and the other bedroom to the south is narrow, and made even more narrow by a looming, dark wooden armoire with deeply carved, mirrored, double doors that open almost to the opposite wall. It is necessary to stand a little to the side to open each door in the small space. Opening both requires a kind of sidestep first one way and then the other. Like the entry-way closet, the armoire is filled in every nook and shelf with the stuff of José's life. In an apartment as small yet rich in adornment as José's, every little space has its assigned task. There are no doors in the place without shelves inside and hooks outside. Finding video-tapes or scrapbooks or items of clothing can be a kind of Easter egg hunt without the eggs.

Finally there is José's bedroom; a large four-poster bed dominates the room with its four big down pillows, its patchwork quilts, feather comforter, and colorful afghans. His walls are covered with the most special of his mementos: old graying family portraits, letters from the governor, special awards. At the foot of the bed against the wall is a large wardrobe, and a heavy wooden dresser squeezes onto the wall by the door. Altogether, it is a cozy, uphol-stered kind of place. A visitor does not so much walk into José's bedroom as squeeze, turn, sidestep, and dance into it, as if the room itself and furniture conspire to force a newcomer into a slightly different way of being. If the twisting and the turning strains the body, there is the puffed and rounded bed almost begging for a backward flop and a groan of comfortable pleasure.

The first time I came to José's intending to spend the night, I was alone, so I suggested I sleep in his bed rather than fuss with the hide-a-bed. José was more than agreeable. The shared comfort of the feather bed gave us a special closeness, which of course did not prevent José from teasing me the next morning about my snoring. Sweeping into the kitchen dressed in a full quilted robe to fix breakfast as I stumbled grumbling to the bathroom, José declared in his most theatrical voice, "Come one, come all! Hear this amazing man! He grunts! He snorts! He makes exotic noises!"

Welcome to José's home theater and cafe. You will be welcomed with thick comforters and soothing sounds. You will be fed generously; out of the small pantry and smaller kitchen, José and his roommate, Miss Beverley Plaza, performer extraordinaire from Finocchio's, work miracles. But then, San Francisco is a city of surprises almost mystical. If you visit, however, count on fighting Miss Beverley for the morning paper, but be warned that she is a diva of prodigious resources, always subtle but always clear. She does, after all, handle living with an empress.

The Diva

I had heard much about José's decades of performances, but with the exception of the quick clip of him singing "God Save Us Nelly Queens" in the PBS documentary *Before Stonewall,* I had never heard him perform. I stepped into the dimly lit San Francisco bar with excitement, but also a little trepidation. He was, after all, seventy-two years old. Operatic music is a challenge at any age. Most singers retire long before seventy-two.

Yet, no matter what condition José's voice was in, I felt as if I were about to witness a piece of history: a performance by the Nightingale of Montgomery Street.

The bar management had set up a tiny stage in the corner of the main room. It was surrounded by tightly packed, round cocktail tables with chairs. I crossed over the stage in two steps and entered the little back room that was serving as a dressing room. José stood before a large mirror applying two very large sets of eyelashes. He was dressed only in a pair of large cotton briefs.

"Hello, my dear!"

José seemed as comfortable in his underwear as he did in street clothes or in his fabulous gowns. He hugged and kissed me affectionately. It seemed a pleasant irony to me that a man who built his professional career on clever pretense and artifice would be so open and unassuming in reality. The gown for tonight was red, trimmed in black lace, and was hanging on the wall behind José. He was to perform the opera *Carmen.* We talked briefly as José prepared. He spoke of his makeup, the show, the accompanist. He teased me with double entendres as he always does. He complained a little about this queen or that queen. He introduced me to a few people who came in to wish him well. He expressed some nervousness about his voice and the notes. I left him to dress and went out to take my seat in the audience.

There was an eclectic mixture of patrons sipping their drinks and waiting for the show to start. Many were middle aged or above. One old fellow had to have been in his nineties. There were a few younger drag queens and a smattering of men in their twenties and thirties. The pianist played a few show tunes as we waited. Finally, the bar's owner stood on the stage and introduced, "The star of stage, screen, and the back rooms of bars, José Sarria!"

To the driving strains of the *Carmen* overture, José emerged from the back room, accompanied by the swish of taffeta that held his Spanish skirts out to a prodigious width. Fringes of black lace contrasted with the deep red of the dress that swept the floor. Bright red and deep black underskirts peeked out from the bottom of the dress. On his head, José wore a large red Spanish headdress that looked a little like a lace fan. Attached to the headband was a tuft of black hair, an obviously intentionally unsuccessful and campy attempt to cover the performer's bald spot. His black, elbow-length gloves glittered here and there with sequins, and he held in his right hand a red and black fan which he fluttered seductively in front of his lavishly painted face. His tightly laced, richly embroidered bodice lifted his bosom into a vision of a true opera diva. On his feet were red-heeled pumps, something he always wore.

When José first began performing in various degrees of drag at the Black Cat just after World War II, he usually wore the same black shoes he wore when serving drinks and food. One night an executive from the Hoover Company, with which José had a part-time job, came to the Black Cat with his wife. As José was preparing to perform one of his comic operas, the woman called him over. "You need some shoes that will add some color to your outfit." She removed a pair of red pumps that she had just purchased in Paris for ninety dollars, a considerable sum in those days, and told José to try them on. To their delight, the shoes fit. The woman gave them to José. He wore the bright red heels from that day on, both while performing and while waiting the tables. They became one of his signature symbols. He still wears red pumps to perform today.

"My name is Carmen, a common cigarette factory worker. I'm supposed to be introduced by a chorus of other cigarette girls, but they apparently are off doing God knows what with their cigarettes. I sing them a song about untamed gypsy love. Now don't worry if I talk on and on. We have a signal. When I say *"C'est toi,"* the piano will start. That way I don't have to tell the silly queen to stop and let me finish. One time I was ready to sing, and he left me standing up here like an idiot, because I forgot to say *"C'est toi."*

The piano started.

"Not yet!"

The piano went silent.

"C'est toi!"

In a rich voice, José began singing the lively "Habanera," its lyrics rewritten in English and telling the story in a condensed fashion. José punctuated his words with suggestive smiles, swirling of his hips, and seductive glances over the fan, drawing his listeners into his funny campy rewrite of the opera. Despite the comic nature of this condensed *Carmen* and its wacky lyrics, José's tenor voice, once he began singing, was smooth and resonant, and beautiful. It seemed to be the voice of a man decades younger than he was.

"Okay, enough of that shit," he declared, stopping abruptly. "Don José, of course, hears me singing and falls madly, passionately, wildly in love with me and wants to do the nasty. I say not without a ring first, and so he gives me one." José kept the surprises coming, demonstrating a mastery of incongruity and comic timing.

José continued on with his singing and his funny, irreverent commentary between, mixing hurried details of the opera's story with contemporary social commentary and spontaneous repartee with audience members, all of it generously sprinkled with playful sexual innuendo.

"So we have secret meetings at the city walls and bullfighters and bull and flowers and gypsies cavorting, and who knows what all. . . ."

After roughly a half hour of alternating between naughty narration and funny, but lovely, singing, José prepared the audience for his death scene. Often José's press releases, both for *Carmen* and other operatic parodies, promise the audiences that they will get to see his "famous . . . and slow . . . death scene" once, twice, maybe three times, depending on the requests from the audience.

"Now it's time for my death scene. This is very good. It's very tragic. Especially the accompaniment." José slipped a small knife into his bodice. José stood waiting for the piano to start. Silence. José glanced back at the pianist, who smiled charmingly. José looked forward again as if innocently awaiting the music. José looked back again.

"Okay, okay, the accompaniment is fabulous as always. *C'est toi!*" The music began. "Goddamn sensitive queen!"

As the pianist played the "Toreador Song," José continued, "Look! The bullfighter has killed a bull! The crowd jumps to its feet in wild applause!" The audience playfully followed José's arm gestures and rose to its feet applauding wildly. After a moment, José shouted, "All right, all right, all right! This is my show. Sit down! A bunch of goddamn drama queens!"

"Well, now all hell breaks loose. There's a bunch of smugglers. I don't know what the hell they have to do with the story, but they sing nicely. I send flowers. Don José decides to leave the military; he didn't ask, I won't tell. He wants to join the gypsy band. I go to a fortune teller and end up with a card of death. Some other bitch tries to take Don José. I decide, to hell with all this mess and go off with the bullfighter. Don José pleads with me to return to him. I say to hell with all men and throw his ring at him."

José made a comic display of trying to remove the ring, finally asking some man in the audience to lick it for him. The man did so. José mugged his delight, moved close to the man, and asked, "Oooh, honey, that was good. What else do you lick?" Returning to the stage, he muttered, "Best sex I've had in years."

José finally threw the ring and began singing his rejection of Don José. Then he broke in with a hasty narration. "Don José doesn't take rejection well. He needs a therapist. He becomes furious!"

José began singing again, this time as Don José. "If I can't have you nobody can!"

"Then he stabs me."

José whipped out the knife, and with a flourish, stabbed himself. He began to stagger into slapstick death throes, punctuated with, "Oh! Ah! Eh! Oh! Oh shit!" He paused as if ready to finally collapse, and then began again to stagger broadly across the stage and into the audience, to the delight of the patrons. He looked to the sky saying, "Oh my dear!" He collapsed onto a handsome man's lap with an "Oh!" of pain and despair. Then he bounced a bit on the man and his second "Oh!" came out in a tone of delight and discovery. He leaned to the man and put his arms around his neck with a decidedly seductive tone of "Oooooh!"

He staggered back to the stage after milking the bit with the audience member, and grabbed his bosom. "And now, I die!" The audience applauded playfully, and José flashed a reproving look. In a more expansive voice, he repeated, "And nooow, I, die!" He began to kneel slowly, emphasizing his age. The audience laughed. "This is opera. We die slowly here. I'm not sixteen anymore, you know." He flopped onto his back and raised his legs, revealing black stockings and his signature red heels. He momentarily spread his legs, drawing out a last laugh, and lay still.

The audience rose to its feet and applauded and cheered wildly.

With the help of his pianist, José rose and bowed flamboyantly. He smiled in mock humility and batted his eyelashes.

"That was pretty good, huh!" he asked the audience. The applause rose again. José knew how to play an audience. "Want to see it again?" Affirmative shouts led to a frenetic search for Carmen's ring. During the search, José pretended to grope more than one patron, all the while wondering aloud where the ring was. The sexual teasing escalated. When one man in the audience playfully groped José back, he invited the man to come on stage and play the part of Don José. The audience applauded its encouragement. The man followed José on stage with an embarrassed grin.

José took the man onto the stage and began to tuck the knife into his belt, pretending to accidentally slip and touch the man at the crotch. "Oooh, I see you already have a weapon tucked away! Now, when I sing"—he sings loudly in the man's face, startling him—"I do not love you! Take back your ring!" José smiles proudly toward the audience at the man's startled reaction to his still-powerful voice. He continued after a pause, "Then you whip it out." The man went for his zipper. "Not that one! The little one!" José touched the man again and declared, "Oh, I see they are both little! I mean the other little one!" José is not one to let an amateur steal his spotlight.

"Then you whip it out. Can you do that, honey? Be brave. And then you say, 'If I can't have you, nobody can!' Then you stick me." José wiggled his eyebrows at the audience. "Here we go."

José made a show of standing waiting for the music. There was silence. He glanced over his shoulder and then at the man with whom he was sharing the stage and repeated, "Here we go." Silence still. He looked again at the pianist, smiled sweetly, and said, *"C'est toi."* He turned back to the audience, lost the smile, and muttered, "Bitch!" The music began.

José sang, threw the ring after a momentary fake toward the man who had licked his finger earlier, and defiantly rejected Don José. Don José pulled out the knife, and with a flourish, stabbed Carmen. José fell into the knife, throwing his arms around his recently cast coactor, and gave a delighted squeal. Quickly pulling himself together and leaning back, he corrected himself in a tone of mock agony, "I mean, oooooh!" Again, José staggered around the stage, dragging Carmen's death out to ridiculous lengths. At one point he nudged Don José aside and said, "Step aside, bitch, this is my big scene."

When he finally grabbed Don José's hand and sank to the stage floor in death, the audience again erupted into wild applause. José stood, took the hand of his new coplayer, and led him in an elaborate series of bows and blown kisses.

As the audience settled down and José patted the other player's butt off the stage, a sense of anticipation overtook the audience. Those who had followed José's career, some since the days of the Black Cat Cafe, knew what was to come next.

"Okay, everybody stand up," José instructed. All attention went to José, and the room grew quiet. "Everybody hold hands. That's not his hand, honey. We don't want any accidents here.

"Now I want you all to pretend we're back in the old days. There across the way is the paddy wagon with all those queens arrested for licking a lollipop in the park or God knows what. There they all are, smiling and waving at us, the silly cunts! We know we have to support them, give them courage, show them that we stand behind them, or somewhere. I shout to them, 'That's all right, girls! You plead not guilty! Just swallow the evidence, and plead not guilty! Ask for a trial by jury!' Then I'd step back into the Black Cat, and we'd all hold hands and sing."

Suddenly serious, José led his listeners with a voice clear but husky with emotion in the song that became his signature in the early days. To the tune of "God Save the Queen"/"My Country 'Tis of Thee," he sang:

God save us nelly queens
God save us nelly queens
God save us queens
From every mountainside
Long may we live and die
God save us nelly queens
God save us queens.

I glanced briefly around the room as we sang, and over to my right was a stooped and wrinkled old man who looked to be well into his nineties. He had been unable to stand for the song, but from his chair he held tightly to hands on either side of him and sang loudly, if not altogether in tune, in a tremulous voice. Tears streamed down his cheeks. I saw José smile briefly at him. The man's eyes brightened, and he sang with even greater gusto.

After the song trailed off, José looked out at the crowd with unabashed affection and said, "Never let anyone make you a second-class citizen because you are gay. You are as good as anyone else, and never let anyone say otherwise. You are a free citizen and have the same rights as anyone. When you go out into the world, keep your weenies tucked and your head held high!"

There was a pause before the ring of applause, more intense this time, and less punctuated with laughter and words. Curious, I stepped over to the old man to ask about his connection to José.

"I was on shore leave with the Navy the first time I heard José. The Navy would publish a list of the bars that were forbidden and why. That's how I found the Black Cat and José." Looking at me through his tears, the old man continued, "It was the early fifties. José was the first person to ever tell me that I was okay, that I wasn't a second-class citizen. I've tried to come watch José whenever I can ever since."

He turned his gaze back to the stage where José was playfully accepting congratulations, hugs, and kisses. The old man lapsed into his own reverie. I left him alone.

Senator Emperor

José is always disarmingly gracious to his guests. When I showed up to interview him one evening at his apartment on Bush Street, an old friend was there. Naturally, José began to talk of him as if he were the most important dignitary in the world and should be included in "the book."

"Through the development of the Court System, as I have become more prominent in the gay community, I have people that phone me and want to meet with me because they're either going to write a story or they're going to start some project and they need my help or they want to know if I know someone who can help them. Such was the case with a young man who was gay and had political ambitions, a very, very smart looking, nice, little Italian boy.

"Jim Mancha came to me because, as I say, he had political ambitions, and because I was the first openly gay person to ever run for office, he felt that I could help him. He was really very charming. However, he played very hard to get. I was able to embarrass him, and make him laugh and get him all rattled up. Since then we have become very good friends.

"So he came, and we talked. I told him that the Coronation was coming up and I thought he should present himself there to the gay community. He was running for the U.S. Senate as an Independent. Well, my dear, we had never had anybody for the Senate yet. And Barney, up in the New England states, had not come out and said he was a fruit yet. So this was unique.

"At the Coronation, I had him speak at the morning breakfast. That opened up some doors for him. People left their names and offered support. I'll open the door, but you have to put your foot in and push it open. It's up to you. God helps those who help themselves.

"So he ran for senator on the third ticket. Needless to say, he's still running.

"He actually did quite well. He made quite an impression. He gathered twenty percent of the vote.

"The next thing I understand, he's running for Emperor of Los Angeles. I thought, 'My God! His political ambitions are out the window, and now he's going to be a gay emperor!' He ran and he won, and so naturally he became one of my sons. Needless to say, Los Angeles is not one of the smoothest of kingdoms to run. He was not happy with the conflicts. He was working for a Latin clinic that catered to children and poor families, and the Court was supposed to help by raising some money. It was all very confusing, a regular Mexican melodrama. Consequently, he resigned as Emperor of Los Angeles. He wanted to keep the title, so he went over to Hollywood and, lo and behold, became the Emperor of Hollywood. That's a step up from senator, I'd say.

"I went down soon after for a garden party he was having. It was going to be a very New-York-who's-who-breakfast-at-Tiffany's kind of thing. He had a little tent put up—very, very *elegawnt*. He had a string quartet to play music.

"But staying at his place was a horse of a different color. I arrived on one of those hot, hot days they have down there, with all my baggage. He showed me where I was going to sleep; it was on a bed that was one foot off the ground. The mattress was I don't know what! I suffer from asthma, and I need to be elevated. I couldn't get my legs to unbend when I got out of bed. I thought it was just hysterical. He's used to living by himself. Cook a dinner, set the table, have everyone sit down to eat; that's not the way it's done in his house. He makes dinner, serves himself. You want dinner, there it is. If you don't have a dish, take one out of the sink, wash it, and put your food on it. I never in my life! I was a guest, and I had to wait on myself. It was not to be believed. It was just not to be believed. He made himself comfortable. When it was time for him to go to bed, it was, 'Good night!' And there I am standing with my finger up my twat wondering what I'm going to do next. Then the dog barked and scared the shit out of me.

"I exaggerate, naturally, but I had a fabulous time there. We grew very close. We decided to meet in New York when we went back for the big Stonewall 25 celebration where I was honored. We went all over New York together. He took me by his father's restaurant in the old part of New York. You almost imagine yourself being a part of Fanny Brice's story. Papa runs the restaurant himself. Papa does not approve of the son being a queen. So it is not mentioned; however

Papa knows it. Papa receives the friends at a polite distance. I also met the mother. They are divorced. She's a very modern woman. Lesbian in tendencies and very charming. We went to the Castillo Center and saw *The Many Emotions of Lenin.* Absolutely fantastic. We saw a short Latin-themed play too: *The Loves of Pancho Villa,* or *He Made Love to a Horse,* or something. Small little theater, but very good. His mother and I had a lot in common.

"I went back to New York later for the New York Coronation. It was also his birthday, and he wanted me to come to his birthday party. He says, 'It's going to be at my father's restaurant.'

"I said, 'Fine.'

"Now, he's never told me not to wear earrings or anything. It was so hot in New York that day, I wore a shirt and tie and slacks. Respectable attire. Papa cooked us a fabulous meal. I met the family, his sister, her children, the aunts. There was one aunt who didn't know how to take me. There was another aunt that I think had visited Greenwich Village more than once. We got along very well.

"One cousin had a boy there who was about eleven years old. Leslie. He was very curious. That one didn't want to go out and play. He wanted to hear everything I was saying. I was telling stories of Finocchio's and some of the things that happened to me on the stage. The aunt that I said was very partial to me, that was her grandson. Then there was the other aunt that sat there, and I thought she was going to explode. She really didn't like me, and she didn't know what the hell was going on. I sensed this, and I thought, 'Well, I've started, I've got to finish.' I told my little stories about how my corset stays were pinching me—I mean, I had a three-ring show.

"After we left, I asked Jim how they had reacted to me. He said, 'My one aunt, she's never been exposed to anything like that. I can't believe you sat in there and told my family drag queen stories. But my cousin really liked you, and my nephew just couldn't get enough.'

"It was a very pleasant dinner. I understand that Papa is going to sell the place and retire. The one sister is going to move away. And my friend Jim is now the Secretary General of the new Patriot Party. He introduced me to Lenora Fulani, a brilliant woman. I appeared with her on a talk show in New York. I wish them well.

"Meanwhile, back on the ranch: I decided in the Court System to take the bull by the horns. As the founder and Grandmamère, I have named people who will succeed me in the system, Heirs Apparent in various regions of the Court System. Now, by definition that doesn't mean shit. The first Heir Apparent was Nicole Murray of San Diego. Jim more or less convinced me that he should be an Heir Apparent down in southern California. They are my eyes and ears outside of the San Francisco area.

"Now Jim is here on a visit as I tell my story, and I thought it would be nice to include him. He had a love when I first met him. It was supposed to last forever and ever. It didn't. Now he's met a man, Tim in New York, and their love is supposed to last forever and ever. I was introduced to Tim, a charming man. He flies out here to Los Angeles, and Mancha flies back to New York. We don't know where the money is coming from, probably being embezzled from the children's clinic."

At this point, Jim jokingly began to lament that José's book would be the end of his career, and that he'd have to sue for libel. José responded, "I want to put in there that he wants to sue me for libel and that you can't sue for libel when it's the truth.

"Tim is thinking of moving out to California. I don't know. We've marked the calendar as to when they met, and we'll see how long this romance stays together. There are romances that do live beyond a year. Of course, with Mr. Mancha, it is not always easy to weather a year.

"There is a Coronation coming up in West Hollywood which Mr. Mancha will host. That is a very thriving kingdom. They've raised a lot of money for charities, for AIDS organizations, children's groups. They've helped a lot of people in that area. So that's it."

Cinderella Did Drag

It was RuPaul, a cultural heiress of José's, who said, "We are all born naked. The rest is drag." Everybody dresses to create an image, and that is what drag is all about. Royal drag, girl drag, boy drag, disco drag, leather drag, yuppie drag, cowboy drag, biker drag, gender-fuck drag, fifties drag: it's about painting a picture with yourself as the canvas. It just happens that some people elevate drag to a level beyond mere image, to a level akin to other arts. And like all good art, it tweaks at society's comfortable assumptions and conventions. In this case, it blatantly but affectionately bends the rigid gender roles that burden far too many of us. No one does this better than the queens and dykes of the Imperial Court System. The living art they create moves beyond dressing up. Theirs is an illusion of splendor that borders on the magical.

When José began the Court System, he wrote away to Washington, DC, for the requisite paperwork for obtaining nonprofit status. The instructions included the usual requirements for such organizations: a board of directors, a slate of officers, a promise to keep things nonpolitical. The hitch for José, however, was the need to elect a president and vice president and the other usual officers. José does not do usual. And an annual installation of officers sounded downright dull.

Not one to be deterred by official details and expectations, José decided to elect each year not a new president, but a new empress. Eventually the slate of "officers" included an emperor, dukes, duchesses, and assorted czars, czarinas, jesters, and keeper of this and that (as José would say). There was to be no stuffy installation of officers each year. José's organization would hold an annual Coronation. The new Royal Court would automatically become family and heirs to Her Royal Majesty, Empress One of San Francisco, José I, the Widow Norton. José jokes each year about the birth pains while delivering her new children. "Some of these queens are not small!"

A former partner of mine had been involved in the Sacramento Court for a time, the Court of the Great Northwest Imperial Empire, so I had attended two coronations before I even knew who José was. I was only a year out of the closet and still looking for my Marlboro Man when I fell in love with a little queen and ended up escorting her to the royal event. Go figure!

By the time I received my first invitation to the Coronation in San Francisco, I had "gotten over myself," the queen's phrase for letting go of insecure judgments of other people's differences, and through an open-minded study of gay history, had learned to admire and appreciate the audacity of the drag queens. I felt genuine excitement about attending the Coronation at the mother court for the whole international system. Not only was I to attend, but I would escort the Dowager Empress herself, which is an ego-boosting privilege until you find yourself migrating unwillingly to the back of a throng that is working its way toward greeting the Widow. Then it becomes an ego-testing experience. Not that I took any of it personally, mind you. But I digress. But while I am digressing, let me mention that I tried drag once. Aside from having shoulders that made Joan Crawford's look akin to Twiggy's, I ended up looking like my mother: 'nuff said—end of Michael's drag career. Okay, end of digression.

I picked José up from his job at the reprographics shop at two in the afternoon, and followed his directions for the quickest route to his place on Bush Street. As we turned off of Leavenworth onto Bush, we asked Joshua to find us a parking place as we always do. Friends I tell this to are skeptical, but after two-plus years, I have become a believer. We found a spot two cars away from José's front door. Whenever José or my son Mack is in the car, we find a parking place within the block. When I am alone, I usually have to park two to four blocks away. Very cute, Joshua.

Waiting for us in José's apartment was Empress Coco LaChine, a past empress of the Imperial Court of New York, along with a good friend, Bopsie. They were chattering excitedly about their day of shopping at one of San Francisco's most exclusive dress design shops. I remember thinking that they both must have very good day jobs.

Watching Coco and José transform from men into female royalty for the night's festivities was like watching a tornado strike a makeup and fabric store. With a jewelry shop next door.

"This one or this one?"

"Should I use the bustle?"

"Oh, no dear, not with that color."

"I love the thing you do with shadow. You'll have to show me sometime."

"Well, it's not Bob Mackie."

"Where is my purse?"

"Too much?"

"Can you zip me, dear?"

"Never too much!"

"The gold one, I think."

"Perfect with that new wig!"

As a man, Coco is attractive. As a woman, she is almost frighteningly beautiful. Her Asian features take on a regal power and a deep allure. To see Coco in full dress is to understand the artistry of drag. Braids in her deep brown wig curl and loop around each other, almost, but not quite, stealing the focus from her tall, shimmering tiara. José, in contrast, becomes the mother you always wanted: warm but strong, funny yet nurturing, clever but kind. And with great hair.

José's gown for the evening was Victorian in style, as befits the Widow Norton. The material was a rich red and gold velvet. A built-in bustle was topped by a red bow with trailing ribbons. There was a short train. A length of red velvet swept across the front of the dress like bunting. Bunting indeed!

As we cinched José in, he chuckled and told the story of the gown. While his mother was in Panama, the canal opened. All of the members of the Kopp family for which she worked participated in the Panama Exposition to some degree. Included in the celebration was a beauty pageant. One of the Kopp daughters won runner-up for the title of Panama Canal Princess. Decorating the staging area were beautifully rich waves of gold and red velvet bunting. When the celebration ended, José's mother, never one to let nice things go to waste, took down the bunting, washed it, and saved it. When she died, José inherited the material. This year, a friend, Lee Raymond, designed and assembled the gown. Not only did he create a fabulous dress, he understood the fun of its origins: thus the bunting front and the sleeves.

Once he was securely in the gown, José reached over and lifted up one of the billowy pumpkin sleeves to reveal the seamed edge wrapped snugly around his upper arm. It was made of plain white canvas folded around the edge of the material into a strip about half an inch wide. Stamped on the strip in black letters were the words, "U.S. Air Corps. Rose A. Miller." They reminded me of the inventory lettering on the green canvas tents we used to check out of Special Services when my father was in the army. He lifted the other sleeve to reveal, "KLPM Set 3 SMGM Sept 1914."

"The seams of the bunting," José said with a smile.

José has a talent for juxtaposing things that other people think ought not to be juxtaposed. He is like a one-man wrecking crew for conventions. Never tell José what he can't do.

At the appointed time, a sleek, black limousine awaited us out front, provided by T. S., a wealthy businessman and club owner from Sacramento who is a strong supporter of the Court System and of the gay community. Nothing less for the Dowager Empress would do.

By the time we arrived at the San Francisco Gift Center Pavilion, the glass entrance was already reflecting a thousand jewels and sequins. Those lingering out front turned to watch Her Imperial Majesty Empress One, José, the Widow Norton arrive on my arm. Soft greetings to "Mamá" replaced previous conversation. The crowd parted, and we entered.

We checked in at the reservations desk and found our table. The softly lit hall was designed in a contemporary industrial style, with green fence-like metal railings and poles, and an abundance of glass panels. The walls, cut and sliced with overhangs, balconies, and alcoves, were painted a light beige. The various levels of the main floor and the four balconies on one side gave the place a compelling but pleasing asymmetry. The lighting was patchwork and mostly indirect, soft white with occasional green, blue, or amber. The sides of the stage were bordered with curved walls of thick glass blocks that hid the backstage entrances. Round, linen-draped tables crowded together on the main floor. The long, smooth bar bordered one wall of the entry hall between the front doors and the main room.

José did not linger at our table once we located it. She set down her purse, greeted the old friends who were to share our round space, and then walked up the few steps to a wide walkway near the end of the bar and began greeting her subjects and children. Most of the gathering royalty came to pay their respects to Mamá.

"Mamá, how are you?" A kiss on the extended hand of the Empress.

"Ah, Mamá, you look divine!" A wide, gentle hug that does not muss wig or veils.

"Hello, Mamá." A sideways air kiss in respect for the carefully applied makeup.

The polite deference was sometimes answered in kind and sometimes peppered with teasing innuendo or campy repartee. Occasionally the Grand Empress's calm would be broken by a high squeal of delight at the sight of an old friend whom she had not seen for months or years. "Ohhhhh, my Dear!"

The milling about of royalty could have rivaled visually any grand ball at the palace in czarist Russia. Finally the music began and the fantasy crowd settled into its seats for the ceremony. The Imperial Color Guard presented the flags of Canada, Mexico, and the United States. Representatives of each country sang the national anthems, with the exception of Mexico because José was out of voice, a fact that foreshadowed the later events of the evening. The Reverend Donald Fox of the Night Ministry of San Francisco gave the invocation. Then began the introductions of the Imperial Family of San Francisco and the visiting royalty of courts from across the United States and Canada. As the emcees chanted the names and the royalty began parading up the ramp, I began to feel as if I were caught up in some fabulous illusion.

Sweeping sequined gowns brushed across the shiny floor. Huge jewels glittered against necks and ears and wrists and bosoms. Rhinestone tiaras shot out knifelike white lightning flashes from a hundred meticulously coifed wigs. Bracelets clicked and capes swished. (As did some of those who wore them.) Trains, bustles, bows, and inflated sleeves seemed designed to brush crowds of commoners aside. Seeming breasts rose up like mirages from shaved male chests and heaved their necklaces, brooches, and pendants into shimmering shards of multicolored light. Boas of every color puffed around the chimeras of femininity.

"Her Most Imperial Highness, Empress One of San Francisco, José, the Widow Norton, Founder of the Imperial Court!"

"Alexis de Moné, the Aurora Borealis Empress Twenty, Absolute Empress for Equality, Colorado Springs, Colorado!"

"His Most Imperial Majesty, Emperor Twenty-five After Norton, Steve Valone of San Francisco!"

"Her Most Imperial Majesty, Empress Thirty-one Cockatielia of San Francisco!"

"Absolute Empress Twenty-nine, Anita Martini of San Francisco!"

The outrageous names. The jewels. The music. The hair braided, curled, teased, combed, tied, clipped, and ribboned bigger than any French Court fantasy. Delight. Absolute delight. Formal tuxedoes with blue, green, black, and red bow ties and cummerbunds mingled with sequined coats, leather jackets, colored metallic tunics, and long-tailed period cutaways. Top hats and leather biker caps and feathered caps and Easter-like bonnets shared the view-blocking duties.

"Oh, my dear, did you see her gown?"

"Darling, how do you stay so divinely thin? Love you. Mean it!"

"Tootles, sweety! My machine will contact your machine. Lunch, okay?"

"Her Most Imperial Majesty, Empress Seven of New York, Coco LaChine, the Celestial Dragon Empress of New York, Third Heir Apparent to the Widow Norton, Her Majesty Empress José One!"

Walking constellations on the runway. Smiles. Prom queen waves. Applause. Hurrahs. Music swelling.

"Empress Seven, Donna Do You Wanna of the Imperial Court of Calgary!"

Flowers in hair. Flowers on lapels. Flowers on wrists. Flowers behind ears.

"The Celtic Hope Emperor, Brian K. Stoner!"

"The Crystal Vision Empress Aramis, of the Palace of Miracles and Visions, the Imperial Court of Iowa!"

Eyelashes curling up and out. Makeup out of fantasy and glamour out of dreams.

"Doctor Jorge Alvarez Michel of the Kingdom of Tijuana!"

"Nicole the Great of San Diego, Heir Apparent One to Her Royal Majesty Empress José Norton One!"

Skirts draped over petticoats and hoops. Faux furs and spandex. Royal sashes dappled with shimmering jeweled pins and insignias, like military insignias crystallized.

"Her Most Serene Imperial Majesty Judy Jive, The Silver Jubilee Empress Twenty-five of the Mother Court of Canada, Vancouver, British Columbia!"

Dream weavers in drag.

"Her Royal Majesty Richelle Von Wah, Rhinestone Empress Twelve of Vancouver, British Columbia!"

Grace walking above the crowd. Gliding in the spotlight. Visions out of night dreams floating past eyes fully awake but enchanted all the same.

"His Most Royal Majesty Peter Christie, Emperor Twenty of the Royal Court of the Great Salt Lake Empire, the Double Diamond Stud Emperor, Heir Apparent Sixteen!"

Short-haired women in impeccably tailored suits. Bowler hats and top hats. Suspenders. Shiny leather boots. Bow ties, long ties, neck scarves.

"His Most Royal Imperial Serene Majesty Emperor the Golden Phoenix of the Dogwood Empire, House of Style of the Imperial Sovereign Silver Jubilee Court!"

White blousy shirts with puffy sleeves or no sleeves. Black trousers tightly hugging tight rounded bottoms. Neatly trimmed mustaches, beards, goatees. Vests. The royalty, the crowd swirled into one sweet hallucination.

"Emperor Jim Mangia, Emperor for Life of Hollywood, Imperial Court of Los Angeles and Hollywood, and Heir Apparent Four!"

Jeweled scepters. Laughter.

"Mama Karen De Vander Vogue, Emperor Fifteen and Empress Twenty-five and a Half of Vancouver, British Columbia, Heir Apparent Eighteen to Empress One José Sarria, Founder of the Imperial Court System!"

"Princess of Imperial Harmony Ginny Knuth!"

"Prince of the Butterfly and Galactica, Fritz Hall!"

"Lady-in-Waiting to Her Imperial Majesty Empress One José, the Widow Sarria-Norton, Mrs. Anna Kaya Nikolayevna Romanova Tchaikovsky Anderson Manahan, Princess to the Jade Dragon Empress of Russia, Shelby!"

"Gary Haubold, Prince to the Owl Empress Frieda!"

"Jerry Coletti, Emperor Seventeen After Norton, the Leather Lion Emperor!"

Marquesses, Countesses, Dukes, Duchesses, Archdukes, Knights and Dames to the Order of the Garter, Crown Princes and Princesses, Czars, Czarinas, Imperial Viscountesses, the Lord High Chancellor, the Lord High Executioner. Ducal Courts and Empires. Leather chaps. High heels. Tailed coats as effulgent as the gowns they escorted. A kilt. A white-faced Sister of Perpetual Indulgence, those omnipresent guardians of the gay soul. Fantasy. Dream. Illusion more real than the fantasies we call life.

Amber lights.

Blue shadows.

Rampant masculinity and extravagant femininity divorced from gender. Men, women soaring into fancy. Dreams. Fantasy. Romance. Castles in the heart. Locked out from so many myths, these are the rainbow chasers who weave their own.

*   *   *

I awoke from my own dream when I saw that José, José the man and my friend, was becoming ill. I tended to him as the best I could. Cleaned up. Water. Napkins. They asked for a doctor. He ordered club soda and bitters. His handsome young lover had a Jewish mother who was proud he married a doctor. José's nausea improved only a little. We went out for air. José wanted to stay. He was embarrassed. I wasn't. Just concerned. The doctor gave instructions for treatment at home. The limousine pulled up, ordered by old friend Bob Golovich. We somberly went home to his apartment, the Empress and I. I walked to the store down the block for medicine. José slept sitting up in the chair next to the hide-a-bed I was on. A little fear. Reality is not all it's cracked up to be. Goodnight for now, Camelot. The Empress will be back in the morning, be assured.

To Oz?

During one of the semesters I taught at a Sacramento community college while I was researching and interviewing for this book, I was asked, out of the blue and out of a previously silent classroom, by a young woman in the first row, "So, Mr. Gorman! What is it about gay men and *The Wizard of Oz?*" Thirty or so pairs of eyes focused on me. It seemed lots of inquiring minds had the same question, but without the chutzpah to ask insistently during a quiet moment in English 1A. Never a teacher to discourage genuine curiosity, I searched my gray cells for record of a study on the subject. It was an unsuccessful split-second search. I fell back on my natural insight, born of years of watching *The Wizard of Oz* since its first showing on television, and even more years of humming "Somewhere Over the Rainbow" whenever things got tough.

I answered, "That's easy. Most of us little gay boys felt as if we were growing up in black-and-white Kansas, when what we really wanted was to live in that Technicolor place where people wear funny hats and pink taffeta and burst into song and dance whenever they wanted without anyone thinking it was weird or sissy."

"That makes sense," she replied with a smile. "My friend Chad couldn't answer that. I'll tell him what you said."

The class went casually back to work in their response groups for the Process Analysis essay.

(To those GUPPIE—gay urban professional—queens who object to being so stereotyped, I challenge you to listen at your next party celebrating your new redwood deck or new hot tub or new accountant or whatever, and count the number of references to Oz in the conversations. And if you don't then chill about it, I say that you're just still angry that they dropped a house on your sister! And the next party of yours I attend, I will be sure to keep my ruby slippers handy for a quick exit.)

Speaking, or rather writing, of exits, let it not be said that José Sarria does not have his index finger on the wrist pulse of the gay world, especially if the pulse rates have anything to do with anything outrageous or flamboyant. And he can be counted on to be less than subtle in his expressions of the knowledge. Such was the case when the Dowager Empress and Grandmamère decided to leave Baghdad by the Bay to move in with Pierre in Phoenix.

José was not about to leave his beloved city by quietly packing his things and driving up the South 101 onramp. There are always production values to consider. It took some time and some gentle persuasion to get the permits for the use of the City Hall steps and for the flight of a hot air balloon over the city, but, undaunted as usual, José managed. He, apparently, was less flustered by the process than the city officials. The mayor at the time jokingly threatened to station himself at the window of his City Hall office with a gun and take shots at the balloon.

The crowd that gathered on the steps of City Hall observed an eclectic mixture of characters ready to honor the departing Widow Norton. There was Aunty Em. There were emperors. There was Dorothy. There was Emperor Joshua Norton I. There was his widow. There were, of course, the Scarecrow, the Cowardly Lion, and the Tin Man. There was San Francisco Board of Supervisors President John Molinari, and City Attorney Louise Renne. There was Glenda the Good Witch, the Wicked Witch of the West, and an array of Munchkins from Alameda County. Towering over all of them was a huge, brightly colored hot air balloon similar to the one that carried the Wizard of Oz into the Emerald City and then back out again. The Wizard stood ready to reprise his exit.

The San Francisco Gay Freedom Day Marching Band and Twirling Corps struck up a rousing tune, and the festivities began. José welcomed the crowd. Supervisor Molinari read a decree from the City and County of San Francisco. City Swing offered its music, and a soloist sang. The characters on the stage performed a rollicking comedy with song and dance that mixed the legend of the first imperial couple with the legend of Oz. Finally, another woman sang what has become the anthem of the gay community, "Somewhere Over the Rainbow." Unable to resist, the crowd joined in.

What happened next has itself become a matter of urban legend. Ask some who know the truth absolutely, and they will tell you this: the Empress José I, the Widow Norton, camping lines of Dorothy's from the end of *The Wizard of Oz* and dressed in full Victorian mourning drag, climbed aboard the gondola of the balloon with the Wizard, waved a royal goodbye, blew royal kisses, and gradually rose into the blue sky over San Francisco as the Munchkins chanted a high-pitched "Bye! Bye! Bye! Bye!" The crowd waved until their arms hurt and watched until the balloon disappeared past the Golden Gate Bridge and into the green hills of Marin County.

In the other version, the San Francisco weather, fickle as a drag queen in diva mode, turned cold and windy at the last minute. Conditions prevented the safe flight of the balloon. Like Dorothy, the Widow missed her ride. She, of course, worked the unexpected circumstances into her routine, waved a royal wave, blew royal kisses, and made her way toward the South 101 onramp while the Munchkins helped hold the balloon as it deflated.

Believe what you will. This is, after all, the life of the Empress.

Get Me to the Church in Drag

When the Court System first began, José had a personal hand in most of its events. As the organization grew and spread across the country, and even over the borders into Canada, José's influence became more tangential. Yet because he established a strong foundation at the Court's inception, he is generally pleased by what he hears of the various courts across the land. Because he cannot possibly travel to every court in the system, he loves hearing reports about the activities of his far-flung "children," as he calls them. Sometimes he tells of their exploits with so much enthusiasm it would be easy for the listener to erroneously assume that he had been there.

"The influence of the Court has shown up in the most unexpected places. I love the story of a Lutheran church in Rhode Island. The Rhode Island Court had helped this small church with fundraisers, and they had also been giving regularly to this community church as a Court. That was their project, to help this church, this community.

"The founder of the Rhode Island Court, Ralph Martino, got a phone call from the minister who said, 'We wish to thank you for helping us as you have. We want you to come all dressed and participate in a celebration. It's our way of saying thank you.'

"Ralph got on the phone. 'Come on, girls! We've gotta go to this thing for the ones we've been helping.'

"But they said, 'Oh, I can't go,' or oh, this and the other. Making excuses.

"And Ralph says, 'You *gotta* go! They want us to go. We have to wear all our paraphernalia. The cars leave at such and such a time.'

"They had a good showing, thank God. Those who did not go felt very, very bad. So they all got in their cars, and off they went with tiaras and capes, driving through hill and country vale.

"They arrived at the church to be greeted and were told to wait a minute, that there was to be a procession that they had to be in. The church was packed. The organ was playing. The church leaders were all lining up and getting their robes on. Then the procession began with the head pastor and the incense and altar boys, and the choir. Then in came the founder of the Court with feathers in his crown, and the Empress, and the Grand Duchess, and the Viscountess, and the other Empress, and the other Emperor, and the Lord Duke of this, and the Lord Duke of that. They were all walking regally in their capes and their gowns; it was a Cecil B. DeMille Hollywood production.

"They all finally sat down when they were asked to sit down, and the service began. They had their best robes and their best candles. It was very, very good, very majestic. They asked for all the queens of the Court to come up, and they were all blessed. They blessed their crowns and they blessed their robes. They blessed them, that God would give them long life. It was very emotional.

"This is what I have intended for the Court to do, to bridge differences.

"At the end of the service, they thought that was it, but there was a luncheon downstairs. There they were, all corseted up, so they could hardly eat, but they were stuffing themselves anyway. Everybody was commenting on how beautiful the gowns were. They had a beautiful Sunday!

"While they were in Rhode Island, they were also able to break the social barrier in Newport at a big social fundraiser. I think it was called 'The Vanderbilt Fund Raiser.' It was arranged through Ralph, who was an interior decorator. This one woman, a client, said, 'We would like to have some entertainment. Couldn't you please come out and do something? We'll pay you.'

"Well, what queen wouldn't want to walk down the marble staircase in the Vanderbilt mansion in Newport!? My dear, we had about twelve of them appear! They did their numbers and then got paid. They've gone back two times already. They are now known for their entertainment. They raise money by being paid for entertaining at parties and events in the straight community. They've worked with famous stars. Bridging the differences. This is the Court of Rhode Island; it's one of my favorite Courts."

The Great Idaho-Utah War

Although José is an entertainer always, and although he loves to tease and make people laugh, he is very clear about what he thinks is right and wrong and what should or should not be done within the Imperial Court System. As a leader he is both charming and effective because he is able to combine his keen sense of values with his humor. He prefers to disarm conflict with laughter, and he sweetens his admonishments with irony and camp. Many times, though, he does not even need to lecture. His actions speak quite clearly enough.

"A group of us from San Francisco was in Boise, Idaho for the Coronation of their new emperor and empress one year in the early 1980s. After we arrived, we heard about a conflict in the local Court System. It seems that Pocatello, Idaho wanted to form a Barony. But because Pocatello was so close to Utah, the Utah Court claimed its territory for themselves, whereas Boise said, 'No, it belongs to us.' And so there was this fight going on, basically between the Court systems of Utah and Idaho.

"I did not stick my nose into it at first, because I had never done that. They asked me though, 'José, what are we going to do?'

"And I answered, 'Utah has no business coming in and dictating in Idaho, and Idaho does not have any business going into Utah. Pocatello belongs to Idaho, and that's the end of it.'

"I made this decree, and that was going to be the final word on it.

"The Coronation was an elaborate affair, as usual, and the new empress and emperor for that year sat on beautiful, large thrones after they were crowned. The thrones were actually movie props. They were borrowed through a queen who worked for a film company. The Court told him they needed thrones for the Coronation. At the time, this company was filming a picture there, in which these thrones were being used.

"He told the Court, 'Well, as long as nothing happens to them, you can borrow the thrones over the weekend, but I've got to have them back on Monday for the picture.'

"So the chairs were set up at the Coronation, and on the day of the ceremony everything looked great. It got underway smoothly.

"Without telling anyone, I had made some arrangements myself for the ceremony. During the Coronation, I had a young man come running in and interrupting with an urgent news bulletin from the battle raging at the Snake River. Nobody knew I was going to arrange this little charade, so the runner took everybody by surprise. They started whispering, wondering what the hell the runner was talking about. The runner announced that there was a big battle raging between the Utahans and the Idahoans over Pocatello. This was the first big battle, he explained. The opposing sides had met on the Snake River and were fighting. The bulletin was from the commanding general of the Idaho empire's armed forces.

"People started to get it and laughed. After the runner left, the Coronation got underway again. Half an hour went by, and pretty soon here comes the man running in with another news bulletin from the commanding general. I threw in all kinds of crazy crap, whatever I could think of.

" 'It seems that the turn of the tide and the direction of the winds and moon's position are influencing the battle, and the tide is turning. Idaho's forces are suffering great losses, and there are many handsome men in need of good nursing!'

"Again the runner left and the ceremonies again got underway. By this time people were beginning to look for the updates on the imaginary battle. When the third message came, the Utahans were on the run; the Idahoans were chasing them out, vowing that it would be the last time they would ever invade the land and try to steal the property of the Imperial Court of Idaho. Cheers greeted the news.

"Well, during all this commotion that I caused at the Coronation, the new empress, a heavyset girl, backed up to sit on her throne, and the throne started to fall off of the platform. Trying to catch her balance, she grabbed the other throne. Down went empress and her throne and the emperor's throne.

"I stood and began screaming, 'Assassination! Someone has attempted to assassinate the Empress!'

"The place was in total turmoil. It was a big mess. People weren't sure whether to rush to help or laugh. Now, the worst part was that the thrones were broken, and the queen who lent them to the Court had to return them to the set for the picture to continue. Well, my dear, the repair of the chairs was going to cost in the neighborhood of five or six hundred dollars!

"I said, 'There must be some queen who can glue those sons of bitches together without having it cost that kind of money.' But that wasn't the bad part of it. Those chairs were being used in the scenes that were then being filmed, and for every day that that film was not filmed, it cost thirty thousand dollars. A day. So a delay cost quite a bit of money.

"We did get the chairs repaired and back in a week, but the picture was held up. It ran way over cost. It was such a typical deal between queens! Go ahead and take it, but I absolutely have to have it back right away. How many times does a queen take something out of the store without the boss's permission, and prays that it's going to come back, and something happens? It doesn't come back, and the boss finds out.

"I made quite a big interruption in the Idaho Coronation, but, except for the broken chairs, it was fun, and the message got out. That solved the conflict over Pocatello."

Mr. DeMille?

My very first exposure to José was on television, watching the documentary *Before Stonewall* on Channel 6, Sacramento's PBS station. I had not been out of the closet for very long, and I knew very little about gay and lesbian history. I watched with fascination a man from my parent's generation who had been out of the closet before I was born. That documentary sparked my interest in gay history and my desire to discover a heritage I never knew I had. What was for José a retrospective of his life, for me was a beginning.

"I was called by Robert Rosenberg, the codirector and coproducer of the documentary film *Before Stonewall*. He contacted me because he wanted to do a history. I've always been contacted about these things; I've never had to push to get into the media. I wasn't supposed to be as big a part of the film as I was. I ended up, I think, a very big part of it. I said yes because I've always believed that was important—preserving our history—because, you know, everybody thinks it all came down from the mountaintop on tablets. Nobody ever knows the real story of things, how they came to be.

"We filmed. We got people from the old days at the Black Cat together at the Valencia Rose. And in that group of people, 75 percent were gay. It was a Black Cat reunion: the pianist, Hazel; the man who sang with me, Eddie Paulson; Henry Vondekoff; Sol Stoumen; Phyllis Schuenberger; and her husband. And those people were the real people of the Black Cat.

"So we got together and had a fabulous time. We talked about the early days while the camera recorded us. We made the film, and later he sold it to PBS.

"People want to use me for projects once they find out what a part of the gay community I am, that I am a familiar face. It's like this Halloween [1996]: the picture of me that became the posters and billboards for the city's big Halloween street party. I was contacted by them because they knew I would be good publicity. I said yes.

"Another time I was contacted for a movie was at the big twenty-fifth anniversary celebration of the Stonewall Riots in New York. I was one of the twenty-five early activists to be honored on the stage at Stonewall 25. I remember you almost gave me a heart attack when you appeared on the media platform right at our feet."

I had agreed at the last minute to travel to New York to cover the international event for *The Latest Issue*, Sacramento's gay newspaper. The publisher had intended to go but was thwarted by circumstances. I did not have time to tell José I would be there before he left, so when he saw me at his feet on the media platform a few feet below the downstage edge of the stage, he was more than a little surprised.

"When you hissed my name I thought I was losing it."

I noticed his surprise only because I was close and I had grown familiar with his mannerisms. A slight muscle jerk and two raised eyebrows and a quick eyes-only glance around were the only evidence that he was startled. Always the stage veteran, he quickly recovered and stayed in character as the Widow Norton with a dignified smile in my direction when he finally noticed me—with some relief.

"That honor was arranged primarily through Nicole Murray, one of the three cochairs of Stonewall 25. The organizers figured that twenty-five people should be honored. The early activists.

"I do not approve of the way the committee operated everything. There was a lot of controversy. There were a lot of typical queens getting a soft job and living high on the hog for a couple of years, because that Stonewall 25 took a couple of years to plan. I find that very, very mean. And they were even talking about not inviting the drag queens involved because people up to that time, and even up to today, didn't want to give the drag queens any credit."

There was considerable argument during the planning for Stonewall 25 about the participation of drag queens. There were those who claimed that drag queens are bad for the public image of the gay community and should not be allowed to officially participate. After all, a million people from all over the world were expected to show up for Stonewall 25, and the event would make the news internationally. Others just wanted the drag queens kept in a low-profile position. The irony of this antidrag prejudice is that the Stonewall Riots were initiated by drag queens who had been harassed by police one too many times.

It was June 28, 1969, the day after the funeral of Judy Garland, a woman deeply admired by most gay men. Her theme song, "Somewhere Over the Rainbow" had become the unofficial anthem of the gay community. She had for years been a favorite subject for impersonation by the queens. The drag queens at the Stonewall Inn in New York's Greenwich Village were already depressed that evening. The New York Police Department chose that night to carry out one of its routine gay bar raids, but when the police entered expecting the usual peaceful acquiescence from the queens, the first and easiest targets of such raids, the men in blue were instead faced with angry men in dresses who had had quite enough of this regular badgering, thank you. This time the drag queens fought back, and the three days of the Stonewall Riots began.

Many assumed that the queens who had participated in the riots would lead the parade at Stonewall 25. Because of the controversy, it was decided that a more "acceptable" contingent would head the parade instead. The queens would be identified, but not at the front of the parade. True to their wonderfully defiant natures, the drag queens, José among them, decided to lead the parade anyway, down an alternate route. The New York Police were faced with controlling two parade routes that day. The two halves came together at Central Park, and the celebration continued.

"It was the drag queens who were already leading the parade. It was the drag queens who had the balls to start the riot at Stonewall. Honey, they had nothing to lose. Their reputations were shot. They lost their jobs. They had to revert to doing drag, to be street hustlers, or whatever they were because nobody wanted them. I mean they were outcasts. That was not going to happen with me and I and made damn sure of it. But people had to accept me on my terms. I did not accept them if they did not accept me. The world has accepted me on my terms.

"I marched the full length of that damn parade. It was a very hard fight all the way around. I was well honored. It was more good than bad.

"While I was in New York, I got into a tea on the lawn at Gracie Manor with the mayor, and I entertained him. Naturally there were parties all over New York that week. I was invited to more than I could attend. At one of these parties I met Beeban Kidron, the director of the movie *To Wong Foo, Thanks for Everything! Julie Newmar,* which was about to be filmed. She was an up-and-coming director.

"I said, 'Oh, Mr. DeMille! Here I am!'

I love the way José switches the gender of his subjects with impunity! Familiarity breeds camp.

"And she had seen me perform before.

"She said, 'Well, you are an actress!' She said, 'I am going to make sure that there is a place for you in my movie.'

"I said, 'Would you really? All you have to do is send me my ticket. No, for a chance to be in the movie, you don't even have to send me the ticket; I'll pay my own way.'

"I made a show of it, a big joke. You know, it was a cocktail party, a New York cocktail party. It was fun. I met all these people, the people from *Out Magazine,* and *Genre,* and *The Advocate,* and *Frontiers.*

"I wasn't sure if the director was serious. At the party I asked Coco, Coco LaChine, my 'daughter' and past Empress of New York. I said, 'Coco, what's happening?'

"And she tells me, 'You know, they contacted me about *To Wong Foo,* the motion picture.'

"I said, 'Oh, really? She said she was going to use me. Can you find out?'

"She says, 'I will, José.'

"Evidently Coco mentioned me. The director said, 'Oh, yes!' So Coco gave my name to the casting department at Warner Brothers, and I didn't hear any more.

"She calls me up, and she says, 'Be on the lookout. They are going to be calling you for a part. It may not be a speaking part, it may not be very big, but you're going to be in it. I'm in it! I got a part in it!'

"And so I said, 'Well, my dear, if *you* got a part in it, then *I'm* going to be in it!' And sure enough, they phoned me at work and said they were going to give me one day in New York for filming, and I said, 'Well, to fly back to New York for one day is hardly worth it,' not knowing how much money they were going to pay me.

"'Well,' she said, 'We could maybe make it two . . . we *might* squeeze in three days.'

"I said, 'Oh fine.' Never mentioned money. I don't like to mention money. I don't mention money. Definitely. So I said, 'Okay.'

"So this was on a Friday, and I had to catch a plane on a Saturday. So I flew in. I arrived. Monday morning I had to be on call for a rehearsal at six o'clock in the morning. I was there. They still never mentioned how much I was going to make.

"Well, Coco said, 'You'll make something like three-fifty an hour.'

"And I thought to myself, 'Three dollars and fifty cents an hour?! Lord! I'm in the hole already!' I didn't realize it was three *hundred* and fifty! Well, I nearly died when I got my check! They extended it to three days' pay, and I'm on the screen not even a minute. I played one of the judges for the drag contest at the beginning of the film. They actually filmed an awful lot of the way judges should act. The little bit in the film was all that was left. They didn't put it all in. In fact, in the picture it doesn't really tie us together with the contest. Really, when you look at it, they are performing, and we were the judges, and they should have shown us marking scores down on the paper, and then carried on. Well, we were too animated, or not animated enough, or there was too much paper—I mean it was all kinds of things. And they finally got that small bit.

"They paid me a salary, and I get royalties. I got my first royalty of $200 on November 23, 1995. Later I received a residual check for the video version. I'm still receiving checks. Remember, the picture was paid for within two weeks or three weeks after it was made. It was good! It was big! It had no lesson to teach. It wasn't on a moral issue. It was just a fun movie. That's why people liked it.

"That's how I got there—it's through my connections. It is not who you know, it's who you do.

"No, it's really who you know."

Bridges

Much has been written and spoken about building bridges in these middle years of the last decade of the century. We've had a president who made "a bridge to the twentieth century" the keystone of his second campaign for the White House. Like rain seducing mushrooms out of their spores, that phrase forced countless columns and editorials with bridge metaphors to pop from the soil of our psyches, or at least those cultural outlets of collective psyche we call writers. In this atmosphere of rhetorical bridge building, I found it deliciously appropriate that San Francisco, the state, and to some extent the nation, became embroiled in discussions over what to do about replacing the Oakland side of the San Francisco-Oakland Bay Bridge, one of the most photographed bridges in the world. It was damaged in the Loma Prieta quake a few years back. The governor, showing his usual aesthetic taste, wants the span replaced with a flat, gray, soulless causeway kind of thing. Others with more, shall we say, taste and vision, want a gossamer cabled roadway in the sky. The difference is a few measly millions, and the final decision will be with us for nearly another century.

(Yes, I know this is beginning to sound like an editorial with a bridge metaphor, but it all relates. Trust me.)

As I read the media accounts of the controversy over design, I couldn't help but think of José. (No, really.) What he would say about the choice between beauty and practicality would sound something like, "Well, my dear, why can't you have both? Big hair and big bridges are good for the soul. Of course, you also need a good corset to keep it all from falling apart."

José is no couch critique of things bridgely either. He has been intimately involved in that two-part span across the bay. It all started with the Widow Norton's deceased husband Joshua.

Joshua Norton I, Emperor of North America and Protector of Mexico was not just a figurehead ruler during his heyday at the end of the nineteenth century. He regularly issued proclamations, and presented his vision for the City by the Bay. Like any true madman, his visions were rarely mundane or small. Often they elicited chuckles and affectionate shakes of the head. One of Norton's wilder ideas was to build a bridge spanning the bay between San Francisco and Oakland. Some laughed indulgently and said, "Impossible."

There is an appropriate literary quote for what happened subsequently. It comes from the Fairy Godmother in the Rogers and Hammerstein musical *Cinderella:* "And because these daft and dewy-eyed dopes keep building up impossible hopes—impossible—things are happ'ning every day!"

The San Francisco-Oakland Bay Bridge opened on November 12, 1936.

*   *   *

It was a Sunday night at the beginning of November when the Widow Norton gathered her friends and family (and a few reporters and camera people) on a pier thrusting from the Embarcadero into the chilly bay waters. Looming over the scene were the dark gray girders and cables of the Bay Bridge. With Mama Norton were her various royal children and heirs: Emperor Marcus, First Emperor of San Francisco after Norton; Empress Sable Clown, Twenty-first Empress of San Francisco and reigning empress at the time; Emperor Matt Brown, Emperor Fourteen after Norton and reigning monarch, and a plethora of former monarchs and current dukes and duchesses. The sparkle from the jewels of the cross-dressing royalty served as foreshadowing of the sign to come.

Dressed in Victorian widow's black with hat and veils, the Widow Norton walked in a stately manner to the end of the pier. In a voice vibrating with serious supplication, she called out to the heavenly Norton, her beloved dead husband, "Joshua! Send me a sign to let me know you are watching over us and over your beloved city!" She lifted her hands toward the bridged envisioned by Norton so long ago. Like a middle-aged, female Moses, she waited, frozen in prayer. Suddenly, the bridge burst into light, its graceful outlines twinkling with thousands of starlike points of light. It swept like an artist's brushstroke to heaven. The now-silhouetted widow nodded to the dramatic message from beyond, and stated with a grave smile, "Joshua has heard my call."

* * *

Today, the Bay Bridge is a visual tribute to the city that has become a type of signature, along with its sister bridge, the Golden Gate. Both are massive icons whose cultural and spiritual value rises far beyond their practical boon to cross-bay transportation. Foolish notions often thrive in San Francisco. The bridge became so beloved over the years that the city held a celebration of its fiftieth birthday in 1986. As a part of honoring the span, the city fathers and mothers decided to illuminate the sweeping, cabled lines and flying roadway of the bridge with thousands of lighted bulbs.

Sometime before the night of the appointed lighting of the bridge, the Widow Norton, José I, announced that her beloved deceased husband Joshua intended to send her some sort of a sign of his eternal devotion and desire for his widow. The time he revealed for this miraculous sign happened to correspond to the date and time of the bridge lighting, the city being simply tools in the hands of the cross-time communications of the Emperor, of course.

Not satisfied with a simple, one-night declaration of Joshua's love and devotion, the Widow Norton raised her arms that evening on the pier and loudly proclaimed, "I hereby claim this bridge in the name of my dear and beloved husband, the Emperor Joshua Norton. For now and forever, may the lights of the bridge form a beautiful halo to shine over the bridge and the City of San Francisco!"

She subsequently revealed to the chilled crowd on the pier her plan to push the city to keep the bridge perpetually lit in honor of the Emperor. She officially began her campaign to raise the thousands of dollars the city number crunchers said it would take to install permanent lighting and pay the electric bills. She also proposed renaming the span the Emperor Norton Memorial Bridge. Thus was born the campaign called "Light Up the Bridge." Some called it a foolish and impractical idea, but the city councils of San Francisco and surrounding towns became caught up in the romantic audacity of the campaign. Corporations too sent in their donations, as did thousands of individuals with a love of things beautiful.

Though the bridge has not yet been rechristened the Norton Bridge, in 1997, as of this writing, the bridge is still lit with countless magical lights every night of the year, a shining gateway to a shining city.

"The world is full of zanies and fools . . ."

Two Old Farts

Sometimes these days there are reminders that José is no longer a young man. There was the Coronation he and I had to leave early because his stomach was distressed. There was the trip to Canada that was marred by a hospital stay, and the wheelchair he rode in when I picked him up at the San Francisco airport. But like everything else in his life, José faces age with wry humor. One day when I met him to work on this book, he had just come from a chance meeting with an old friend.

"Standing at the corner of Hallidie Plaza, which is Fifth and Market, I see my old friend from the Black Cat. Levi was his last name, but that's what we called him, Levi. He was a very attractive young man, and he did drawings. His father owned a big smoke shop right where Hallidie Plaza is. He was a very wealthy Jewish gentleman who took a great liking to me, not realizing that I was gay. Levi worked at his father's store, and he worked very hard to not let his father know he was gay. And I said, 'Well, of course your father knows you are gay, you damn fool. How can you hide it, with that big bundle hanging out in front of you and carrying on like you do!'

"And he would say, 'No, my father doesn't know that I'm gay.'

"So just to upset him, I'd go into the smoke shop, and I'd say, 'Well, hello dahling!'

Well, here we are now, and the smoke shop is gone. Papa is gone. In fact, Levi drank a lot, and first he got his license revoked so he couldn't drive. So he said, 'Well, screw you!' He bought an airplane and he flew around, until finally he had too many accidents with the airplane, and now he's grounded. He travels around by Muni, the subway. He's a fabulous man.

"So there we met the other day, and we both suffer from asthma and sinuses. His is pretty bad, a lot worse than mine, because he did smoke. So we are always comparing notes about what the doctors are doing for us and how we are getting along. And of course, he's just one year younger than I am. So we're just standing on the corner watching the parade go by, commenting on things that we see, talking about what was, and about the doctors, and how we would manage to get to be a hundred. I was mentioning to him about how young people seem so different these days, how they want us to support them. I may have reached an age, but I'm not paying for it. If they think I'm going to support them . . . I'm too old to start supporting someone.

"He said, 'My dear, when we were young they were looking to support us. Now we are looking to support them.'

"The bus comes, and he turns to me and says, 'Do you want me to help you up onto the bus?'

"I said, 'You damn fool! You're the one who needs help, not me.'

"So we got up onto the bus and we stood there. You see, the bus was full. Neither of us looks our age. He has beautiful white hair, but he looks young. People look at us if we sit in the senior citizen's seats like we are committing some kind of crime, so I said, 'Let's stand up.' We stood for a while, and finally I got a seat. Well, we decided that we needed to go do some shopping. Since he lives up in this area, I said, 'Let's go together. We can go to Cala.'

"He said, 'Sure, and I can help you push your cart.'

"We got off the bus at California Street and walked down California Street to Cala. I suggested we share a cart, but he said, 'No, you push your cart, and I'll push my cart.'

"I said, 'Fine.' We went into the store, and I was talking to myself, 'Let's see, I need . . .'

"He said, 'Are you talking to yourself or are you talking to me?'

"I said, 'No, I am not talking to you.'

"It was hysterical. Here we are on the street; we're both two old farts, and he has the nerve to say, 'Shall I help you onto the bus?'"

His World

I sat quietly on José's hide-a-bed couch and leaned my head back, tired and peaceful. I thought about the many nights I had spent there in the apartment getting to know the man. I let my eyes roam around the room, taking in the now-familiar knickknacks, posters, paintings, pictures, and awards. Here and there my eyes would pause, and I'd smile, or chuckle, or sigh quietly. I had come to have a personal connection to José and his crazy world, and I felt profoundly privileged.

"This is José's world," I thought, "the world that he created for himself."

* * *

When less courageous men would have buckled, José turned his personal trials into triumphs. He created a persona who could side-step the difficulties on the way to some royal ball. The Widow Norton wastes no time on regrets; she has her children to think about, the thousands of proud queens who, following her example, don a dress, sing, and turn their exile into a powerful tool for the good of others, into a life uniquely their own, into a quirky and wonderful celebration of all that is singular.

Self-doubt, bitterness, recriminations: these things José leaves out on the curb to be hauled away. More than anyone else I have known, José is master and mistress of his own world. What he saves, what he frames and puts on the walls of his rooms, nobody dictates, nobody decides but him.

His stories of his life are not so much the offerings of a historian as they are the still-wet brush strokes of an artist. José is his own canvas, his own masterwork. Events that would make lesser men beat their breasts, José sees as the colors he uses to paint. Many would argue with some of his interpretations of events past, but that is their world, and this is his. It doesn't matter. Like all great artists, José's vision is his own. His kingdom, and the wonderful royal personages who people it, are under his rule. On the hills of this magnificent City by the Bay, José has created his own Camelot. And there he lives to this day. Happily ever after.

Order Your Own Copy of
This Important Book for Your Personal Library!

THE EMPRESS IS A MAN
Stories from the Life of José Sarria

_____ in hardbound at $39.95 (ISBN: 0-7890-0259-0)

_____ in softbound at $19.95 (ISBN: 1-56023-917-4)

COST OF BOOKS _____

OUTSIDE USA/CANADA/
MEXICO: ADD 20% _____

POSTAGE & HANDLING _____
(US: $3.00 for first book & $1.25
for each additional book)
Outside US: $4.75 for first book
& $1.75 for each additional book)

SUBTOTAL _____

IN CANADA: ADD 7% GST _____

STATE TAX _____
(NY, OH & MN residents, please
add appropriate local sales tax)

FINAL TOTAL _____
(If paying in Canadian funds,
convert using the current
exchange rate. UNESCO
coupons welcome.)

☐ **BILL ME LATER:** ($5 service charge will be added)
(Bill-me option is good on US/Canada/Mexico orders only;
not good to jobbers, wholesalers, or subscription agencies.)

☐ Check here if billing address is different from
shipping address and attach purchase order and
billing address information.

Signature _____

☐ **PAYMENT ENCLOSED: $** _____

☐ **PLEASE CHARGE TO MY CREDIT CARD.**

☐ Visa ☐ MasterCard ☐ AmEx ☐ Discover

Account # _____

Exp. Date _____

Signature _____

Prices in US dollars and subject to change without notice.

NAME _____

INSTITUTION _____

ADDRESS _____

CITY _____

STATE/ZIP _____

COUNTRY _____ COUNTY (NY residents only) _____

TEL _____ FAX _____

E-MAIL_____
May we use your e-mail address for confirmations and other types of information? ☐ Yes ☐ No

Order From Your Local Bookstore or Directly From
The Haworth Press, Inc.
10 Alice Street, Binghamton, New York 13904-1580 • USA
TELEPHONE: 1-800-HAWORTH (1-800-429-6784) / Outside US/Canada: (607) 722-5857
FAX: 1-800-895-0582 / Outside US/Canada: (607) 772-6362
E-mail: getinfo@haworth.com
PLEASE PHOTOCOPY THIS FORM FOR YOUR PERSONAL USE.
BOF96